BADMINTON HORSE TRIALS

A History of the Three-Day Event

M
R
H

BADMINTON HORSE TRIALS

A History of the Three-Day Event

CAROL FOSTER

FOREWORD BY HIS GRACE
THE DUKE OF BEAUFORT, KG, MFH

INTRODUCTION BY
CAPTAIN MARK PHILLIPS, CVO

BARRIE & JENKINS
London Melbourne Sydney Auckland Johannesburg

Barrie & Jenkins Ltd

An imprint of the Hutchinson Publishing Group

3 Fitzroy Square, London W1P 6JD

Hutchinson Group (Australia) Pty Ltd
30–32 Cremorne Street, Richmond South, Victoria 3121
PO Box 151, Broadway, New South Wales 2007

Hutchinson Group (NZ) Ltd
32–34 View Road, PO Box 40–086, Glenfield, Auckland 10

Hutchinson Group (SA) (Pty) Ltd
PO Box 337, Bergvlei 2012, South Africa

First published 1980

Set in VIP Bembo
Printed and bound in Great Britain by
Fakenham Press Limited, Fakenham, Norfolk

British Library Cataloguing in Publication Data

Foster, Carol
Badminton Horse Trials.
1. Three-day event (Horsemanship) –
England – Great Badminton – History
I. Title
798′.24 SF295.7

ISBN 0 214 20631 9

DEDICATION

To my mother

FRONTISPIECE

'. . . the perfect setting for such an event . . .'

Contents

List of Plates

Colour (*between pp. 96–7*)

Monochrome

Foreword

I must congratulate Miss Foster on the excellent and interesting account which she has given in the manuscript of her book on the Badminton Horse Trials. It brings back happy memories, especially of those early days, and the first time I had ever watched a Three Day Event at Aldershot in the Olympic Games. The first time we put on the Event here at Badminton was, I think, the most exciting, wondering if there would be any entries and if anyone would come to watch it. We have been extremely fortunate in two respects, first the support which we have always been given by the members of the Royal Family, and secondly in the standard of efficiency shown by the three directors, Colonel Trevor Horn, Colonel Gordon Cox-Cox and Colonel Frank Weldon. We have been favoured by the weather except for three extremely wet years, and I hope the Badminton Horse Trials will carry on for many years to come.

13th June 1979

Beaufort.

Badminton, Gloucestershire

Introduction

by Captain Mark Phillips CVO

Being asked to prepare an introduction for this book, a comprehensive illustrated history of the Badminton Horse Trials which were inaugurated in 1949, is to put one in mind of one's own experiences at this great event.

My parents tell me that I attended the very first Badminton but was left sitting under a tree, in the charge of a nanny, while they went off to walk the course. In later years I remember being totally overawed by the size of the fences and seeing such great characters as Sheila Willcox and Laurie Morgan compete.

In my Beaufort Pony Club days the Badminton fences still seemed unjumpable but it was always my ambition to ride at Badminton, as three-day eventing was the natural progression from Pony Club one-day events. Thus in 1968, the year of the Mexico Olympics, I had my first Badminton ride over a course which was to prove the biggest that I have ever ridden there. My horse, Rock On, gave me the most fantastic ride over the big course, even though the fence where the Keeper's Rails are now had eliminated a good many of the earlier riders, and the Coffin, about three from home, was the biggest I have ever seen. It was a good introduction! Since then I have had two further classic rides both on Columbus, once in 1974 when he won, and again in 1979 when he never felt like making a mistake.

Badminton week has always been preceded for me by a week's concentrated training with Bertie Hill: there is just so much you can do for yourself but then you get to the stage when you need someone on the ground. I usually arrive at Badminton on the preceding Tuesday afternoon and ride quietly around the trade stands after a pipe-opening gallop before leaving Devon in the morning. Early on the Wednesday morning, before the briefing, I do some dressage for the first time and in the afternoon I take my first walk round the course, looking purely objectively at the fences to try to gain an overall impression. On my second walk round on the Thursday I make carefully calculated decisions on how to ride each fence, and on the third and final inspection, on the Friday, I walk the course exactly as I am going to ride it: even with the course stringed, one can save precious feet – ten feet are equivalent to one second.

Riding-in for the dressage is just as important as the test itself. I find the secret is only to pick up the reins just before the test: some people tend to ride the best out of their horses before they enter the arena. There is a tremendous atmosphere in the dressage arena at Badminton; you can always feel the horses lift as they enter the arena and the art is to try and control this to the best advantage.

There is enormous tension before all stages of the event; you wouldn't be a good competitor if the butterflies didn't flutter a bit. Nowadays the competition is so close that you can't afford to relax for a single solitary second, and I think this means that the approach to the event has to be much more professional now than in years gone by.

Badminton has more than its fair share of critics who condemn the fences for being too big, but I feel most strongly that these criticisms come from people who don't really know. The fences *are* big, but they must be so for Badminton to maintain its prestige as the greatest annual event of its kind in the world. The great thing is that the fences are very, very fair and beautifully built. Frank Weldon is very good at building 'jockey stoppers' rather than 'horse stoppers'.

There are many ways in which Badminton has changed over the years, the most obvious being its enormous growth and increase in popularity. The courses themselves have changed, in that after 1968 the general concensus of opinion was that they had got big enough. So Frank Weldon began to build more riders' problems: 'bounces', fences at angles and combination fences. In the interests of television and the public the courses have now settled into a pattern, around basically the same track, with excellent made-up take-offs and landings.

The crowds of course are now very large, but I cannot see them getting much bigger, simply because there will be a limit to how many people can be fitted into the Park. I am never really conscious of the crowds when riding, except that when approaching the Lake you seem to descend into a bowl of people with a puddle in the bottom! Occasionally you hear a clap or cheer but this only helps you on your way.

As far as the organization is concerned, there isn't another event to touch Badminton. Everything is now provided free for competitors and their grooms, thanks to Whitbread, and everyone goes to tremendous trouble to help. It's all part of what makes Badminton, 'Badminton'. Nearly all similar events in the world are modelled on Badminton, which has been the pioneer in experimenting with new rules, administration techniques and types of fences.

The future of Badminton? I can only see it getting better and better. For the competitor the Badminton prize money has always led the field, but I think that it will be raised still further now and that this will help prevent good horses from being sold abroad.

The Badminton Horse Trials have, and always will have, an atmosphere all their own. Like the Derby, it is *the* event. It is still – and should be – our 'Olympic Horse Trial' and, personally, only an Olympic Gold Medal takes precedence over victory at Badminton.

AUTHOR'S ACKNOWLEDGEMENTS

The author wishes to thank the following people for their assistance in the preparation of this book:

His Grace the Duke of Beaufort, Major Derek Allhusen, Miss Joanna Boswell, Mr Raymond Brooks-Ward, Mr Michael Bullen, Mr Chris Collins, Mr Bertie Hill, Mrs Jane Holderness-Roddam, Col. Bill Lithgow, Mrs Wendy Marshall, Mr Richard Meade, Miss Daphne Moore, Miss Flavia Phillips, Capt. Mark Phillips, Miss Lucinda Prior-Palmer, Mrs Victoria Sanford, Mr John Shedden, Mr David Somerset, Mrs E. Straker, Mr Hugh Thomas, Col. Frank Weldon, Mr Martin Whiteley, Mr Dorian Williams, *Horse & Hound, The Field.*

Photographs: Findlay Davidson p. 177; Peter Harding pp. 2, 12, 15, 22, 25, 26, 27, 28, 29, 30, 32, 34, 37, 38, 40, 41, 42, 43, 44, 45, 47, 51, 53, 56, 59, 62, 71, 88, 119, 126, 129, 148, 149, 154, 155, 156, 158, 159, 160, 161, 162, 163, 164, 165, 166, 167, 168, 169, 170, 171, 172, 173, 174, 175, 176, 186, 191, all colour (except 'Clarissa Strachan': Kit Houghton); Clive Hiles pp. 95, 116, 117, 140, 141, 147, 152, 181; Jim Meads pp. 60, 66, 67, 68, 69, 70, 76, 88, 92, 93, 102, 106, 107, 109, 112–13, 114, 115, 119, 120, 121, 122, 123, 138, 142, 143, 146, 147, 148, 149, 150, 178, 179, 180, 181, 183, 184, 185, 186, 187, 188, 189, 190; Reed Photography pp. 144–5

Remaining photographs by the author. Cartoon on p. 151 by Giles. Drawings of fences on pp. 110–11 by Reginald Bass.

1

BEFORE BADMINTON

At the end of the Second World War, there were few people in equestrian circles in Britain who knew, understood or, for that matter, even cared about a branch of riding, popular on the Continent for fifty years or so, known there as the 'Military'.

People were much more interested in getting back to their hunting, and in trying to restore the atmosphere of the 'Golden Age' of the 1930s. For those who enjoyed competition outside the hunting field, hunter trials were much in vogue and show-jumping commanded an interest which was to grow phenomenally (and never to look back) after a team led by Col. Harry Llewellyn on Foxhunter took the Bronze Medal at the London Olympics in 1948.

There was little interest in the Continental training system of 'dressage' (and even a certain amount of suspicion of it). It was considered to be an esoteric form of horsemanship having little in common with the British way of riding. The 'Military' included three main sections, one of which was dressage, and so the possibilities of it catching on in this country were remote in the extreme. The foundation of the 'Military' lay, as its title suggests, in military training and was a test of competence for a cavalry soldier and his charger, in both obedience and endurance. In short, it was a form of training for war, as described by Miss Daphne Machin-Goodall in *The Horseman's Year* in 1965:

All the officers of most of the Continental countries were expected to be proficient in the complete training of their horses. This training was naturally regarded as essential for anyone holding commissioned rank, for it was an excellent method of developing self-confidence, determination, and respect for discipline, and it offered a challenge to nerve and ability; it also taught the rider to adjust himself to the temperament and character of his horse, to cope with unforeseen or difficult situations; through his horse, he ought to develop better judgement as a leader of men.

That is not to say our own cavalry did not train: the famous cavalry school at Weedon, which closed down in 1940, was a great influence and one which many feel is now sadly lacking in the horse world, as the training was strict and rigorous. Cavalrymen were trained in equitation, which was really a form of dressage, and took part in formidable cross-country rides with long, stiff courses; but it was not considered as a competition or event in its own right.

The Military, combined training, horse trials (call it what you will),* tentatively emerged as the ultimate combined competition, the three-day event, at the Olympic Games of 1912 in Stockholm. Although the

'. . . $4\frac{1}{2}$ miles of roads and tracks . . .' Lt. Morgan and Heavy Weather in the 1953 Badminton.

*It is understandable that the sport should have been colloquially called the 'Military' because it was originally confined to Continental armed forces. But why the English word was used when we were the only country not to participate has proved inexplicable. The most common official title is the French 'Concours complet d'equitation', or 'Concours complet' for short. It is certainly more descriptive than the Anglo-Saxon 'three-day event'.

Olympics had been revived in 1896 by the Frenchman, Pierre de Coubertin, it was Count Clarence von Rosen of Sweden who succeeded in having equestrian competitions included from 1912 onwards. Seven nations entered the combined training event, including Britain, but no member of our team completed the course.

After the First World War, in 1924, the Games were held in Paris where Capt. B. de Fonblanque came sixth (individual) in the three-day event, while the fourth place in the individual jumping went to Major P. E. 'Bogie' Bowden-Smith, a name which was later to feature prominently in the introduction of the new equestrian sport to Britain. The composition of the three-day event changed at each Olympics from 1912. The second day usually included a long distance ride – occasionally two with an interval in between – which sometimes included jumping 'cross-country obstacles'. The only constant was dressage on the first day and show-jumping on the last. In Paris (1924) the second day consisted only of a steeplechase.

Berlin, in 1936, brought some measure of success for Britain in the three-day event, over an extremely severe course when the Weedon-trained team collected the Bronze Medal. This is regarded as the first 'modern' three-day event, the format remaining basically the same ever since.

Despite the success, eventing was still very much a military affair and certainly no one in this country – or indeed the world – had thought to emulate it for public 'consumption', so to speak. According to Col. Frank Weldon, current director of Badminton, the system of 'team selection' at Weedon was a question of '"You, you and you will go in for the three-day event and you, you and you will compete in the show-jumping".... Dressage was not considered because most people, including me, thought it was something only foreigners did, in funny-shaped breeches and hats, and it was beneath our dignity!'

There was, however, a small group of horsemen who thought dressage was far from beneath their dignity. In the 1930s, a growing band became interested in 'equitation' – the science of riding – as opposed to just 'riding'. Under the guidance of Col. V. D. S. Williams, described by the late Col. Podhasky of the Spanish Riding School as the 'father of British dressage', the St George's Riding Club was founded at Winkfield, near Ascot, Berkshire and the idea, in 1946, was to start a national equestrian centre. British riders were not ready for such a bold venture, however, and Col. Williams had to wait for some time before he began to see the fruits of his hard-fought labours.

London hosted the first Olympic Games after the War, in 1948 – amidst the inevitable protests at the unwarranted expense – and the full quota of equestrian events was staged at Aldershot. During that August, probably quite unconsciously, the British riding public began to develop a growing, if sceptical, awareness of the three-day event, still very much a military confine. Conditions were ripe for the reception of new ideas: hunting, sadly, was not the same – the halcyon days were gone for ever, and people were looking for something different. The 'new' event was explained in *Horse and Hound* of 21 July 1948:

> The three-day event is a very real test of horse and man. Obedience, suppleness, impulsion and the attributes of the highly schooled animal are called for in the dressage test at Aldershot on the first day; the following day demands 4½ miles on roads and tracks, the negotiating of a steeplechase course on Tweseldown racecourse, then nine miles on roads and tracks, and five miles across country with thirty-four obstacles – including some very solid ones – in seventeen minutes and then a 1,000 metre run-out at a canter. The third day is devoted to show-jumping at Aldershot.

On 7 August, a week before the event, *Horse and Hound* reported: 'One of the best courses ever laid out has been prepared by Mr H. Wynmalen and Brig. P. E. Bowden-Smith [formerly Major] for the cross-country section of the Three-Day Event which will start at 5 am on Thursday, August 12. [This was owing to the very hot summer that Britain was enjoying and the organizers wanted everyone to have completed the endurance before the heat of the day.] There are no tricks about it – it is all absolutely straightforward but none the less difficult.' Another name to appear on the officials' list for the 1948 Olympics was that of Col. Trevor

1936 brought some measure of success in the Olympics. Lt.-Col. A. B. J. Scott, seen here at Badminton in 1952, was a member of the bronze medal-winning team.

Horn, a council member of the British Horse Society (BHS). Completely new to the idea of dressage and the three-day event, he arrived at Aldershot a fortnight in advance of the Games to live with some of the competitors and officials in the barracks allotted to them, and learn what he could. Another person who lived with the three-day event competitors at Aldershot was Major Derek Allhusen. An Olympic pentathlete, he was so impressed by what he learnt of the sport then, that he later switched to eventing, going on to win the Individual Silver and the Team Gold Medal in Mexico in 1968. He recalls that our team were virtually 'babes in arms as far as our knowledge of the three-day event went in those days. People, in general, were not the least bit interested and didn't know, at all, what it was all about.'

The XIV Olympiad duly commenced. The first equestrian event was the dressage on which the late Col. Jack Talbot Ponsonby, in *The Horseman's Year*, commented:

From a spectator's point of view the competition provided one of the finest spectacles of horsemanship ever seen in this country, and it is greatly to be hoped that it may encourage British horsemen to study and practise advanced dressage. . . . Next came the three-day event which is an exhaustive trial of stamina and judgement. . . . The first section, the dressage test, was perhaps an anti-climax after the previous day's event as, of course, the test laid down is far less severe, and these general utility horses cannot be expected to reach such a high standard.

The British appreciation for dressage was awakening, together with an eye for technicalities. *Horse and Hound* reported on the three-day event dressage that 'The results obtained from the different seats and positions of the hands were of considerable interest . . . one individual looked as if he was about to throw his arms round his horse's neck in supplication. . . . The majority did not employ these exaggerated tactics and many fine horsemen who were, indeed, a part of the horse delighted our eyes – in fact they made it look all too easy.' Going on to comment on the condition of the three-day event horses, *Horse and Hound* wrote 'One or two of the horses which looked most likely to stand up to it [the speed and endurance day], were a shade impatient during the dressage test.'

Returning to *The Horseman's Year* commentary, 'The 8 kilometre cross-country course consisted of thirty-four jumps of varying types, many of them placed at very awkward angles of approach. It is impossible here to describe them all, but a formidable concrete wall after a little over a mile-and-a-half caught the eye, as did a combination of fences a little farther on, consisting of a picket fence, a sharp turn to the right, and at once a bush fence and ditch into the lane: out of the lane was a ditch in front of a bank with a rail to the far side. Out of forty-five starters, thirty-three completed this arduous test.' British hopes were high when Major Borwick had a brilliant round on Liberty, but were dashed when Brig. Lyndon Bolton had two falls on Sylveste and the team was eliminated when Major D. Stewart's Dark Seal had to retire lame at the start of the cross-country. 'It came as a rude awakening to find we were not very good,' summarized *The Horseman's Year* in 1959. 'There is nothing which so gets under the skin of an English horseman as to be told he does not know how to ride.'

Throughout the running of these Games there was one man in particular who was a very keen observer, in his capacity as vice-patron of the British Horse Society and vice-president of the Fédération Equestre Internationale (FEI), and also from a personal point of view. He had driven up to Aldershot from his Gloucestershire home on each day of the event to witness, firstly, the dressage and, secondly, the three-day event. As a neighbour of this interested visitor, and also as one who had walked the Olympic course a couple of times, Col. Trevor Horn volunteered to escort him around the course. The enthusiastic 'new recruit' was, of course, His Grace the Duke of Beaufort.

The late Col. Trevor Horn recorded that it was during a picnic lunch on the cross-country day – 12 August 1948 – that the Duke of Beaufort first mentioned the idea of holding a three-day event as an annual competition in this country. Thirty years later to the day, for the purposes of this book, His Grace recalled how the idea of 'Badminton' was born:

In 1948 the Olympic Games were held here (in Britain) and I had never seen the three-day event competition. Of course, it was held in Berlin in 1936 and our team went there, finishing quite well, but it had never been really known to people in this country what was actually involved. I went to see our team take part in the cross-country which was held at Aldershot in 1948 and I was very impressed with what I saw, not only by the size of the jumps and the skill of the riders, but also because it was something which could easily be held at Badminton. We have the room to have it, the Park is big enough, and we have the point-to-point course just up at the end of the Park, so there was no reason why it could not be held here. I immediately went to the British Horse Society and asked them if they would back me if I ran it the following April, and held it here in the Park. They agreed to do so and we set to work building the course.

The 'backing' given by the BHS meant that they gave not only their moral support, but they also underwrote the event should it have to be cancelled. This they did up till a few years ago, when Badminton took out its own insurance, but profits from the event always have been, and still are, donated to the BHS.

The Duke of Beaufort asked Col. Trevor Horn if he would undertake to organize the event, and recalls, 'He was a very fine horseman in his time and we had a very interesting and exciting time building the course.' Such a modest statement of fact after a thirty-year interval, belies the immense amount of effort which went into staging that first 'Badminton'. The reason behind the Duke's generous offer was that he saw in 'three-day eventing' a sport at which we British could excel, given the correct training ground. Thus Badminton became the ground on which to test and prove horses and riders for Olympic competition. At the outset, no one thought further than the 1952 Olympic Games in Helsinki. *Horse and Hound* reported: 'His Grace the Duke of Beaufort has not only given the country a lead, but has provided a practical demonstration of his wish to help in the preparation for the next Olympic Games by the generous offer of his assistance and land at Badminton for a yearly Three-Day Event competition. In this way a team of horses and riders may be trained to partake in the Olympic Games in Helsinki in 1952 with far less difficulty and without encountering the many snags which we were up against in our over-rapid preparations for the 1948 Games.' In that year serious training of unschooled and many unfit horses did not commence until the April. *Horse and Hound* continued in its announcement of the horse trials to be held at Badminton:

> A yearly event in 1949, '50 and '51 should not only provide a great deal of interest, but make it far easier to produce and train a representative team of horses and riders without interfering too greatly with the ordinary life of the riders.
>
> A small committee of the British Horse Society formed to handle the arrangements will consist of The Duke of Beaufort, Brig. P. E. Bowden-Smith, Major P. Borwick, Lt.-Col. the Hon. C. Guy Cubitt and Col. Trevor Horn,

to whom all communications were to be directed. By early September preparations were 'well-in-hand' and at the end of that month details were announced: 'A competition sponsored by the Duke of Beaufort KG MFH and organized by the British Horse Society, which is the governing body in Great Britain for all international equestrian events, will be run on similar lines to the Olympic Games Three-Day Event. ... The entry fee is £2 per horse. ... First prize £150, second £100, third £75. ... The sole object of this annual competition which will be held on his land at Badminton is to find riders and horses suitable for training as a team to compete at the Olympic Games in Helsinki in 1952.' *Horse and Hound* continued to outline the requirements of each year's test, which got progressively more severe as Olympic year approached. Prospective competitors were informed that accommodation would be found for them, their grooms and horses on application and, while horses would be stabled free, they would be charged for forage, etc.

The first organizing committee had a basic knowledge of the new event: among them, the Duke of Beaufort and Lt.-Col. Cubitt were vice-patron and chairman respectively of the BHS, Brig. Bowden-Smith had trained the 1936 team as well as organized the 1948 event, Major Borwick had just competed at Aldershot while Col. Horn had gained some experience at that event. In addition, Mr Charles Cornell was elected treasurer to the first Event and an enthusiastic local sportsman – an ex-amateur NH jockey, Lt.-Col. R. B. Moseley – was asked to be assistant director.

It was a *new* event, though, and the guidelines for the pioneers of this great sport were largely those gained from the experiences of running the Olympic Games here, together with the general regulations of the FEI. The FEI had not then drawn up any regulations for the three-day event, such was its novelty, indeed they did not do so until 1957. Rules for the first Badminton were largely devised by Col. Horn himself, following the lines along which the Continentals had run their events – indeed many of the basic principles, such as maximum height and spread of obstacles, penalty zones, etc. still apply today. However, when he could not find the answer to any point of detail, he made it up – and the whole thing worked perfectly.

If arrangements seemed to be rather hurried and haphazard for the first Event – the first 'office' was a room in Col. Horn's house with the piano doubling up as a filing cabinet – there can be no doubt that, with the distinguished group of ex-soldiers and cavalrymen at the helm, it was organized with military precision.

As director of the Event, Trevor Horn had the major task of making all practical arrangements, from building the course to organizing the catering. Apart from the experience gained during his brief visit to the Olympics, he had no personal knowledge upon which to build. He is remembered, by the many people who knew him, as a charming, unassuming and quiet gentleman, who worked very hard and with great efficiency to achieve undoubtedly successful results. 'His was no easy task,' reported Col. W. E. Lyon in *The Horseman's Year*, 'for it must be remembered he was starting from scratch and yet all the arrangements worked with the precision of well-oiled machinery.' It was his task to plan and build the first-ever course over the beautiful, gently rolling pastureland of Badminton Park, with all its wonderful natural features, in which he must have seen potential and which have become, if not 'household', at least 'stableyard' words! Every inch of each of the five sections of the speed and endurance (there was a Phase E run-in in the early years) had to be plotted and measured with a bicycle and cyclometer. The fences were constructed with help from workers on the Badminton estate and the twenty-one obstacles of the first Event were described in the schedule as 'rigid and as far as possible resembling natural objects (hedges, ditches, farmgates, brooks, streams, road crossings, barriers, etc.)'. Michael Bullen remembers visiting Col. Horn during his directorship: 'He used to spend a lot of time with his poles lying on the lawn. He would fiddle around with them every day, putting them in different directions and measuring them, which was how he came up with his Badminton fences. It was fascinating that, although he had never evented himself, he never made the mistake of building a fence which wasn't jumpable.' He was, of course, an extremely knowledgeable horseman and a great hunting man.

As well as organizing the 'spectacle' of the event, Col. Horn also had the task of interesting the press and public, and arranging accommodation for officials and competitors. The Duke of Beaufort recalls that local hoteliers were very helpful in this respect, while he himself put his own stables at the disposal of competitors – and of course still does – and this side of the organization was taken on by Col. Moseley. Even in the first year, a number of local traders exhibited at Badminton and this, too, together with general arrangements for tentage, catering, etc., all fell on Col. Horn's broad shoulders. But, comments John Shedden, he was one of the 'great people of the old vintage to whom everything came naturally'.

Hard work it must have been but the Duke of Beaufort's enthusiasm and vigour was infectious and, no doubt, as he recalls, it was an 'exciting time' for men who could hardly have conceived what they were starting. As for any who doubted the value of the competition, Lt.-Col. Hance wrote: 'The Badminton Event has been rendered possible through the assistance of the Duke of Beaufort. The fact that he is providing the facilities for, and sponsoring, the show should convince any sceptic of its practical value and of the chances of our team's ultimate success.' Equally significant was the support given to the Event, from the beginning, by the Royal Family. His Majesty King George VI graciously agreed to become Patron to the new event, while his elder daughter Princess Elizabeth, was the first vice-patron.

It was undoubtedly due to the Duke of Beaufort's stature in the sporting world that people did take the new horse trial at Badminton seriously. Views were expressed in *Horse and Hound* that the 'dressage' would put off many potential competitors. At the end of 1948, Lt.-Col. Jack Hance wrote a series of five articles for the magazine, 'Training for Badminton', in which he expressed the fear that 'the terms "dressage" and "show jumping" may lose for those staging the competition the very chaps we want to encourage to compete . . . the type of rider . . . who cuts out the work in a hunt and at the end of the season has a crack as often as possible at point-to-points – is really the man for the job. . . .' He went on to explain that 'dressage' was merely a foreign word meaning training, just as 'chauffeur' meant driver. In anticipating that 'dressage' would soon become part of our language, he pointed out that, just as 'chauffeur' meant a particular type of high-class driver, so dressage 'aims not only at producing a high-class horse, so that amongst its other accomplishments it can get over a country, but also one that is properly balanced, has a good mouth and is obedient to the hands and legs. . . .' The prescribed test – the BHS Test B – was nothing outside the capabilities of the prospective competitor. Col. W. E. Lyon described it as 'a simple test of Riding School training as practised in the days of horsed cavalry. This training has now assumed the dignity of the name "Dressage".'

As for the show-jumping, Col. Hance wrote:

Until recent years even the most enthusiastic of us got 'fed-up' going to show after show, seeing the same horses jumping (or not) fence after fence, wall, gate, triple bars, stile, in and out, and water, any of which jumps would collapse like a pack of cards.... But the jumps at Badminton will... certainly not collapse, although if given a hefty clout they will come down, but the horse will have had a lesson.

That is the second advantage of the whole contest – it will be an education to horses and riders, and spectators alike. It will be a lesson and a privilege to train for such a competition.

In his five articles Col. Hance gave invaluable advice and training hints for intending competitors who, like the organizers, had no guidelines upon which to prepare themselves, while an article by Col. Cubitt built up for the horse world an impression of the fun to be had at 'Badminton '49' as it became known. The British equestrian public were indeed awakening to developments, and with the announcement of times and distances for the speed and endurance section of the first Badminton, also came news that Mrs Home Kidston's six-year-old gelding, Golden Willow – winner of four hunter trials in succession the previous autumn – was entered for the Event, while Major Peter Borwick, member of the 1948 team, gave a lecture demonstration at the Cotswold Equitation Centre, on the preparations needed for Badminton.

John Shedden, rider of Golden Willow and principal at the Cotswold Equitation Centre, remembers the competitors' attitude to the new event:

The announcement of the first Badminton caused a tremendous stir in the riding world. Few people had any idea what it was all about, except perhaps for a small number of the professionals who had looked further afield than the usual type of English riding. In those days a person's horsemanship was based on his ability to ride to hounds and there was no doubt that these new competitions, coupled with this new-fangled thing called Dressage, caused a great deal of suspicion from these hard-boiled, and I regret to say, narrow-minded hunting types.

It was discussed over many glasses of port and the general consensus of opinion was that only the foreigners did this sort of thing and no one had ever seen a foreigner who was any good across country to hounds. However, the fact that the Duke of Beaufort was holding this big new Event at Badminton did make people, out of respect for Master, sit up and take a bit more notice than they would otherwise have done.

It was therefore not surprising when in April 1949, when we all assembled at Badminton, that there was more than the usual excitement. It is a long time ago now, but I am sure that, in retrospect, the riders to the last man were more than looking forward to it. The fun, leg pulls and jokes as we progressed around the course discussing and arguing about the fences and the problems they caused, were tremendously amusing and enjoyed by all!

The worries and reservations of the Duke of Beaufort, Col. Trevor Horn and the committee must have been many as they stood on the launching pad or precipice of the boldest venture ever known in equestrian competition in this country. Without confident publicity, however, they would have been one step down the precipice before they started. Thus, as one exercise, a poster was produced. Visionary in its concept, it proclaimed that on 20, 21 and 22 April 1949 would be staged 'Badminton Three Days' Event: The Most Important Horse Event in Great Britain'.

BADMINTON

THREE DAYS' EVENT

THE MOST IMPORTANT

HORSE EVENT

IN GREAT BRITAIN

APRIL 20th, 21st & 22nd, 1949

1st Day—DRESSAGE, 10.30 a.m. at BADMINTON HOUSE.

2nd Day—SPEED & ENDURANCE, 14 miles, commence 2 p.m., including—
STEEPLECHASE COURSE (2 miles), DIDMARTON CAR PARK.
CROSS-COUNTRY (3 miles—21 Fences), BADMINTON CAR PARK.

3rd Day—JUMPING, 12 o'clock at BADMINTON HOUSE.

AND

TWO JUMPING COMPETITIONS (Organised by B.S.J.A.)—
TOUCH and OUT and OPEN COMPETITION.

ADMISSION to all Car Parks:

Motors, £1 per day. £2 10s., Seasons. Charabancs, £2 10s., 26 seaters.
Pedestrians 1s. each. ,, £3, 32 seaters.

Tickets may be had in advance on payment.

CATERING BY W. OSMOND & SONS, SALISBURY

Full information from: BRITISH HORSE SOCIETY, 66 Sloane Street, London, S.W.1.

2

THE MOST IMPORTANT HORSE EVENT

April 1949 arrived! 'There were two things that worried us to start with,' recalls the Duke of Beaufort. 'One whether we should get any entries, and we got just as many as we'd hoped for, and secondly whether many people would come to watch it, or *anybody* would come to watch it!'

The weather during that first Event could hardly have been more unkind after a promisingly sunny start. The second day was miserably cold and rained torrents, soaking competitors, officials and spectators alike, to the skin. The show went on, however, and the 'customers' went away more than satisfied with the goods. The impact of the Event was immediate; it had been an unqualified success. The leading item in *Horse and Hound* made fitting and far-seeing comment: 'In a historic setting in front of Badminton House the first day, 20 April, of the annual Three-Day Event which, it is hoped, will become a permanent fixture, passed off very successfully supported by a crowd of interested spectators. The big crowds testified to the interest aroused by this first annual Three-Day Event which may well be said to have made history. Nothing of the kind has ever been tried in this country before and it is likely to become the most important sporting event of its type.'

The Horseman's Year made equally evocative comment: 'Badminton itself is the perfect setting for such an event for there is no estate in England which could combine with such harmony the dignified home, the informal sporting atmosphere and the intimate feeling of hospitality as Badminton. I had a feeling as I watched the dressage test being performed in perfect weather and with Badminton House as a background, that I would like horse lovers from all over the world to be there just to see, if nothing else, English country life at its very best.'

As for the competitor's point of view, Miss Vivien Machin-Goodall (the late Mrs Boon), who finished fifth in the first Badminton on her own Neptune and became the first woman to win a three-day event, wrote to *Horse and Hound* in appreciation of the event:

As a competitor in the recent Badminton Three-Day Event I would like to thank the Duke of Beaufort and all those on the committee and stewards who gave unsparing help and time to those of us who were competing.

Nothing was spared to assist us and we received consideration and advice in any difficulty that arose.

The organization and work caused by this event must have been terrific, as it was run so efficiently and smoothly. And although the Test itself was no light matter for us and had entailed months of concentrated hard work, it was an experience which I would not have missed and which I enjoyed thoroughly.

And, from the organizer's point of view, the Duke of Beaufort recollects that 'All three

People stood on their cars to obtain a better view.

days were well-attended and financially we did make quite a nice little profit over it!' It was, in fact, about £100; by 1978 the net profit had increased to nearly £50,000, with the total contribution to the British Horse Society over the years amounting now to over £200,000.

Badminton obviously won many 'converts' for the sport and the previous chapter has already dealt with the scepticism of the British equestrian public in general. Who, then, were the people who were willing to 'have a go', as Brig. Bowden-Smith had put it? Basically, they were people interested in seeing Britain widen her equestrian horizons; the people active in the St George's Riding Club of the 1930s; and people who recognized that, in Britain, we had in our horses and riders rough, uncut stones which, with care and skill, would become the brilliant gems of future years. And beyond it all was the quest for gold; Olympic Gold!

The two names which featured at the head of the results sheets in 1949 and 1950 were, in fact, the principals of two of the country's leading equitation schools: John Shedden of Cotswold and the late Tony Collings of Porlock. 'We naturally thought,' says John Shedden, 'that as we were the two people who were supposed to be the leading instructors, we ought to be represented at Badminton.' As the country's leading instructors, they clearly set a very good example.

Dorian Williams recalls that his father, the late Col. V. D. S. Williams, leading light behind the St George's Riding Club, welcomed the three-day event as much as anyone: 'He felt that the struggle he had had, almost fighting a losing battle, in interesting people in dressage from the mid-thirties onwards, might benefit as a result of the three-day event.'

Qualifications for the first Badminton were, understandably, negligible, the only conditions being that riders be British, over seventeen years of age, and that horses should not exceed ten years – a special clause to admit only those horses which would still be eligible, if selected, for Olympic competition in 1952. No other qualifications could have been imposed; there was nothing on which to

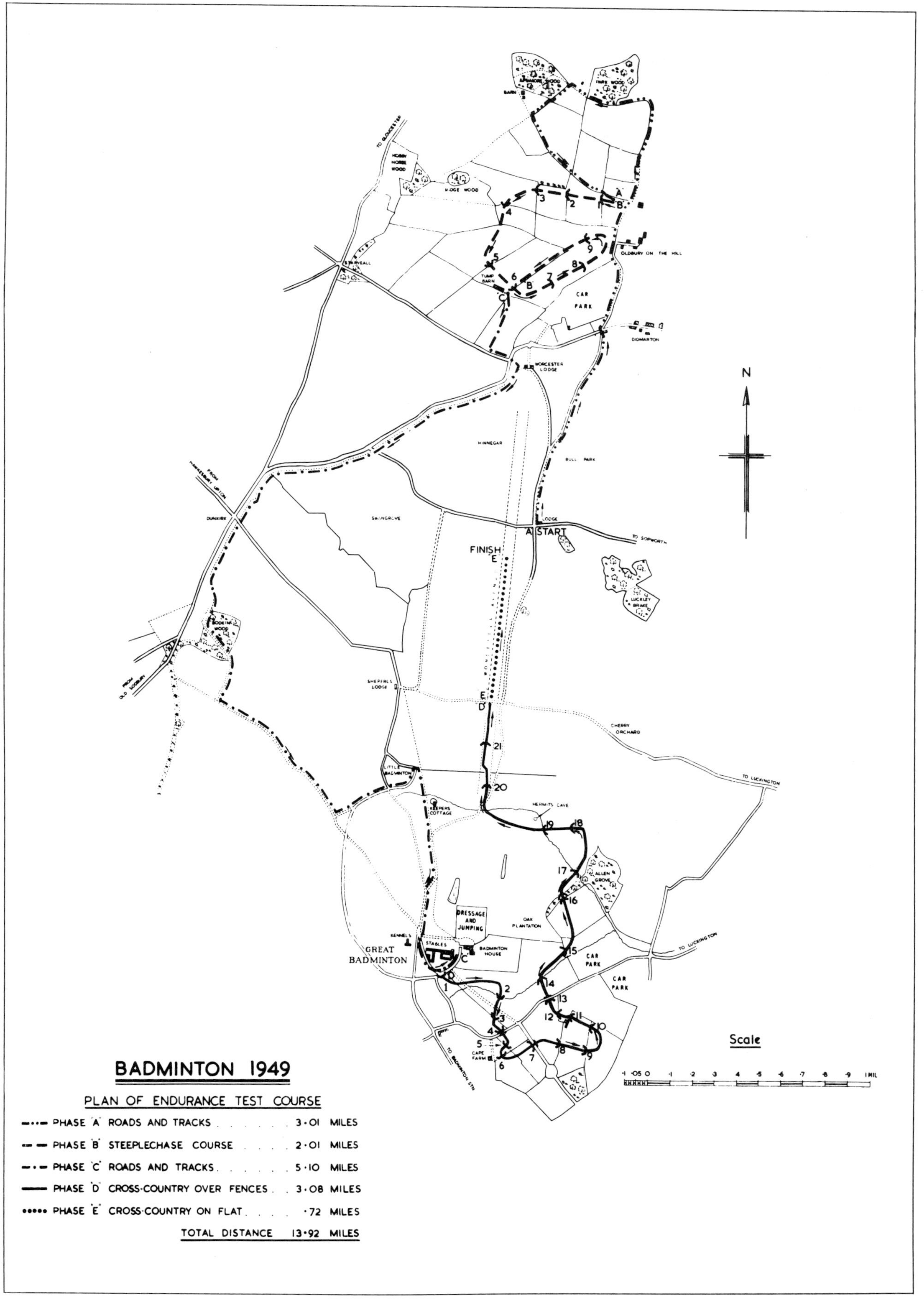
N
FINISH
E
A START
GREAT
BADMINTON
STABLES
DRESSAGE
AND
JUMPING
BADMINTON
HOUSE
KENNELS
OAK
PLANTATION
HERMITS CAVE
ALLEN
GROVE
CAR
PARK
CHERRY
ORCHARD
TO LUCKINGTON
TO SOPWORTH
LODGE
LUCKLEY
BRAKE
HINNEGAR
BULL PARK
WORCESTER
LODGE
DIDMARTON
OLDBURY ON THE HILL
RIDGE WOOD
TO GLOUCESTER
LITTLE
BADMINTON
KEEPERS
COTTAGE
CAPE
FARM
TO BADMINTON STN
Scale
BADMINTON 1949
PLAN OF ENDURANCE TEST COURSE
PHASE 'A' ROADS AND TRACKS . . . . . . 3·01 MILES
PHASE 'B' STEEPLECHASE COURSE . . . . 2·01 MILES
PHASE 'C' ROADS AND TRACKS . . . . . . 5·10 MILES
PHASE 'D' CROSS-COUNTRY OVER FENCES . . 3·08 MILES
PHASE 'E' CROSS-COUNTRY ON FLAT . . . . ·72 MILES
TOTAL DISTANCE 13·92 MILES

base a horse's or rider's suitability for the event. It is pertinent only to add that any rider who had cast aside all reservations and launched forward into the first Badminton was the most suitable type. Also relevant, in the light of current showings, is that, although not eligible for the Olympics, a quarter of the entry were ladies.

Forty-seven people ventured to enter the first three-day event at Badminton. Of these, for various reasons, only twenty-two declared to start, two of the non-starters being cobs; there was clearly no particular *type* of horse which could be pin-pointed as suitable for Badminton, as is still the case today, but the ultimate winner in 1949, Golden Willow, was an indication of the type which people then, and many people now, considered to be basically right; the class thoroughbred.

The first British steps at dressage were somewhat insecure: many horses were clearly not ready to accept a double bridle while a number of riders were not sure how to perform a simple change of leg or perform an accurate serpentine, the latter owing to the stiffness of these dressage-green horses. Some riders had so little control that their horses meandered through the test, some attempting to jump out of the arena, and one actually doing so, landing practically in the judges' tent!

Badminton in 1949 was a wonderfully informal affair, with both the dressage and show-jumping sections taking place in front of Badminton House. Straw bales and wagons were the grandstand seats and, for the show-jumping especially, it was difficult to gain a vantage point. Behind the 'ringside seats', people stood on their cars to obtain a better view.

Mr David Somerset, heir to the Duke of Beaufort, who was, at the time, in his own words, 'pretty ignorant about horses', remembers the 1949 Event 'as just a sort of hunter trial', such was the relaxed atmosphere of the whole competition. The crowds, though perhaps considerably more than expected, were a house party compared with the hundreds of thousands of modern times. Unlike today, it was not necessary to rope off the cross-country course and riders were able to take their own lines, thus making up time and gaining bonus marks.

People's memories of those first events, leading up to the reason for their being, the Olympic Games, are many and varied, but there is one thing shared, probably by all, and expressed by Col. Bill Lithgow. 'The whole atmosphere at Badminton was superb: I fell in love with it from the word go!' Richard Meade remembers the first Event as 'a very friendly, small affair', with crowds on the course sufficiently scanty to allow 'a picnic by one of the fences the other side of the Luckington Lane'.

Making his début in 1952 as a potential Olympic rider was a very successful point-to-point and National Hunt jockey, from the West Country, who had been introduced to eventing by Tony Collings, who reckoned that, with a good grounding in dressage, he could become a world-class event rider. Today Bertie Hill is still regarded as one of the great *natural* horsemen of all time. Thrown in at the deep end, Bertie's introduction to eventing was two rides at Badminton, on Banbridge Boy and Stealaway, and he remembers the Event 'in those days was informal and great fun; everyone knew everyone else'. He then went on to represent Britain in Helsinki, making history with his team colleague Reg Hindley in being the first two civilians ever to represent Britain in Olympic three-day eventing. He made an auspicious start which must have more than repaid Tony Collings's faith in him, finishing eighth individual at Helsinki on (the then Major), John Miller's mare Stella. A groom to the Olympic horses in 1952, Wendy Marshall (then Jones) sums up the atmosphere among the riders as 'more of dedication than competition'.

There was obviously still a strong military entry, and it was in 1952 that the commanding officer of the King's Troop, Royal Horse Artillery, first stumbled upon 'Badminton'. His position today makes the account of Col. Weldon (then Major) particularly interesting.

Col. Bill Lithgow competing at Badminton in 1961. '. . . I fell in love with it from the word go . . .'

41

The informality of the early events. The Royal party mingles with the crowd as Major Rook and Starlight gallop by.

In his typically blunt, dry manner, Col. Weldon tells his own story:

The only reason that I got interested was that I was sent to command a small mounted unit in London called the King's Troop, RHA, and I was searching for something I thought was worthwhile for the young officers to do on their government horses in summer.

In the winter we went hunting in Leicestershire where we kept our horses for nothing at the Army Remount Depot. That was fine but in the summer they went show-jumping and although they picked the smaller shows round London, halfway through any competition a cattle-truck would drive up and two or three horses belonging to a garage owner called Mr Payne would come down the ramp, to be ridden by a sixteen-year-old boy called Alan Oliver.

Every now and again one of the young officers would jump a clear round, but in the end Alan Oliver would usually finish first, second and third. So I didn't think that was very profitable but it was no good encouraging them to go racing, as I was doing, as their horses were hardly suitable.

Then one evening, an old general came to dinner and told us that he had been to Badminton and what a good thing it was. I couldn't think of what he was talking about, because the only thing I could think of connected with Badminton, involved a high net, small racquets and balls with feathers on. However, when he mentioned the steeplechase and cross-country it made me prick up my ears and the next day I sent one of the subalterns down to the British Horse Society headquarters, which in those days were in Sloane Street, to find out what this Badminton thing was all about.

He brought back a schedule and sure enough there was the steeplechase and cross-country, but I said 'Hey! What's this dressage you have to do first?'

That worried me a bit, but I said 'Come on. We'll have a go at this', and two or three months later, in the spring of 1952, two young officers and myself set off for Badminton. The two boys on their government chargers got safely round and returned to London delighted with their exploits. The major, I regret to say, had not taken nearly as much trouble to prepare as he should

Bertie Hill, one of the great natural horsemen, seen here riding Banbridge Boy in 1952.

and although he was riding a much classier horse, which jumped a bit out hunting, spent a week in Tetbury Cottage Hospital after a crashing fall at one of the easier cross-country fences. That was bad for morale and persuaded me to take it more seriously in future!

How seriously he then took it on his legendary Kilbarry, leading the British team to success after success during the 1950s, forms a golden chapter in the history of British eventing. But Col. Weldon's last remark is also indicative of one of the major factors which has shaped eventing from the easy, happy-go-lucky atmosphere into the very serious business it is today. Though today's riders obviously only compete because they *enjoy* eventing, and indeed it is still the most amateur of sports, their attitudes have had to become more professional. Eventing is big business and the top horses are worth thousands of pounds. With ever-increasing standards, riders must work hard and be totally dedicated to keep at the top. While not suggesting for a minute that the riders of the early days did not take Badminton seriously, it is no longer a game for all and sundry on their favourite hunter or retired point-to-pointer: it is an exacting test for *eventers*, the new type of horse which has emerged over the last thirty years.

Such an impression had the first Badminton upon the horse world that the very next year Col. W. E. Lyon wrote in *The Horseman's Year*, that 'After the first and highly successful effort in 1949, we have come to expect the machine to run perfectly smoothly, in other words, we now take it all rather for granted, forgetting the fact that it all calls for endless forethought, careful planning and hard work on the part of, first, the Duke of Beaufort who, by his generosity and enthusiasm, makes the Event possible; then Col. Trevor Horn who, as chief director, aided by a small but select army of helpers, worked unceasingly to make it a success.'

From the little acorn, the sapling was growing fast. In 1950, only one year after

Reg Hindley on Speculation. He and Bertie Hill were the first two civilians to represent Britain in the Olympic Three-Day Event.

Britain had seen its first national three-day event, an estimated 20,000 people attended Badminton; and this, it can easily be forgotten, when travelling was not quite so easy and fast as it is today, although one could catch a train from Paddington which stopped at Badminton. By special arrangement with British Railways, express trains delivered spectators in time for each day's programme and those travelling from London could be back in town by eight o'clock the same evening, having dined on board train. The huge crowds also caused the now age-old problem of spectators being unable to locate their cars at the end of the day. Having experienced such difficulty in 1950, Mr Peter Bedford, formerly from Warwickshire, attached a 'landmark' to his car the following year, consisting of drain rods and a sweep's brush. So grateful were other spectators for Mr Bedford's ingenuity that there apparently followed quite a party.

What was more surprising at Badminton in 1950 was the unprecedented interest that people were taking in dressage. Whereas previously, spectators around a dressage arena had been the exception rather than the rule, it was reported that a crowd 3,000-strong took the keenest interest in watching the 1950 competitors perform their tests. Enthusiasts were educated in what 'to note at Badminton' by Col. Trevor Horn in a prelude to the 1950 event in *Horse and Hound*. Of course, not for long was Badminton the only horse trial in Britain, and one-day events soon sprang up, thus providing, as they do today, a basic introduction and schooling ground for three-day events.

Despite the obvious success of eventing as a sport for both spectator and competitor the 1950 Event brought a note of pessimism from some observers. Badminton had repeated its earlier success but British three-day eventing was halfway along the road to the Olympics and many considered that not enough young potential riders and horses had emerged. On paper it was hoped to select sixteen horses to

Bertie Hill's Helsinki mount, Stella, seen here ridden by her owner, the then Major, John Miller at Badminton in 1952.

go into initial training at Porlock, in the October prior to the Olympics. This would be narrowed down to ten for final training from April onwards, together with six selected riders. In 1950, however, there was nothing like the number of horses on hand from which the selectors could have chosen the desired quota.

The dressage was much improved among the top horses in 1950 but the remainder were only average and some not even that. Tony Collings, on Remus, managed to maintain his dressage lead throughout the event to win by a short neck from the 1949 winner, John Shedden, this time on Mrs Fanshawe's King-pin. Remus failed on speed across country, however, and, at ten years old in 1950, it was felt he was not really Olympic material. *Horse and Hound* evaluated the various tests at Badminton for the now critical audience, noting the value of the dressage in the three-day event 'both from the point of view of marks, and of the muscling up and suppling of the horse for the second- and third-day tests, not to mention his hardiness and instant obedience'. All the winning animals had done a good test. 1948 Olympic rider Brig. Lyndon Bolton on Letham commanded the most wonderfully graphic description, surely, of what performing a dressage test is all about. They 'swept into the ring and carried out the movements with breathtaking panache. What a showman!' Finishing the dressage equal fourth, and the second day in a strong position, he was unfortunately disqualified in the show-jumping. Indeed, while the best riders were undoubtedly concentrating on their dressage, the show-jumping was a very, very weak link. Only one person managed a clear round in the first ten – John Shedden on Golden Willow who finished fifth – but he incurred time faults in doing so, as indeed did five others in the top bracket, including the winner.

The 1950 Badminton had a lesson to teach. Without the greatest dedication to schooling and training, no amount of the traditional

John Shedden on Kingpin – just beaten into second place in 1950.

British skill, fitness and courage would produce the desired result.

There was one other observation; a greater number of high-class horses was needed to swell the reserve of potential mounts from which the selectors could choose. *The Horseman's Year* explained the dilemma: 'It is a lot to expect of a private individual these days, that he or she will surrender a good hunter, point-to-point horse or promising 'chaser to train for the job, especially if that person cannot ride in the event.' This question of the owner riding possibly bears no more significance today than in 1950, but *The Horseman's Year* went on to suggest another scheme, the emergence of which we are only just beginning to see now, as we enter the 1980s. Although there has always been an Olympic equestrian fund (the British Horse Society sought between £7,000–£8,000 to train and send a team to Helsinki) 'The answer is that the money to buy suitable horses must come out of the Olympic and International Equestrian Fund. It's all too easy except that the fund is not sufficiently endowed to be able to send teams abroad to gain experience, and also to buy horses and the two things are interdependent.... Therefore more and more money must be raised to swell the fund by every means possible!' A cry just as applicable today as then, but one which now, increasingly, the new Horse Trials Support Group with schemes for both individual and company sponsorship is answering. It is now *becoming* possible for the national body to purchase horses, but it is an expensive business and one in which we are at a severe disadvantage since, unlike many other countries, our own government allows no allocation of funds to strengthen our Olympic effort. It is still now, as then, an entirely voluntary exercise.

The British Horse Society, as the National Federation, fostered and nurtured the growing sport: they too had taken a bold step in backing the first eventing venture at Badminton, but now it was beginning to pay dividends. They lent support not only by giving technical advice, but also by donating prize money and awards to the spreading number of one-day events. But more than this, they were investigating ways to encourage the right type of horse to be trained – and possibly looking further ahead, to be bred – with combined training in mind. In *Horse and Hound* ('Explaining policies', 1951), Capt. Tony Collings wrote 'It [the British Horse Society] is also anxious to instigate the holding of Prix Caprilli tests (dressage and jumping) and working hunter competitions (judged on conformation, ride and manners, and jumping) calculated to interest people in this form of training, and encouraging them to keep the type of horse required for the three-day event.' This, in the long-term policy, would bring to the fore the potentially ideal Olympic horse and rider.

The Olympic Games were the goal towards which Badminton aimed and upon which the whole concept of the three-day event was based. After the 1950 Event, although even by then it was a case of 'a rose by any other name ...' for the equestrian world, confusion had arisen among the general public between the new horse event and the well-established racquet game which had also had its origins at the home of the Dukes of Beaufort. To keep the records straight the Badminton Three-Day Event was retitled, announcing the direct link between the original and its imitator. From the 1951 Event, the ever-increasing crowds flocked into the Park to witness the success or failure of our riders at the Olympic Horse Trials, Badminton.

3

THE OLYMPIC HORSE TRIALS

An Olympic team Gold Medal is the ultimate prize 'beside which,' says Col. Frank Weldon, 'all other international aspirations pale into insignificance'.

There is simply nothing to match the prestige and honour of success at the Olympic Games, the unique gathering of the world's finest athletes and sportsmen although, to quote the well-known words of Baron de Courbertin, the founder of the modern Olympics, 'The important thing in the Olympic Games is not winning, but taking part, for the essential thing in life is not so much conquering as fighting well.' To win, however, is the pinnacle of achievement.

As previous chapters have explained, it was to form a staging camp on the difficult track to the Olympic pinnacle that the Duke of Beaufort's visionary experiment at Badminton ever took place. The idea, wrote Trevor Horn in 1953, was to 'find and train a team to compete with honour if not success at the Games in 1952'. Honour was most certainly upheld; but more of that later.

The road to the 1952 Games was long and difficult, holding many pitfalls for the unwary. No one expected overnight success; training horses is a task of years, not months, but with the unique facility at Badminton, as well as the growing number of one-day events, hopes for our riders' success must have been raised when, in 1951, Badminton opened its gates 'to the world'. For the first time it was a truly international event with, as the programme described, the 'team championship of Europe' staged concurrently with the 'individual championship open to the world'. The success of the first two Badmintons must have given the committee great confidence to accept the added burden of holding such a championship, but, though not entirely misplaced, the committee's confidence extended beyond our riders' capabilities at that stage; nor could such confidence be placed in the April weather, which played havoc with the course. In a nightmare situation, Col. Horn and his team slaved under appalling conditions. *Horse and Hound* reported:

Mr Ted Marsh on Wild Venture.

> It is no exaggeration to say that nothing but a bull-dozer determination and an absolute conviction that the Trials must at all costs be held enabled the Duke, the organizing committee of the British Horse Society and all those who worked on the courses, to stage it. The first cross-country course to be built became impracticable owing to the state of the land, so a second was prepared and succumbed to the same fate as the first one. The third was not finished until the evening of the first day...!

Happily for the organizers the show went on, but unhappily for British riders and their Olympic hopes, the first international Event was carried away convincingly by the Swiss on their totally obedient dressage-trained horses. Commenting on the Swiss victory, *The Horseman's Year* wrote: 'It was most noticeable, particularly at the "queer" fences,

Jane Drummond-Hay, here on Abbeyfeale, finished second in 1952.

such as the pond jump, the "coffin" ... how in hand, on the bit and entirely obedient were these foreign dressage-trained horses in the hands of their equally dressage-trained riders.' Experience has taught us that this strict discipline – to the extent of making the horse a slave to his dominantly dressage-minded rider – does not suit the temperament of highly couraged British horses which have been bred from generations of racehorses and hunters; it merely serves to break the noble spirit rather than channel that incomparable quality, willingly to serve and display brilliance. However, the problem in 1951 was that many horses had never been given even a basic schooling as youngsters. They had been taught to run before they could walk and their subsequent training was described in *Horse and Hound* as 'either superimposed or too fragmentary'. This, of course, was not true of all of the British horses, some of which put up creditable dressage performances, notably Happy Knight (ridden by its owner, Miss Jane Drummond-Hay – now Whiteley), which finished second overall, nineteen points behind Capt. Hans Schwarzenbach on Vae Victis. The Olympic Three-Day Event was still, however, a male preserve and, while Miss Drummond-Hay could not be considered for selection, her horse became one of the very few genuine Helsinki possibles. Indeed, the selection committee had to cast its net far and wide in its search for horses which had substance and quality, the sum of which was Olympic potential. Polish could be added during the winter months of training planned under Capt. Tony Collings at his Porlock establishment. Slowly the right type of horse was emerging and Badminton was beginning to show its worth. Lionel Dawson wrote in *The Horseman's Year*.

I really believe that this year's Event [1951] has convinced the vast majority of the value of Badminton in reference to the Olympiad. It has also, I believe, established the meeting as a permanency on its own merits which will attract many who have no Olympic ambitions and will produce dividends for those who can produce a suitable horse. The Duke of Beaufort, to whom this splendid outing is entirely due, announced that it will be held next year, Olympiad notwithstanding. The Olympiad is, however, our present goal.'

As Badminton led the field in the organization of eventing, the British Horse Society delegated responsibility for the selection of a team to the 'Badminton Committee for Combined Training Matters' whose task was simplified by being able to refer to performance at their own event – a facility not available to the selectors of the 1948 Olympic team. Nothing was left to chance, and, while Tony Collings had been appointed trainer and manager, he recognized his own inadequacies in the field of dressage training, and Herr Richard Waetjen, who had trained the highly successful American team in 1948, was engaged to look after this part of the training programme. The Olympic 'possibles' started preliminary training in October 1951 – the Great Auclum one-day event having provided a selection test for those to go into training – and arrived at Porlock in January 1952, allowing seven months of concentrated work. Experience was the one vital factor that these riders needed and Tony Collings persuaded local shows to include FEI show-jumping competitions in their programmes to enable the Olympic horses, which were all novices in this field, to gain the experience of jumping in public. The winter months were spent training over cross-country fences and throughout the whole seven months the dressage training continued steadily. In April, of course, there was Badminton and from then on a full programme of public appearances was arranged, leading up to the team's departure in July, including the one-day event at Sherbourne and outings to dressage tests and show-jumping competitions.

From the outset lack of funds was a major problem. The British Horse Society could act as nothing more than an advisory body and the entire cost of producing horses and riders, and sending them to the Olympics was borne by voluntary contribution. 'In principle this policy is all wrong of course, but it will probably go on for ever,' wrote W. E. Lyon prophetically. The estimated cost of the venture was £7,000–£8,000 and, above all, a handful of 'ideal owners' was needed of the type described by Col. Lyon in *The Horseman's Year* as 'a saint-like patriotic, private person who either possesses or buys a horse for the sole purpose of contributing to the prestige of the British nation in the Olympic Games'.

Although in 1949 Col. Lyon thought that such characters lived 'vaguely in the regions of that mythical Castle in the Air', several did descend into the realms of reality and by 1951 a number had generously volunteered their horses. The selection was still much scantier than that from which foreign rivals would have had to choose, but it was generally felt that, despite the lack of training, the British horses were of a better type than those available in other countries. Thus, from the beginning, we had the best material with which to build.

In the long term, although the ultimate test for a potential Olympic horse would be to prove its ability at Badminton, it was soon realized that eventers could not live on Badminton alone. A plan had been submitted to the British Horse Society in 1951 by the South Berks. Hunt for the running of a scaled-down version of the three-day event, less taxing for horses, competitors and organizers, but they needed a guarantee from the National Federation. The late Henry Wynmalen, as Master of the Woodland Foxhounds, was asked to look into the scheme, but he went one step further than this and himself organized the first-ever one-day event. Following his action, Tony Collings and Col. Guy Cubitt, then chairman of the British Horse Society, and until his death in 1979 still involved with Badminton, particularly as a member of the committee of appeal, set about persuading other people to hold similar events, thus giving the Olympic possibles opportunity to improve their performances.

The type of long-term, team training into which potential riders entered in 1952 would not be practicable today, even if desirable. Then it was a question of concentrated, expensive training or getting nowhere. The 1951 event had shown that our riders and horses still had a long way to go before they could compete on equal terms with their foreign rivals and, as the best knowledge was restricted, it was necessary to collect the best of the riders together to gain the benefit of that limited expertise. Now riders themselves are so much more knowledgeable of the requirements of the three-day event, and will turn to the experience of trainers to iron out particular problems and improve the general performance. One such trainer is, of course, Bertie Hill, who was amongst the six riders who collected at Porlock in January 1952. The others were Mr Reg Hindley, the team captain, Com. John Oram, Major John Miller, now Crown Equerry, Major Lawrence Rook, now chairman of the Horse Trials Group Committee, an FEI Technical Delegate and member of the Badminton Committee, and Capt. Michael Naylor-Leyland, who has been Technical Delegate at Badminton over the past few years. Major Rook recalls: 'I well remember Tony Collings's dedication to one goal, the Olympic medals at Helsinki. He drove us very hard and we were practically never off a horse's back, running up a mountain or doing something which ultimately made us fitter or better prepared to attain that goal. He had the good sense to realize when we were getting stale, and allowed us to break training, but made quite sure we made up for it later. We ate, thought and dreamed of nothing but the Olympic Games to come, and Tony Collings saw to it that we had few outside distractions.'

These six riders, with their eleven mounts, rode at Badminton in 1952 under strict training orders. It was to be used purely as a schooling ground, to save the horses for the greater task in hand, a system which Bertie Hill strongly believes prolonged a horse's three-day event career. The whole atmosphere was relaxed and relationships between trainers, team and grooms remained on a good, even keel. The idea was, however, to present horses and riders with the type of fences they would be likely to meet in Helsinki and alterations and additions were made to the course as a result of Tony Collings's and John Shedden's visits to events in northern Europe. Col. Lyon reported in *The*

Major Lawrence Rook on Starlight: an Olympic 'possible' in 1952.

Horseman's Year that 'in order to conform with the sort of conditions likely to be met with in the Olympic Games, several new fences were put in a wood – all fairly close together and at odd angles needing a bold, handy and obedient horse'.

By the time the Olympic possibles arrived at Badminton, by invitation of the Duke and Duchess of Beaufort, a week before the event for special training, all the horses had a good deal more eventing mileage under their girths. The one-day events had done their job, as had various dressage and show-jumping competitions which had been organized with the Olympics in mind. The riders had improved markedly and the general concensus of opinion was that our team would put up an average dressage performance at Helsinki which would enable the team to go into the second day in a healthy position.

The most vivid recollection of the very happy pre-Badminton week is given by Mrs Wendy Marshall (then Jones) who had been invited to join the Olympic team as groom by Tony Collings, with whom she had worked on the teaching staff at Porlock prior to travelling with Col. Harry Llewellyn's show-jumpers:

My fellow girl grooms and I lived in Badminton House under the scrupulous attention of housekeeper and butler. We had all home comforts and wonderful food – we were *always* hungry! Our day began at 5 am and ended at 7 pm with the usual routine of pre-breakfast ride on our particular horses – in my case, Bambi V – for one and a half hours in the Park, home for a rub-down, skip-out of stables, and morning feed. The horses were left to rest, well rugged-up whilst we had our breakfast.

At 10 am the team rode under the supervision of Capt. Collings and Richard Waetjen, whilst we cleaned the stables thoroughly before the horses returned. Whenever we could we liked to watch the horses working, but this was not always possible.

Great courtesy and consideration was shown by the Duke and Duchess of Beaufort – even to the extent of giving us each a large bar of choco-

Capt. Michael Naylor-Leyland competing in the pre-Olympic Badminton.

Bambi V with Bertie Hill up. 'She would attack her work . . . her ears laid flat against her neck.'

late for our journey to Helsinki! The concern foı our welfare was constant and I admired the Duke's ability to remember the names and faces of all whom he encountered. It made one feel special and part of a great occasion.

On the day of the competition, it was agony watching whether Speculation or Starlight became over-exuberant in the dressage test! These particularly highly couraged horses were inclined to explode into squeals and bucks.

Bambi V became marish and would attack her work with enormous ability, her ears laid flat against her neck. She would sometimes return to the stables in this mood after work and I had to groom her with great tact, and equally tactfully leave her comfortable and warm, and strictly undisturbed if she was to finish eating her subsequent feed.

Speculation was a difficult feeder. Many bottles of beer and milk and eggs were coaxed down his throat before any event. He could smell a competition days before and his appetite would vanish.

The team members were extremely kind to us and even-tempered at all times. My memories of Com. Oram who rode Bambi and Michael Naylor-Leyland include wonderfully witty repartee if I became a little short-tempered under pressure of work! Invariably amusing, it made me remember that their responsibilities were far greater than mine!

Richard Waetjen's private dressage display on his own mare before the Royal Family was an example of skill and discipline executed against the background of the green Park and Badminton House with no sound but that of the touch of the horse's hooves on the fresh grass of the new arena, while the morning the royal visitors inspected the horses in the stables was particularly memorable. Each groom was instructed to present her horse to the Queen, but no one could tell us whether one curtsyed or bowed when holding the end of a halter rope – Olympic girl grooms were unique!

The preparation of the team was not without problems. Major Miller sustained a heavy fall over a small, unfixed show jump, breaking a vertebrae, but undeterred he returned to complete Badminton two months later. At the very last minute, literally on the day the team departed for Helsinki, Michael Naylor-Leyland contracted chickenpox and could not compete, while possibly the worst tragedy was that which befell his prospective Olympic mount, Savoyarde. Wendy Marshall was in charge of this mare, which was, in Tony Collings's opinion, possibly their most brilliant performer, but which, tragically in training, stepped on a low horizontal railing which snapped back and staked her deeply in the groin:

Her life hung in the balance for a week after her injury and each of us took turns to be with her day and night until the crisis was over. She lost a great deal of condition and was very weak for a long time, finally recovering in the summer. When she was at Badminton with the other horses she still looked very thin and ill. My routine was to feed, nurse and keep her contented and she derived much benefit from the sun and rest and excellent grass in the Park where I would lead her as often as possible to graze.

However, during the three-day event, when the stables were open to the public, a lady was horrified at the sight of poor Savoyarde collapsed in her usual morning rest, stretched full out in the deep golden straw. She certainly did look a wreck and the good member of the public, unwilling to accept any kind of explanation, rushed off to report the matter to the RSPCA. She obviously thought that the poor little mare had been worked into the ground and horribly neglected!

Eventually she was persuaded otherwise.

Tony Collings reported that, from the beginning, the team seemed to get more than its share of bad luck, but the cruellest misfortune was yet to come. Nineteen teams started the competition on 30 July 1952 – the final selection for Britain being Reg Hindley on Speculation, Bertie Hill on Stella and Lawrence Rook on Starlight, and, wrote Capt. Collings, 'I do not think three fitter horses entered the competition.' The dressage scores were slightly disappointing for the British who had felt reasonably confident in their performance but nevertheless they finished the first day in ninth position. More remarkable was that we, the British team, lay just half a point behind the Swiss who had beaten our riders so convincingly at Badminton the previous year.

On the second day Britain scaled the heights and plumbed the depths. After promising performances by Reg Hindley with Speculation and Bertie Hill with Stella, who each finished with bonus points on the speed and endurance section, the British camp realized they were making a very strong challenge for the Gold Medal. Lawrence Rook was the last to ride in the whole competition and the position was clear. In mounting excitement came the news, first that he had gained maximum bonus on the steeplechase, and then that he had successfully negotiated the difficult quarry fence. five from home. When Rook came into view four minutes up on time and galloping effortlessly with only one easy fence to jump, the British were ecstatic.

For a fleeting moment we had visions of a Gold Medal for the team and Individual Medal for Lawrence Rook – when tragedy entered the scene. Rounding a slight bend, on the right-hand side of which there was an overhanging branch, Rook pulled over to the left and, in doing so, Starlight pecked badly at a small and quite blind irrigation gutter that ran at right angles to the track. He blundered, half recovered, then put his foot in another little gutter and turned 'end over end'. Rook was, for the moment, completely knocked out. But all was not yet lost. Starlight was quickly caught and two friendly Finns carried Rook to his horse, where he recovered sufficiently to be helped back into the saddle. With his rider still dazed, Starlight galloped on to clear the last fence and, despite the delay, the score board two miles away showed a bonus of sixty.

The drama had not been played out. Completely stunned by the fall, Lawrence Rook lost his way and began to wander off the course of the run-in Phase E, missing an apparently unimportant turning flag. But rules are rules and Rook's elimination meant that the team award was lost. Ironically, Bertie Hill and Reg Hindley put up competitive performances in the following day's show-jumping to leave them seventh and thirteenth respectively. There was consolation to be gained, however. Had it not been for Lawrence Rook's desperate misfortune, the British team would most certainly have been in the medals. They had competed with honour, if not success, just four years since the first Badminton had put eventing on the map and pointed the way to the Olympic Games.

There was no time to dwell on misfortunes. The greatest attribute an event rider can possess is resilience in the face of setbacks and the next task in hand was Badminton 1953, again host to the European Championships and starting the four-year Olympic cycle leading up to Stockholm in 1956. This was the first Official International three-day event, the Concours Complet Internationale Officiel (CCIO), to be held under the auspices of the FEI and, while individual entries were made from seven different countries, those fielding teams numbered a disappointing three: Great Britain, Ireland and Switzerland, the latter no doubt out for a repeat of their 1951 performance! They were never given the chance, however. The British team was on the threshold of the door to unrivalled international success throughout the 1950s and, although dropped from the team, literally at the eleventh hour because his horse could not be relied upon in the dressage, Major Lawrence Rook and Starlight went part of the way to making up for their Helsinki disaster by winning Badminton convincingly with a score of +5.3! Not since Capt. B. M. Chevalier and Aiglonne had won the 1948 Gold Medal with +4, had a plus score been recorded in a three-day event

The Hon. Patrick Connolly-Carew seen here in 1962 on Ballyhoo.

Miss Iris Kellet on Glentoi in 1951.

and *Horse and Hound* reported, 'It is almost unheard of for a horse to finish a three-day event with a plus score!'

The vacant place in the team was filled at the last minute by an ex-racehorse which had been Hobdayed and his rider, the commander of the King's Troop, Royal Horse Artillery. The horse, Kilbarry, and his owner, Major Frank Weldon, had just won the first one-day event at Stowell Park, but their inclusion in the team was to have far-reaching effects on British eventing which remain to the present. The new combination, though entirely self-made, amply justified the selectors' confidence by finishing second to Lawrence Rook, and with Reg Hindley at sixth and Bertie Hill completing on Bambi V, the British were the only team left in the race to take the European team honours. *Horse and Hound* reported: 'This, our first major victory in this type of international competition, augurs well for the future of British success in this form of sport, and in the opinion of the foreign riders who competed at Badminton, British horses and riders would now more than hold their own in world-wide competition.'

Sadly, while Badminton had given life to British international eventing, the 1953 event was the first and last at which an Official International competition was held. The lack of team entries was indicative of the fact that, owing to the severe European winters, continental riders were unable to prepare their horses to three-day event fitness by early spring. Thus, while Badminton had become our National Championship, our international selection trial, and the most important event for many foreign riders as well as British, apart from the Olympic Games, it can never again hold European or World Championship status.

Horse trials were catching on like proverbial wildfire and, as chairman of both the British Horse Society and the Badminton Committee, Col. Guy Cubitt saw a need for a new controlling body for combined training matters. In the autumn of 1952, Mr Neil Gardiner, an early convert to the sport and founder of the Great Auclum one-day event, was invited to chair the new Combined Training Committee whose initial task was the administration of one-day events, but after the 1953 European Championships at Bad-

A competitor of very long standing, Harry Freeman-Jackson on Brown Sugar in 1954.

minton, they also became responsible for international team selection. The new committee's first project was to send a team to the 1954 European Championships in Switzerland but they were to suffer a crushing blow in the spring of that year. Before Badminton Tony Collings was dead, the victim of a plane crash over the Mediterranean. Combined training had lost not only one of its staunchest supporters but the very kingpin around which the international wheel revolved. If it could be said that the Duke of Beaufort was the architect of British eventing, and Col. Horn and the Badminton Committee dug the foundations, few would argue that Capt. Tony Collings, as the first trainer and manager, laid the foundation stone upon which all our subsequent international successes have been built. In 1963 Lawrence Rook wrote: 'I remember when Capt. Tony Collings was killed . . . everyone said how much combined training was going to miss him, and I think that only now are we beginning to realize how true those words were. Tony Collings could borrow horses from anyone. I think he "charmed" them out of their owners before they realized what had happened, carried them off to Porlock and set about training them.'

Badminton went ahead on 21–23 April 1954 under the new directorship of Col. Gordon Cox-Cox. 'Now in its sixth year,' wrote Mrs V. D. S. Williams, in *Horse and Hound*, 'the Trials have a triumphant career and are now world-famous; this has been in no small way due to the generosity, drive and initiative of His Grace the Duke of Beaufort.' The reserve Olympic horse, Bambi V, ridden by his owner Miss Margaret Hough, produced the best dressage test and, although they finished the speed and endurance in second place to Major Weldon on Kilbarry, two mistakes by the latter in the show-jumping let Miss Hough through to win. The Weldon–Kilbarry combination was showing its strength and the Combined Training Committee saw in Major Weldon the very qualities for which they were looking. He was immediately invited to become both team captain *and* manager. Neil Gardiner wrote of him:

> Frank Weldon was the first Englishman to go into the top class of international three-day events entirely on his own efforts and without any of the British Horse Society training that others received. Already members of the King's Troop,

Her Majesty the Queen, the Duke of Beaufort and Col. Gordon Cox-Cox who took over the directorship in 1954.

which he commanded, were in the money at most of the events that they could get to. It was clear that the success of the King's Troop was due to the leadership of their Commanding Officer who left nothing to chance and saw to it that his officers were organized.

The burden of taking on the job of both captain and manager would have daunted a lesser person but Col. Weldon's organizing capabilities are legendary; as of course is the success achieved by the British team he led, which was invincible in international competition. In 1954 with Kilbarry, Crispin and Starlight they won the European Championship at Basle and Bertie Hill took the individual title. 'Badminton' and the European Championship moved to Windsor in 1955 by special invitation of HM the Queen, and this time Kilbarry, who gave the best show of his life in the dressage, went on to win convincingly with a score of +4.676. Bertie Hill came third on Countryman II which he later had to make the heartbreaking decision to sell, in order to buy sheep and cattle to stock his new farm, but which happily was bought by HM the Queen, so the partnership continued. Starlight, although performing a sketchy dressage, finished the Event to leave the British team in championship position again.

1956 was, of course, Olympic year and, although the main Games took place in Australia, quarantine restrictions on horses in that country meant that an alternative venue had to be found for the equestrian games, which were staged at Stockholm in June of that year. After Tony Collings's untimely death the new Combined Training Committee set up a selection sub-committee under the experienced chairmanship of Brig. Bowden-Smith. Col. V. D. S. Williams was appointed trainer and took the responsibility for dressage schooling and Col. Jack Talbot-Ponsonby agreed to supervise jumping instruction. Neil Gardiner wrote, 'Col.

Frank Weldon – pictured here on Young Pretender in 1962 – was the first Englishman to go to the top class of international three-day events entirely on his own efforts.

Weldon, as captain and manager, came in for the lion's share of the work. His job carried with it a good deal of the work of a trainer in that he was responsible for the fitness of horses and riders. As manager the responsibility included the welfare of the whole party.' From 1954–7 HM the Queen made available the facilities at Windsor for the international team to train for six weeks before any major competition with a tactful temporary move away from there prior to the 1955 European Championships, and from here the attack was launched on the 1956 Olympics.

Badminton, of course, was the final selection trial. Frank Weldon confirmed his value as team captain by winning for the second year running and, as he had won the event at Harewood the previous autumn, the Badminton victory meant three successive three-day event wins. A remarkable record. Bertie Hill won his ticket to Stockholm by finishing fourth on Countryman and

Below: *Her Majesty the Queen presents Frank Weldon with his prizes after his second Badminton win.*

Lawrence Rook remained in the team, but Starlight was out, having become completely out of hand in the dressage arena. 'Probably the most promising novice horse seen for years', Mr E. E. Marsh's Wild Venture was in instead, and became Major Rook's Olympic mount.

At last, after eight years of planning and an inordinate amount of work by numerous people following the Duke of Beaufort's example, an Olympic Gold Medal really began to look like reality. The conditions in Stockholm were atrocious and each member of the team very nearly came unstuck; Frank Weldon and Lawrence Rook by taking a line into the trakehner which they had discussed but not actually walked, and Bertie Hill when Countryman became straddled across the same fence. Fortunately, Col. Cox-Cox, an extremely knowledgeable horseman, was on hand and instructed a party of Swedish soldiers to pull Countryman back off the fence. Put at it again, Countryman flew the fence as though nothing had happened. Luck had undeniably played a part but, thankfully, this time *for* our team rather than against it. The team Gold Medal was safely in British hands for the first time: but for his one mistake, Frank Weldon would have won the Individual Gold.

The value of Badminton had been undeniably proved and the seal was set on the charter which proclaimed Britain on top of the world in three-day eventing. Badminton, by this time, had undergone another name change. The 'Olympic Horse Trials', conflicted with the prerogative of the Olympic Association and it became known, in 1956, as it is today – the Badminton Horse Trials.

The Golden Age of the 1950s was nearly at an end. With triumph came disaster and in the autumn of 1956 Frank Weldon lost Kilbarry, who died instantly of a broken neck in a fall at the first fence of the Cottesbrooke one-day event. He had never finished out of the first three in any international competition and, although Col. Weldon rode several other horses, including Young Pretender, who was second to Merely-a-Monarch at Badminton, and Samuel Johnson, who was second at the European Championships at Harewood in 1959, there was never another to touch Kilbarry's brilliance. Lawrence Rook announced his retirement from three-day eventing and Countryman was sold to David Somerset, who himself began to compete at Badminton. A eulogy for the team was best expressed by Dorian Williams: 'Surely, to be able to produce three horses like Kilbarry, Wild Venture and Countryman happens to a nation only once in a lifetime.'

'To produce three horses like Kilbarry, Wild Venture and Countryman happens to a nation once in a lifetime . . .'

1956 marked both the end and the beginning of an era. Combined Training was making its own way as the stature of eventing grew and, through the profits from Badminton, was making money for the British Horse Society. The organization and the system of team selection was becoming more recognizable to modern eyes and, when qualifications were introduced for Badminton in 1958, it was an indication that the whole thing was being taken a mite more seriously. New riders were appearing to consolidate the British position. Unbeatable in her time, Sheila Willcox won three consecutive Badmintons – an unequalled record – and led the 1957 team to victory in the European Championships in Copenhagen when she herself

took the individual title. To her chagrin women were still barred from the Olympic Three-Day Event and the supreme title thus eluded her. Another rider to make his début at that time was Major Derek Allhusen, whose brilliantly consistent mare Laurien saw him regularly in the prize money at Badminton. A reliable team horse, Laurien finished fifth and third (individual) in two consecutive European Championships to help the British teams to win and take second place respectively.

In the early 1960s, British eventing entered the doldrums: there were no team wins for ten years. Even Badminton looked in danger of folding; but that is another story. One thing that has not changed over three decades is the role which Badminton plays today as much as it did in 1949. Each year the Selection Committee still looks at the Badminton results to choose its team for the following autumn's Official International event, be it World, European or, of course, Olympic Championships. A new horse will most certainly have had to complete Badminton before it can be considered for international competition, while with the old horses, whose competitive days are numbered, the Selection Committee may use its discretion and invite them to miss Badminton. If there is a good reason for doubting a horse's continued good performance, such as the terrible mental stress imposed by the problems at the World Championships in Lexington in 1978, then without question the selectors will need to see the horse complete Badminton before it can again be considered for the British team. Therein lies our strength. Despite foreign misgivings, each year we have our international test – quite literally the 'Olympic' horse *trial* – to test, prove and reaffirm that the horses we field are more than capable of the task in hand. As we look forward, in the immediate future, to Moscow, and further ahead to Los Angeles in 1984, there is a threat which hangs over the future of the equestrian Olympics. Recent years have seen more and more difficulty in distinguishing amateurs from professionals and there are some who would like to see equestrianism dropped for once and for all from the Olympiad. One may be inclined to say, 'What does it matter? We have World Championships.' The undeniable fact is that the Olympics have an atmosphere and charisma quite unlike any other competition.

Col. Lithgow recollects: 'I have heard Richard Meade say that he wouldn't have gone on if it hadn't been for the Olympics and I'm sure that a lot of people feel the same way. Everything else is a lead-up to the Olympics; that's what makes it all worthwhile.'

Our Olympic and international record is testimony to the influences of Badminton on eventing in Britain.

British international wins

OLYMPIC GAMES

Team Gold Medals

1956, Stockholm	Major Frank Weldon on Kilbarry Major Lawrence Rook on Mr E. E. Marsh's Wild Venture Mr Bertie Hill on HM the Queen's Countryman II
1968, Mexico	Major Derek Allhusen on Lochinvar Miss Jane Bullen on Our Nobby Mr Richard Meade on Brig. M. Gordon-Watson's Cornishman V Sgt. Ben Jones on Mr M. Whiteley's The Poacher
1972, Munich	Mr Richard Meade on Major D. Allhusen's Laurieston Lt. Mark Phillips on his and Miss F. Phillips's Great Ovation Mrs Bridget Parker on Cornish Gold Miss Mary Gordon-Watson on Brig. M. Gordon-Watson's Cornishman V

Individual Gold Medal

1972, Munich	Mr Richard Meade on The Poacher

EUROPEAN CHAMPIONS

Teams

1953, Badminton	Major Frank Weldon on Kilbarry Mr Bertie Hill on Miss M. Hough's Bambi V Mr Reg Hindley on Speculation
1954, Basle	Major Frank Weldon on Kilbarry Mr Bertie Hill on Mr E. E. Marsh's Crispin Major Lawrence Rook on Mrs J. R. Baker's Starlight Miss Diana Mason on Tramella
1955, Windsor	Major Frank Weldon on Kilbarry Mr Bertie Hill on Countryman II Major Lawrence Rook on Starlight Miss Diana Mason on Tramella
1957, Copenhagen	Miss Sheila Willcox on High and Mighty Mr Ted Marsh on Wild Venture Miss Kit Tatham Warter on Pampas Cat Major Derek Allhusen on Laurien
1967, Punchestown	Major Derek Allhusen on Lochinvar Mr Richard Meade on Barberry Mr Martin Whiteley on The Poacher Sgt. Ben Jones on Miss A. B. Whiteley's Foxdor

Sheila Willcox on High and Mighty – unbeatable in her time.

Derek Allhusen and his brilliantly consistent mare, Laurien, seen here at the Vicarage Ditch.

1969, Haras du Pin	Major Derek Allhusen on Lochinvar Mr Richard Walker on Pasha Miss Pollyanne Hely-Hutchinson on the Hon. Mrs Hely-Hutchinson's Count Jasper Sgt. Ben Jones on the Combined Training Committee's The Poacher
1971, Burghley	Mr Richard Meade on The Poacher Lt. Mark Phillips on Great Ovation Miss Debbie West on Baccarat Miss Mary Gordon-Watson on Cornishman V

Individual awards

1953, Badminton	Major Lawrence Rook on Starlight
1954, Basle	Mr Bertie Hill on Crispin
1955, Windsor	Major Frank Weldon on Kilbarry
1957, Copenhagen	Miss Sheila Willcox on High and Mighty
1962, Burghley	Capt James Templer on M'Lord Connelly
1969, Haras du Pin	Miss Mary Gordon-Watson on Cornishman V
1971, Burghley	HRH Princess Anne on Doublet
1975, Lumuhlen	Miss Lucinda Prior-Palmer on Be Fair
1977, Burghley	Miss Lucinda Prior-Palmer on Mrs H. Straker's George

WORLD CHAMPIONS

Team award

1970, Punchestown	Mr Richard Meade on The Poacher Lt. Mark Phillips on Mr Bertie Hill's Chicago Mr Stewart Stevens on Benson Miss Mary Gordon-Watson on Cornishman V
Individual award	Miss Mary Gordon-Watson on Cornishman V

4

THIRTY YEARS... AND BEYOND

After thirty years as our leading horse trial, Badminton is now in its 'second generation'. Those names which were making equestrian headlines in the 1950s for their international successes which came via Badminton, are now doing the 'desk jobs': and, thanks to their knowledge and experience, as administrators of the sport they know no equals.

To take a brief look, we need go no further than to plot the careers of the members of the invincible 1953–6 team. The captain and manager, Col. Frank Weldon, has, of course, been director of Badminton since 1965; Major Lawrence Rook is chairman of the recently renamed Horse Trials Group Committee (formerly the Combined Training Group), as well as being one of the most respected FEI officials; and Bertie Hill is a highly respected trainer of event horses, including those belonging to H M the Queen. Major Derek Allhusen, who rode for Britain internationally from 1957–69 with considerable success, now breeds and trains horses and coaches riders; while chairman of the Selection Committee, Col. Bill Lithgow, competed at Badminton in the 1950s while commanding the King's Troop, RHA, although, he freely admits, the best he ever did was to get to the last fence on the cross-country before being eliminated!

It is a strength to the horse trials system to have this wealth of talent at the helm and it is equally true to attribute this strength to the innovative mind of the Duke of Beaufort. Without his tremendous foresight in 1948, Britain would most certainly not be in the same advanced position today. From Badminton stemmed the whole eventing tree, and it is indeed arguable that Britain's lead was responsible for the blossoming of the sport world-wide. Television commentator Raymond Brooks-Ward has ventured to say that without the Duke of Beaufort's idea, eventing would have taken at least another ten years to catch on in Britain. The consequences of such a delay can be left to the imagination.

Sunday morning veterinary inspection: now shown on television.

As it was, the flame lit by Badminton was soon kindled. As early as 1952, Capt. Tony Collings, who was selected to train the Olympic team for that year at his Porlock establishment wrote:

> It is little short of miraculous the way Badminton has developed from a sporting local fixture to an event of national and even international importance, in the space of four years – and even more miraculous, in spite of this expansion it has never lost its delightfully sporting character. As a result of the Three-Day Event, 'tabloid' one-day events began to spring up all over England and in the space of four years this country was awake to the possibilities of 'Combined Training' as a new equestrian sport.

Had Tony Collings lived, he would no doubt have thought it even more 'miraculous' that, by 1963, a total of 1,113 riders started in twenty-three events; fifteen years later, in 1978, seventy-eight events saw a total of 10,886 starters, and it is forecast that by

1985 or so there will be an estimated 20,000 starters in some 140 *affiliated* events, let alone the vast number of unaffiliated riding club-type competitions. He would have been equally pleased to see that, as we enter the 1980s, eventing still has a 'delightfully sporting character' about it.

The second generation is also appearing in another, truer sense. Some of those old names are appearing again on the entry lists: the sons and daughters of the pioneers are now themselves competitors.

Derek Allhusen is also responsible for another, unique, second generation. His brilliantly consistent mare Laurien, on which he finished second at Badminton in 1958, produced a son, Laurieston, which finished second at Badminton in 1972 when ridden by Richard Meade, and achieved the ultimate in 1972 with the same rider, by winning both Team and Individual Gold Medals at the Munich Olympics. A second son of Laurien, Laurieman, is now beginning to show his breeding and is no doubt a name to watch. Another double in this respect which cannot go unmentioned, although the sire did not shine at Badminton like his son, is that of Sheila Willcox's Fair and Square which sired Lucinda Prior-Palmer's brilliant Be Fair.

Eventing is, indeed, the most 'amateur' of sports in that the majority of people from all levels of the sport are able to carry on with their own business or employment. Richard Meade and Chris Collins are two very good examples at the top level, and this state of affairs largely reflects our system of team selection and training which, of necessity, does not attempt to regimentalize our international riders as, of equal necessity, it did in the past. Team trainers as such are definitely out with the British nowadays, partly because some riders will agree with their views and others will disagree, but chiefly because there is simply not the time nor the inclination to go into six weeks or so of concentrated training. Today's riders simply cannot afford to be away from their business or yard for such extensive periods. Col. Bill Lithgow, who has been involved with our international teams for over a decade as *chef d'équipe* and is now chairman of the selectors, believes that the present system is the one best suited to us. He adds a proviso: 'But of course, what you may be absolutely certain of is, as long as you're winning your system is dead right; once you start losing, everything from the colour of the farriers' socks upwards is wrong and furthermore is directly responsible for your not winning! We have got to start winning again!'

Badminton is as much the international selection trial today as it ever was. Col. Lithgow explains the procedure:

With slight adjustments each year, we meet about a week after Badminton, not before. I always think it's important to let the dust settle and really do your 'homework' first. We also arrange for such extracts from the Badminton video tapes as we think will help the meeting. At Badminton I walk the course the day before the cross-country, probably twice, so I really know it, and then I watch the event on the competitors' close circuit television, otherwise you simply don't know what's gone on. It's also convenient to be able to bob out into the 'box' and see a horse finish, or talk to someone. In any case, we let things settle for a week and sit and think and do our sums, before holding a Selectors' meeting to pick the short list. A week or so after that, Peter Scott-Dunn, our vet, the *chef d'équipe* and myself meet the riders on the short list at Peter's house. We see each rider individually and they're asked to bring along anyone they like – owners, trainers, anybody they feel can help them – and we discuss their training plans. Now this procedure is established, it is a tremendous help, particularly with the new ones, in forming a good working relationship and, we hope, mutual confidence. We ask exactly what a rider's plans are, what he's going to do about inoculations, when is he going to start fast work, what events is he thinking of doing? At the same time we tell them what our programme is and what we require of them. One likes it to be 'no holds barred' and, hopefully, at the end of it all, both sides know what the other's doing. The horses mostly go out for a fortnight to three weeks after that and have a rest. We get them together again for the International Horse Show in mid-July, asking them to compete in the Horse Trials Dressage, which is a chance to see and talk to them again, and at the same time it gives them a target at which to aim. We have a Concentration Period at Wylye about a week or so after, by which time they should have started their fast work and we can get a look at them to

Sheila Willcox on Fair and Square, sire of Lucinda Prior-Palmer's Be Fair.

see how it's going. The part that, hopefully, we can influence most, is the fitness. A lot of people argue that the riders know their horses best. This is so but I refuse to believe that, certainly the young ones, can possibly know all there is to know about fitness. But at the same time, with Herr Bachinger from the Spanish Riding School doing dressage training for those who want him, and other trainers of the riders' own choice, it's also very much a get-together to build up team spirit. We have a final work-out at a horse trial about three weeks before the international competition concerned, a few days of rest and then back to Wylye for another week before departing for the event a few days in advance.

Some people ask, why this preoccupation with the team award? Quite simply, it is the most difficult, and therefore the most worthwhile, award to win. Any country can produce a brilliant individual combination, but it is something more – indeed a great achievement – to be able to field a team of consistently good performers. Hugh Thomas, who rode in the British team at the Montreal Olympics, values the team competition and 'from a purely selfish point of view, I value the distinction – if it is one – of riding in a British team. Somehow, to be selected for a British team and to represent one's country as a part of a team, is more worthwhile and more interesting than doing it individually.' 'Veteran' of four Olympic Games, so far, Richard Meade has voiced a more practical consideration. Without the team competition, raising money for our international ventures could become even more difficult than at present. Supporting a team is thought to be more patriotic!

In 1954, under pressure from the British Horse Society, the FEI allowed teams for the continental championships to consist of four riders, with the best three scores to count. Also from around this time ladies were permitted to compete at European level; but both allowances were excluded from the Olympic rules until the 1960s. In 1968 Jane Bullen (now Holderness-Roddam), riding her Badminton winner, Our Nobby, was not only the first lady rider to represent Britain in the Olympic Three-Day Event, but also came home having helped the team to win the Gold Medal.

Through Badminton, riders 'qualify' for international competition but over the years, of necessity, it has become more difficult to qualify for Badminton itself. As early as 1953, *Horse and Hound* opined: 'The time is rapidly approaching when some standard must be worked out to qualify entries for Badminton', but it was not until 1958, when Badminton had established its permanency and Britain her supremacy in the field, that it became necessary for competitors at Badminton to have proved themselves to some extent at the increasing number of one-day events. In 1980 qualifications change yet again, necessitating horses and riders to have proved their cross-country jumping ability at advanced level. Competitors at Badminton are the cream of the country's eventers.

As riders have become more knowledgeable and experienced in the sport of eventing, so courses have been designed in a more technical, sophisticated manner than hitherto. In the early days of Badminton, although the fences surprised the horse world because they were so totally different from anything encountered in the hunting field, the courses were, basically, galloping and straightforward. They have always been designed with a view to the fences likely to be met with at the forthcoming international championship, but it is particularly since Col. Weldon took over the designing of the course in 1965 that the technical combination fences, the 'riders' fences', have come to the fore.

Having had the onerous task of organizing the first-ever horse trials in Britain, Col. Trevor Horn steered the Event through until the year after the 1952 Olympics before handing over command to another local man, his brother-in-law, Col. Gordon Cox-Cox. Under the directorships of Col. Horn and Col. Cox-Cox the courses were, if anything, dimensionally larger than those of today, although the timbers themselves were much smaller and fences were not so sturdily or substantially built. There was never a bad fence, however, and, although neither man had ever competed in horse trials himself, each was an extremely knowledgeable, experienced cavalryman who had a feel for what a horse could safely jump. Col. Horn's 'Badminton impressions' in *Horse and Hound*

Above: *The Duchess of Beaufort, with Col. Trevor Horn, makes a presentation to Col. 'Babe' Moseley to mark ten years' service to the Event.*

after the 1953 Event provide impartial contemporary comment on his course of that year as well as interesting comment on riders' attitudes:

I had the pleasure of showing the whole course to Count Ranieri Di Campello, vice-president of the FEI, who walked it with the competitors on the previous Tuesday afternoon. . . . His comments throughout were enthusiastic, and in fact he expressed the opinion that the course was in every way first-class, and exactly what was wanted for the start of a new Olympic training period.

The fences were quite big enough and the problems of how to negotiate each one were exactly what was required – i.e., that the rider should be given a course over which he would have to concentrate more on how each fence should be taken than merely his pace.

The comments of our own Olympic competitors and also of those foreigners who had

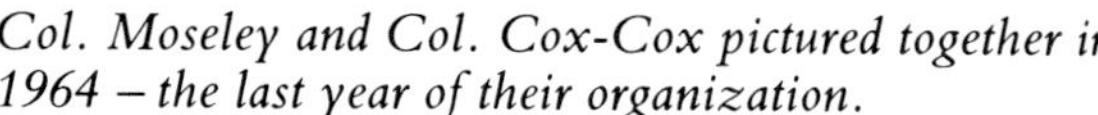

Col. Moseley and Col. Cox-Cox pictured together in 1964 – the last year of their organization.

either competed at Helsinki or at other similar events amply bore this out, and no adverse opinion was expressed by any rider.

Once again, it cannot be too strongly stressed that this competition is the most difficult in the world to win, and again it was noticeable how those walking the course on Tuesday, especially the newcomers, were apt to treat the fences in rather a casual manner, whereas the old hands studied each one most carefully.

Throughout the directorships of both Col. Horn and Col. Cox-Cox, they were ably assisted by a man whose rotund figure, for many, came to epitomize Badminton. He was Col. 'Babe' Moseley, who was assistant director from 1949 and one of eventing's most enthusiastic recruits, having been a top amateur National Hunt rider. He was held in the highest esteem; a very shrewd judge of horse and rider, he also had a keen eye for a course. Col. Lithgow tells a story which 'epitomizes him best'.

The last time I saw him before he died, there had been trouble over the venue for the Junior European Championships (Col. Moseley was chairman of the Junior Selectors and their chief protagonist in the early days when many of us doubted the wisdom of launching the young into international competition so early), as the country which was supposed to have staged it had opted out. He had had quite some difficulty in fixing it up at home and I remember saying to him how pleased he must be to have arranged things. He looked at me and said, 'Yes, I'm very determined. VERY determined.' Those were the last words I ever heard him speak and that was him. A great man. He did everything slightly larger than life, but his services to eventing and his kindness to all of us concerned in it were simply tremendous.

Throughout its history Badminton has been run by truly efficient ex-cavalry officers whose methodical background has led to an organization of military precision.

'The end of Badminton, 1964, was tinged with sadness . . .' [recorded Dorian Williams in *The Horseman's Year*], '. . . it was the last Badminton to be organized by Col. Cox-Cox and Col. Gordon "Babe" Moseley. It is hard to imagine Badminton without them, and certainly they have done a sterling job over the years. Nor incidentally has one ever seen either of them rattled, even in the downpours of 1959 and 1963.'

Badminton was at a crossroads. Since the Gold Medal at the 1956 Olympics, Combined Training had had more downs than ups, and there had been conflict in high places. Lack of success internationally was having an effect on the sport and Badminton was suffering as a result. David Somerset recalls:

When Col. Cox-Cox decided to retire he asked me if I would be director. I said I certainly would be director in name but the only condition would be that Frank Weldon came in with me, because I had no idea how to build fences and anyway I didn't have a lot of time with my business in London. So I went to see Frank Weldon who had come to live in the area. Some people were against him, but he had always been a great friend of mine and he agreed to come in. I quickly changed my name from director to chairman of the committee and left it all to him. Of course he made a tremendous success of it both from the point of view of a competition and as a financial success.

Col. Weldon himself explains the position:

For eight long years nothing would go right for the British team. While there were never many spectators in the early days at Badminton, public interest had started to wane even more. The three-day event was losing money and there was a grave risk that it would have to shut down altogether. Well, it's always better to take something on when it's at rock bottom because if it cannot get worse, it can only get better.

It was my job, I wouldn't say to commercialize it, but to try to make it viable because it is quite frightening how expensive it is. It now costs between £120,000 and £150,000 to lay on. The first and most important factor was to try to help our team to start winning again because nothing succeeds like success.

Everyone likes to be connected with the winning side and is more likely to pay to come and watch them. My two predecessors had both done a fine job starting from scratch but inevitably had never ridden in such competitions nor attended many international events, which I had been fortunate enough to do. The first step, therefore, was to try and build the sort of cross-country courses that competitors would meet abroad, not only to give them the experience but to make it possible to pick the most suitable, because Badminton has always been the main selection trial, the target to aim at for our potential international teams.

That was the start, but at the same time I tried to make the competition more exciting for spectators, to encourage them to come by making the obstacles look far more alarming or difficult than in fact they are.

Obviously there are a great many other factors which help to account for the popularity of the event in which a lot of people are involved. Publicity is one of them but it could not take place at all without the Duke of Beaufort's beautiful Park, which provides such a superb setting, and right from the outset Her Majesty has been one of the most ardent regular supporters.

There is the social aspect as well, but what brings the general public in, and not just the rich or the privileged classes? What brings *this* in,

concludes Col. Weldon, giving a summary rub of his thumb and forefinger,

is the people from the town and countryside around not just Bristol and Gloucester, but stretching as far north as Carlisle, who come, I'm sure, primarily to watch brave horses and riders do things they would love to do themselves, if only they had the nerve.

Although the old system was that each Badminton became progressively more difficult over the four-year Olympic cycle, competitors at the 1965 Event had a bit of a shock. Martin Whiteley explains:

I think there is no doubt that the courses got a bit easy towards the end of Gordon Cox-Cox's time; the early sixties were slightly easier. I think everyone had a very, very severe shock in 1965, which was Frank Weldon's first year. I happened to take a comparatively novice horse that year, which was The Poacher, and we were in the Little Badminton event where you jumped exactly the same course. The year before, which was 1964 – and after all had been the Olympic year, so in theory everyone expected a big difficult course – had been comparatively straightforward, and lo and behold we arrived in 1965 expecting a fairly simple course and it was markedly more difficult.

Frank Weldon had set his stamp on Badminton!

The Little Badminton event was one of the first things to go under the new directorship in an attempt to streamline the whole show. It had all become rather cumbersome: the Little Badminton section of the Event had been instigated in 1959 to prevent the ever-increasing entry from having to be spread out over two days of dressage. The division was made purely on the amount of money won by horses in combined training events: the tests remained of equal severity. For this reason many competitors felt slightly inferior and, as Frank Weldon was determined not to have poor relations, it was phased out. Martin Whiteley was one rider who enjoyed the Little Badminton event, and in fact won it twice: 'I would much rather have won the Little Badminton than have been 10th in the Great: it was merely for the less experienced horses.' The basic question, of course, was extending the dressage over two days; once Frank Weldon had persuaded the Duke of Beaufort to have two days of dressage, there was no point in having a Little Badminton.

Since 1956 the horse trials had carried with them a show section for children's ponies and hunters. Always well subscribed, the entry lists reveal many of the names which return to Badminton now as competitors in the three-day event, while one or two horses competed in both the show classes and the event, in different years of course. These were trimmed from the schedule immediately and 1965 saw the last of the showing classes at Badminton. The one addition to the horse trials which has remained since 1949 is the international show-jumping which takes place on the Saturday and Sunday afternoons, on the latter after the finish of the three-day event jumping test. It is one time in the year, however, when the show-jumpers are very much the second cousins to the eventers.

Inevitably there have been many changes over thirty years, if not so conspicuous as the Little Badminton and the show classes. As standards have risen in sheer technical know-how, so courses have become more complex over the years and the standard of dressage has been raised. This is not to say that today's competitors, in terms of sheer riding ability, are better than the riders of the 1950s or 1960s. Col. Bill Lithgow summarizes: 'Each in his time had "what it takes", which is really what it is all about, and born in a different time would, I am sure, still have got to the top.'

The changes to the dressage test have been multifarious and, while in the first few years the degree of difficulty waxed and waned depending upon the Olympic cycle, the first

HRH the late Princess Royal presents an award to Toby Sturgis . . .
. . . seen again in 1974 negotiating the Giant's Table.

Table of Penalties for Late Arrival on Route

"A" 3 miles in 22′ 30″	"C" 5 miles in 38′ 0″	"E" 1,270 yards in 3′ 30″	Loss of points (five points for each commenced period of 5 seconds)
22′ 31″	38′ 01″	3′ 31″	5 points
36″	06″	36″	10 points
41″	11″	41″	15 points
46″	16″	46″	20 points
51″	21″	51″	25 points
56″	26″	56″	30 points
23′ 01″	31″	4′ 01″	35 points
06″	46″	06″	40 points
11″	51″		
16″	56″		
21″	39′ 01″		
26″	06″		
31″	11″		
Over 24′ 36″ disqualified	Over 42′ 4″ disqualified	Over 4′ 12″ disqualified	

Table of Loss and Gain on the 2 Miles Steeplechase
To be completed in 5 minutes and 30 seconds
Time limit : 11 minutes.

Loss of points (10 points for each commenced period of 5 seconds)		Gain of points (3 points for each commenced period of 5 seconds)	
Counting from ::		Counting from ::	
5′ 31″	10 Pts.	5′ 29″	3 Pts.
36″	20 Pts.	24″	6 Pts.
41″	30 Pts.	19″	9 Pts.
46″	40 Pts.	14″	12 Pts.
51″	50 Pts.	9″	15 Pts.
56″	60 Pts.	4″	18 Pts.
etc.		4′ 59″	21 Pts.
Over 11′ 0″ disqualified		54″	24 Pts.
		49″	27 Pts.
		44″	30 Pts.
		39″	33 Pts.
		No further points awarded beyond this time	

Table of Loss and Gain of Points on the 3-mile Cross-Country
To be made at the speed of 492 *yards a minute and to be completed in* 11 *minutes.* Time limit : 22 minutes.

Loss of points. (10 points for each commenced period of 5 seconds over and above the allotted time)		Gain of points. (3 points for each commenced period of 10 seconds, under the allotted time)	
Counting from :		Counting from :	
11′ 01″	10 Pts.	10′ 59″	3 Pts.
06″	20 Pts.	49″	6 Pts.
11″	30 Pts.	39″	9 Pts.
16″	40 Pts.	29″	12 Pts.
21″	50 Pts.	19″	15 Pts.
26″	60 Pts.	09″	18 Pts.
etc.		9′ 59″	21 Pts.
Over 22′ 00″ disqualified		49″	24 Pts.
		39″	27 Pts.
		29″	30 Pts.
		19″	33 Pts.
		09″	36 Pts.
		8′ 59″	39 Pts.
		45″	42 Pts.
		39″	45 Pts.
		No further points awarded beyond 8′ 39″—45 points.	

major change, in 1953, was the alteration in the scoring of each movement from a scale of 0–10 good marks to 0–6. It was a move introduced by the FEI and used at Badminton for the first time in a major competition. The late Henry Wynmalen, who was judging the dressage that year, wrote that the new system 'cannot be accepted as fully reliable . . . My co-judges at Badminton and I came to the unanimous conclusion that the new system cannot be fairly worked. The system is insufficiently graded to allow of a fair appreciation as between one performance and another and the final results do not reflect, as they should, the judges' considered opinion of the precise respective merits of different performances. The final results are, to a certain extent, a gamble.' The Technical Delegate agreed with Mr Wynmalen and, while the next year the scoring was reverted to the system which had served for half a century or so previously, in 1956 judges' marks were again awarded out of six good marks per movement and this system prevailed until 1977. The test which evoked greatest criticism was that of 1973. A new test set by the FEI and being used for the first time at Badminton, it united competitors in their disagreement with it. The test was totally unsuited to event horses, with flying changes of leg and extensive counter-canter. HRH Princess Anne has been quoted as saying that the test retarded Goodwill's dressage by a year. In 1974 there was a new test.

The modern test and that of 1949 make a very interesting comparison. Note how much more advanced the test has become and also the use of expressions 'short' for collected, and 'ordinary' for working. Note also the 'turn on the haunches', now better known as 'pirouette'.

TEST "B" ...

			Judges Marks 0—10	*Co-efficient Marks*
1—A	...	Enter at ordinary walk.		
G	...	Halt, salute, proceed at ordinary trot to	10	5
2—C	...	Track to right.		
K M	...	Change of rein at extended trot and maintain the extended trot to	10	15
3—E	...	Ordinary trot.		
F H	...	Change of rein at extended trot and maintain the extended trot to	10	15
4 & 5—B	...	Ordinary trot.		
F	...	Short trot sitting.		
A	...	Down centre.		
X	...	Circle right between X and B, on returning to X circle left between X and E, each circle to be 7 yards diameter. Proceed at short trot to	10	20
6—G	...	Halt, left turn on haunches. Proceed at ordinary walk to	10	15
7—H	...	Track to right.		
M K	...	Change rein at extended walk	10	15
8 & 9—K	...	Ordinary walk.		
F X M	...	Counter change of hand on two tracks.	10	30
10—C	...	Turn up centre.		
G	...	Halt, right turn on haunches. Proceed at ordinary walk to	10	15
11—H	...	Track to left.		
E	...	Shortened canter (left).		
A	...	Extended canter.	10	25
12—C	...	Shortened canter.		
E	...	Circle left 10 yards diameter.	10	25
13—A	...	Turn down the centre and serpentine 2 yards on either side of centre line without change of leg making 5 loops concluding at C on the left rein (See Diagram).	10	25
14—H F	...	Change rein with simple change of leg at X.	10	15
15—A	...	Extended canter.	10	25
16—C	...	Shortened canter.		
B	...	Circle right 10 yards diameter	10	25
17—A	...	Turn down centre and serpentine 2 yards on either side of centre line without change of leg making 5 loops concluding at C on the right rein.	10	25
18—M K	...	Change rein with simple change leg at X.	10	15
19—A	...	Turn down centre gradually reducing pace to halt at X.		
X	...	Rein back 6 paces, proceed at ordinary walk to	10	30
20—G	...	Halt, salute, leave arena on right rein at free walk gradually extending reins.	10	10
		Total	180	350

N.B.—Unless change of rein is notified, all movements will be carried out straight round the Arena.

F.E.I. THREE-DAY EVENT DRESSAGE TEST (1975)

		TEST	MAX. MARKS
1	A X	Enter at working canter Halt — Immobility — Salute — Proceed at working trot	10
2	C S EBE EV	Track to the left Medium trot Circle to the left 20 metres diameter Medium trot	10
3	V A L	Working trot Down centre line Circle to the left 10 metres diameter	10
4	LS	Half-pass (left)	10
5	C	Halt — Rein back 5 steps — Proceed at working trot without halting	10
6	R BEB BP	Medium trot Circle to the right 20 metres diameter Medium trot	10
7	P A L	Working trot Down centre line Circle to the right 10 metres diameter	10
8	LR	Half-pass (right)	10
9	C	Halt — Immobility 5 seconds — Proceed at working trot	10
10	HXF F	Change rein at extended trot (rising) Working trot	10
11	KXM M	Change rein at extended trot Working trot	10
12	C HSXPF F	Medium walk Extended walk Medium walk	10
13	A	Working canter — Circle to the right 10 metres diameter	10
14	AC	Serpentine 3 loops, the first and the third true canter, the second counter-canter	10
15	MXK K	Change rein at extended canter Working trot	10
16	A	Working canter — Circle to the left 10 metres diameter	10
17	AC	Serpentine 3 loops, the first and the third true canter the second counter-canter	10
18	HXF F	Change rein at extended canter Working trot	10
19	A L	Down centre line Working canter to the right	10
20	G	Halt — Immobility — Salute	10
		Leave arena at walk on a long rein TOTAL ...	200

Collective marks:	
1. Paces (freedom and regularity)	10
2. Impulsion (desire to move forward, elasticity of the steps and engagement of the hind quarters)	10
3 Submission (attention and obedience, lightness and freedom of the movements, acceptance of the bit)	10
4. Position, seat of the rider, correct use of the aids	10
	240

One of the biggest changes in the scoring came with the abandonment of the bonus system under which riders could positively wipe out a bad dressage score by gaining marks for completing the speed and endurance under the standard time. The scale of penalties and bonus marks is given on p. 56, reproduced from the 1949 programme. In 1953, helped by a change in dressage marking, Lawrence Rook was the first to finish with a plus score, and from then on, as people improved at dressage and became more adept across country, they would often finish with plus marks in double figures. The system ended with the 1970 Event, by which time the record had long been set by Sheila Willcox, who won the 1957 Event – her first of three consecutive Badminton wins – with a bonus score of no less than 79·37! A dedicated and ambitious competitor, Miss Willcox excelled at dressage but she also never missed an opportunity to take a short cut and make up time across country. Scores were calculated by setting a standard speed, below which bonus marks would be awarded and above which penalties would be added. The current system, which came into effect with the 1971 Event, is based upon the Optimum Time which would have gained maximum bonus marks under the old system; now it merely incurs no penalties. The cross-country should still, of course, exert the strongest influence, although at some events the best dressage horse automatically goes on to win. Badminton is not one of these. Each phase exerts exactly the right influence over the final results: not many competitors will manage a fast, clear round across country, but those that do are almost bound to feature in the top twelve.

Another major development, in 1969, was the innovation of the ten-minute compulsory halt between Phases C and D. It is a built-in safeguard for the horses, enabling them to be examined by a panel of three experts – including a veterinary surgeon – who would order the horse to withdraw if they considered it not in a fit state to continue on the most gruelling phase of the speed and endurance day. Before the ten-minute halt was instituted, it was up to a competitor to pace himself according to the time he would require in the 'box'. This would mean that he would need to go a little faster on Phase C than stipulated. Col. Bill Lithgow recalls an amusing incident from pre-compulsory halt days. 'In comparison with all the "to do" which goes on in the "box" now, with buckets of water and vets, etc., I remember my first year. I was riding behind the very distinguished Brig. Bolton who was on the short list for the 1948 Olympics. He was riding Flanagan, which he afterwards sold to Pat Smythe who show-jumped it in the Olympics. I remember his groom coming up to him while he was riding round waiting to start Phase D, and saying, "Shall I sponge him down sir?" "Sponge him down!" he retorted, "Certainly not, he wouldn't get sponged down out hunting would he?" '

Major Derek Allhusen sees the compulsory halt as an enormously important development which not only helps the horses, but also takes much responsibility out of the rider's hands. In the past a team member might have felt compelled to continue for the sake of his colleagues and in spite of his better judgement.

So much for the changes in the competition. It is the commercial aspect of Badminton which has shown the greatest development over the past fifteen years. While there have always been trade stands – even in 1949 local shops and businesses supported the new event – nowadays it can only be described as a mini-Game Fair. The trade stand area is always full to capacity – both with traders and visitors – and, as stands are limited to a maximum of 150, there is now a long waiting list: no one wants to pull out.

The enormous crowds at Badminton are, of course, one of the major changes. Obviously attendance has grown gradually over the years but in 1953 it took the Badminton Committee by surprise: 'The organization this year was inadequate to cope with the enormous crowds that came. One police-officer remarked that in his opinion the number of cars was even greater than on Gold Cup day at Cheltenham,' reported Col. Trevor Horn. The fact that Her Majesty again attended the trials, in her Coronation year, may not have been entirely coincidental! Col. Weldon now fears that:

Attendance has grown gradually over the years. The view of the dressage and show-jumping arenas from the top of the House in the early 1950s.

paradoxically the only risk to the future of the Trials may stem from its very popularity. For ten years there had been an encouraging regular increase in attendance of about 20 per cent each year. It was comparatively easy to estimate how many more of the expensive items like grandstands and loos would be required each time, as well as of the multitude of other 'goods and services' essential for dealing with big crowds, like traffic control and car parking, programmes and catering, even litter baskets and arrangements for lost children. At the same time, in spite of inflation, it was possible to keep prices fairly steady because of increased sales.

Attendance had just about reached its convenient limit, when for two years, 1976 and 1977, it levelled off with only a fractional increase and everyone breathed a sigh of relief, hoping that this would set the pattern for the future. It was not to last long, though, for in 1978 there was suddenly the biggest annual increase ever, of 25 per cent. Car parks overflowed, the loos were inadequate and all the services were stretched to the limit, but mercifully the weather was fine on cross-country day and the good-natured crowds seemed to enjoy themselves.

Luckily an extensive new area has just been put down to permanent grass, conveniently close to the trade stands, which should relieve the car-parking problem for at least a couple of years, even at the same rate of growth. Sooner or later, though, the limit will be reached and already there is a serious risk of damage to valuable farmland in the event of wet weather.

The day may not be too far off when the number of spectators has to be artificially restricted in one way or another – a far cry from the days, fifteen years ago, when Badminton Horse Trials was scratching to survive.

'You have got to remember,' reminds Raymond Brooks-Ward, 'that when Badminton started it was a happy band of amateurs doing a happy amateur thing and they would be the first to admit, if they were alive, that no way could they do that now, as a part-time job, like running a point-to-point. It is now such a huge event that you have to have a full-time dedicated professional in charge, which Frank Weldon is.'

It cannot be entirely coincidence, although other factors must have played a part, that two years after Frank Weldon took over the course building, the British team won the

Cornishman, one of the greatest event horses to represent Britain, seen here with Mary Gordon-Watson in 1969.

European Championship for the first time in ten years. Badminton had re-established the standard required of an international horse and rider. A year later came the ultimate prize, the Olympic Gold Medal, and from 1969 to 1972 British riders won not only every official international award, including the Olympics, but every individual title as well. Raymond Brooks-Ward comments: 'I think Frank Weldon was the man for the times, just like Churchill was the man for the war time. Frank arrived just at the time when Badminton was moving to a professional organization.'

If Kilbarry, Wild Venture and Countryman are the horses to be remembered from the 1950s, those names which are engraved indelibly on the records of the late 1960s and early 1970s are The Poacher and Cornishman: the latter one of the most brilliant event horses ever to represent Britain. Although, sadly, he never won Badminton – his highest place was second in 1971 – his international record speaks for him. Having been a member of the Olympic Gold Medal-winning team of 1968 with Richard Meade, he went on to win, with his owner's daughter, Mary Gordon-Watson, the Individual European Title in 1969, the Individual World Title in 1970, and he was a member of the winning European team in 1971 and finished a second Olympics as a member of the second successive Gold Medal team.

As well as the undoubted attraction of royal patronage, the television coverage of Badminton which began as early as 1952 must, too, have had its effect upon the popularity of the sport. Doyen of equestrian commentating, Dorian Williams was involved from the very beginning:

In 1947 I had become the commentator at the International Horse Show at the White City. Because commentating was rather a new role in the horse world, I was automatically invited to do the commentary at Badminton, but of course when I really became involved was when we started televising the Event. Understandably, the early producers had no knowledge whatever of horses, so one had to help an enormous amount in how to try to cover the Event on television. In those days we used to do two hours on the Friday afternoon non-stop (in the early days the trials were held over the Wednesday, Thursday and Friday, then Thursday to Saturday) – there was nothing else on! It was a great challenge as, in those days, I used to do the public address as well. I was a sort of one-man band, doing both commentaries at the same time, as well as conducting interviews! Then I'd do a five-minute spot for radio at the end of the Event. As far as the television was concerned, we used to film an awful lot of footage, then I had to dash by train to London, edit the film and put it out at nine o'clock as a 45-minute programme. It really was very exciting and, as the result of our experience, I can say quite honestly that there is no country that can cover a three-day event like British television. Badminton lends itself beautifully to the medium, but it's by far the most exhausting job in the television year because we are televising, not necessarily live, but from the first horse on the cross-country course at just after one until the last horse finishes at, perhaps, five. Of course the difficult thing is that so much has to be edited and we therefore have to make sure that we can give clean breaks in the commentary to enable cuts to be made. This means very carefully not speaking too soon when the picture starts and then leaving four or five seconds at the end, when you know your particular horse is going out of vision, because that's where the breaks will come.

Raymond Brooks-Ward, who came in to assist Dorian Williams in 1957 explains the technicalities:

There are two outside broadcast units; one out in the country by Luckington Lane, to cover that particular area, and the main camera unit down by Control. What people often don't realize is that our producer, Fred Viner, sitting there in the scanner, never actually sees a horse jump, and neither do the commentators. We sit in the commentary box overlooking the main arena which is desperately empty during the cross-country, with four television sets. Those sets show what we call the 'off air' picture; the picture which is being broadcast; another 'off air' picture which will come up with the slow motions; and the other monitor shows the Luckington Lane complex, so that while we're commentating on a horse going over, say, the Irish Bank or the Coffin, on the other set we can see a horse going out to Luckington. What one has to be careful of, as a commentator, is not to look at the other picture and say 'God Almighty, look at that!', when that is not the picture going out! We keep a master score card which enables us to keep viewers up to date, otherwise the Grandstand coverage can be very confusing. But we keep updating our results throughout the afternoon and are able to give viewers a summary of the number of fallers, the number eliminated, the number that have actually got round, and anybody inside the bogey time for the course. Usually on the Saturday evening we do what we call a 'pull-together programme' on BBC 2, which is when we bring all the highlights together and top and tail it with an interview. We do the same thing on the Sunday afternoon when we have about twenty-five minutes of the most exciting cross-country and we finish by doing probably the top five or six in the show-jumping phase to complete the edited programme. In 1978, for the first time, Fred Viner televised the veterinary inspection on the Sunday morning which was very interesting and had never been shown before.

With up to sixteen cameras required to cover the cross-country and the miles of cable which must be laid around the course, Badminton is one of the most expensive outside broadcasts on the BBC's budget. Because of this expense it is unfortunate that no coverage is given of the dressage and, although undoubtedly people are now more aware of the requirements of the three-day event, television cannot give a thoroughly accurate picture. On the other hand, over the past few years particularly, it has helped people to understand the sport: 'Even a few years ago,' recalls Raymond Brooks-Ward, 'people would say, "well, why isn't Princess Anne competing against Harvey Smith?". They didn't understand that they competed at two different sports. I think the message has got over now.'

TV commentator Raymond Brooks-Ward broadcasts 'live' from the cross-country course on Saturday evening.

Another major development in the commercial side of the Event was the introduction of sponsorship by Messrs Whitbread & Co., in 1960. Through his friendship with the Duke of Beaufort, chairman of the company, Col. Billy Whitbread felt that he could help the Event by giving his support. It was an enlightened move in the days when sponsorship was in its infancy, and £100 was immediately added to the value of the first prize. Keeping pace with inflation, prize money has increased over the years and Badminton is still the most valuable three-day event in the world to win, with a first prize in 1978 and 1979 of £1,500. To the winner also goes the handsome Whitbread Trophy, while prizewinners down to twelfth position are awarded charming silver replicas of the Trophy. But it is not just with the winners that

1960 saw the first year of the valuable Whitbread sponsorship.

Whitbreads are concerned: they pay all the bills for the keep and accommodation of each competitor's horse and groom, which is a very great contribution – naturally appreciated by competitors. While the Badminton Committee would obviously like to see that their Event remains the richest in the world, David Somerset, the chairman, goes further in saying that he would 'like to see the prizes enormous. Ten years ago it would have been very nice to win £1,500 but now it's nothing; you can't even buy a small car. It keeps the horse for perhaps a few months at £40 per week livery. I think it's absolutely idiotic when people say that you must keep the prize money down otherwise you'll get the professionals in. You will never get professionalism in three-day eventing because a horse will only do two or three big events a year, so no-one is going to go in for it for the money they earn. Even if you put the first prize at £5,000 it wouldn't be worth their while.' This is yet another assertion of the amateur status of three-day eventing and a reminder that money to train and prepare horses and riders for international competition is no more forthcoming today than it was in 1949. In 1978 much research and work was carried out by members of the then Combined Training Committee to devise ways and means of raising money for eventing and also for guiding horse trials into the 1980s. Mr Martin Whiteley chaired the British Equestrian Horse Trial Fund Raising Committee, which looked into ways of raising money for the purpose of buying and keeping horses for our international teams, while a working party consisting of Mr Hugh Thomas, Mr Michael Tucker and Mr Bruce Tulloch looked into the eventing crystal ball and came up with concrete proposals which will ensure the continued good health and growth of the sport. A major move is to plough the greater proportion of the Badminton surplus directly back into the sport, through the Horse Trials Committee. Martin Whiteley explains his committee's action:

Plainly the biggest worry about the future of eventing is escalating costs. I was lucky enough at one time to have three event horses, and certainly never would any of those cost me more than £7 to £8 per week. Now, even one event horse is an extremely expensive pastime. Because of the value of the horses I am afraid more and more that the owners are not going to be the riders. The owners in a sense have got to be rich. Very few of the riders are going to be able to afford to own these horses. Therefore, it does become extremely important that we should generate some system of finance to try to help both owners and, obviously, riders with the training, possibly with the keep, and, if necessary, with the ownership of horses. The Horse Trials Fund Raising Committee discussed, and argued, and eventually worked out two different schemes; one, for lump sums, to buy horses which would otherwise leave the country. We felt that this money should come from companies' sponsorship and the horses we buy should then run in the name of the British Equestrian Federation. Equally, if a company is prepared to put up the money, ask advice from the selectors and buy a horse, we are absolutely delighted that it should own the horse, and it would run in the company's name. We have hopes that some fairly big lump sums will come in this way and we have already bought one horse and I hope very shortly will be buying another. Secondly, quite separate, and in a way much smaller in terms of money, we felt there really was a role to be played by a group of individuals who were interested in the sport and could afford to pay £100 a year for minimal returns. This is how the Horse Trials Support Group came into being. We initially said that we would have a target of 200, by the Olympics, and I wrote some 400 letters and others wrote about

Another aspect of Whitbread's support.

another 100. We are now well on the way to our target and this gives us an annual income of several thousand pounds a year to be used for instance for the keep of BEF horses; it's also being used for grants towards keep to certain owners who perhaps feel they can't go on owning a horse for someone else to ride.

In 1979, for the first time, thanks to the Support Group, scholarships of £300 each were awarded to the first six British riders at Badminton, thus enabling them to further their own training and knowledge. This is an extremely important development in the history of British eventing and one which, hopefully, will help to put our riders back on top of the world.

Perhaps the best person to comment on the future of Badminton is Lucinda Prior-Palmer, whose record at the Event is brilliant and whose future must be just as bright. Her only reservation is to who will take over when Frank Weldon eventually retires: 'It will be a nightmare to follow him – imagine having to follow in those footsteps! But I'm sure that that will sort itself out because I believe that Badminton is meant to be the Mecca of eventing; it will go on till World War Three or whatever! To me, in a gloriously ignorant, innocent way, Badminton is timeless.'

5

PREPARING FOR THE EVENT

The three-day event rider and his horse are 'modern pentathletes'. Nowadays competition is such that they must be equally proficient in each section of the event, and in their training and preparation they cannot afford to lose sight of this. Gone are the days, if they ever existed, when huge numbers of marks lost on the dressage could be won back on the speed and endurance phase: riders with cricket scores on their dressage sheets often stay towards the bottom of the results table. At the other end of the competition, the show-jumping – still the weakest link – must be practised and today's riders take their horses off to various competitions during training to help strengthen their finish, so to speak. And in the middle is the speed and endurance, for which they must take a leaf out of the racehorse trainer's book to ensure that their horses are supremely conditioned and fit. 'To succeed in a competition such as this,' said the 1954 programme, 'the rider will have shown himself a complete horseman and horsemaster. He will have had to prove he has the ability to train and ride his horse and adapt his method of riding for the various tests. Throughout the competition he will have had the opportunity to demonstrate all the best qualities of horsemanship and horsemastership.'

This, of course, is the top of the tree. What happens at the roots, the introduction to eventing and the road to Badminton? Obviously there are many routes: many people today arrive via the Pony Club with a horse they have brought on through junior events; others 'retire' to eventing from racing and yet others may be professional instructors or trainers and students of equitation. In marked contrast to the beginnings of the competition, very few competitors nowadays are soldiers. And what of the horse? What makes that paragon, the 'Badminton horse'? – an expression still very much used to describe a horse which is expected to go right to the top in eventing. Although there is obviously no hard-and-fast rule about the breed or type of horse likely to do well, most people will choose a quality thoroughbred for speed and stamina, with perhaps a dash of common blood for substance and temperament. Martin Whiteley's first priority when looking at a young potential horse is 'Can it gallop?', while Bertie Hill looks for the type 'that wouldn't look out of place at Cheltenham running for the Gold Cup'. Frank Weldon asks 'Can it jump?'; although any horse can be *made* to jump if the rider is skilful enough, the true three-day event horse is one that, if need be, will jump *in spite of* the rider. Unfortunately you cannot tell, just by looking at him, if he possesses this priceless quality.

So we have our four-year-old with substance and quality and it is at this stage of the development of an eventer that we in Britain are so fortunate to be able to go hunting. There is no better schooling ground for a young horse – or for a rider for that matter – than to cross a country at speed behind a pack of hounds, facing whatever obstacle presents itself. It teaches a horse to adapt to bad going,

The Duke of Beaufort's stable yard looks reasonably peaceful during the Wednesday evening veterinary inspection.

'. . . to cross a country at speed behind a pack of hounds . . .'

to jump when it may be unsighted by another horse getting in the way, to take ditches without looking into them, and it develops its enthusiasm for going forward. Even when a horse is 'made' and has possibly become far too valuable to risk taking it hunting, a day with hounds can provide the tonic it needs if it has been mentally soured by a bad course.

The mental development is as important as the physical and many, many potentially good young horses are ruined because an ignorant and over-enthusiastic rider pushes them beyond their capabilities until, mentally, they say 'no'. There is no turning back at that stage.

'Proceed with caution' may be the watchwords in the preparation of an event horse, taking it on and up through the various grades by scoring points at British Horse Society-affiliated events. The words of Guerinière, the eighteenth-century riding master, are as true today as they were when written: 'The aim of training the horse is to make him quiet, supple and obedient by systematic work so that he becomes pleasant in his movements and comfortable for his rider.' One of our top trainers, Bertie Hill, estimates to take three years to bring a horse up to three-day event level, at the end of which time it will be mentally stable and physically capable of negotiating the ultimate, which is as different as chalk from cheese from the one-day events with which it will be familiar. Providing a horse has come through its first three-day event satisfactorily, Bertie Hill will hope to take it to Badminton when it is eight years old.

The British Horse Society grading system stems the ever-increasing tides of horses and riders in eventing, channelling only those capable to the top. Before a horse can be entered for Badminton, which, with Burghley, is one of our two championship events, it must have attained Grade 1 status which means scoring a minimum of forty-one points at affiliated events during the course of its career. Grade 2 horses (16–41 points) are eligible provided they have completed at least two advanced horse trials without incurring jumping penalties across country, thus stressing jumping ability as the all-important factor for a three-day event horse. Qualifications to compete at Badminton come in two stages: to enter, horses must have completed at least one three-day event at standard or higher level, which may include a junior official international event and, to start, horses and riders must have completed at least one advanced horse trial in the previous autumn season. Owners and riders must be members of and horses registered with the British Horse Society and the rider's eighteenth birthday must fall within the calendar year of the competition. Horses must be at least six years old. The qualifications are stiff, but so is the competition, and only stringent regulations can ensure that horses are properly prepared throughout their careers.

Once a horse has reached Badminton level, its preparation for the Event takes on a set

'. . . pleasant in his movements and comfortable for his rider . . .' Topper Too and Jane Starkey make a good illustration of the point.

pattern year by year. There are two eventing 'seasons' in a year, the spring and the autumn, and it is after the close of the autumn season that most riders nowadays will let their horses down and give them a rest. If the horses are not turned out completely to enjoy the last part of the autumn, they will certainly go out by day to relax and unwind. They will be fed and kept looking well, while not being allowed to become fat, as this would mean wasting time in the spring just slimming them down. An older, experienced eventer will come up to condition and regain fitness very quickly when the programme recommences, usually at the beginning of the year. The first month or so is confined to steady road work, walking to begin with, and then a mixture of miles of walk and trot. This alone will harden a horse and is particularly good for strengthening the all-important muscles and toughening the tendons in the legs which have to take the impact of all the landings and provide the propelling power for all the take-offs in the event to come: 'No foot, no oss' as the saying goes, and no short-cuts can be taken. Work proper begins in February, providing the road work has proved successful and the horse is ready.

It is all very much a case of adapting to the individual requirements, some horses being able to take much more hard work than others. The training now, in Chris Collins's words, 'has to be an endless compromise between the galloping and the dressage and the jumping and the outings to various small competitions'. Jane Holderness-Roddam concentrates on schooling and dressage during the second month, which is very good for fittening horses, and progresses to a fair amount of athletic exercise type jumping. The jumping work is eased and the faster work increased, with long-distance slow cantering work introduced during the last six weeks and a couple of gallops in the month

... taking the impact of all the landings. This picture of Goodwill, with Mark Phillips up, shows the strain on the forelegs as the horse lands over the wall into the Quarry.

before the big event. Riders will usually try to compete in two or three one-day events before Badminton, as well as various dressage and show-jumping competitions. Bertie Hill is an exception nowadays in that he does hunt his Badminton horses in the weeks before the event, owing mainly to the fact that in his country, the Dulverton (West), there is very little jumping but a great deal of invaluable hill work; probably the best kind of terrain for getting a horse fit, and ideal for teaching a horse natural balance, especially if a fence should be encountered on the side of a hill. Mrs Wendy Marshall, who was groom to the 1952 Olympic team, remembers the training programme at Porlock for the selected riders who included Bertie Hill: 'Anyone who has cantered a horse at the peak of its fitness from the bottom to the top of Porlock Hill will know how fit both rider and horse have to be.' For anyone who has never had the opportunity to do such a thing, or indeed for anyone who has never encountered Porlock Hill in a car, suffice it to say that it has a 1:4 gradient, and leave the rest to the imagination!

This need for supreme fitness cannot be overstressed and it is where the good horsemaster will score every time. For it is not only the work the horse is asked to do, it is careful feeding, and general vigilance for the horse's well-being, that will win events.

While most of our riders follow a system roughly in accordance with that given above, our leading lady rider, Lucinda Prior-Palmer, has, for some years, followed the American system of 'interval training', more commonly used in the preparation of athletes. The basic concept is that, in more conventional systems, pounding away on a horse with tired limbs is more likely to cause its breakdown. In interval training, the horse will be worked hard only on every fourth day, American research having proved that a horse takes three to four days to recover from full work while not reaching the point at which it begins to lose its fitness. Just before full recovery, the horse's body is said to be most receptive to further work, which will then increase its stamina by demanding more from its heart and lungs than they are really ready to give, while not unduly straining them. This same idea is the basis of the programme on the work day, the horse being asked to canter – for just two or three minutes at commencement of preparation – then walked for a shorter period of recovery, but cantered again before the horse has quite recovered. On the days between work days, the rider will do normal schooling, dressage, show-jumping, etc., but will not include any demanding or fast work. Lucinda has certainly proved that her method works, but most people in this country remain unconvinced, confident in the fact that our own methods are grounded in hundreds of years of keeping horses fit – especially for hunting, when, in the pre-horse-box era, horses regularly covered distances which would nowadays make even the staunchest long-distance rider pale! However, maybe the Americans' success in the 1970s will mean that more people take a look at their method. It may yet be proved that horses prepared by interval training are less likely to breakdown: an ever-present worry with event horses.

. . . the good horsemaster will score every time . . .
Lucinda's horses always look in the peak of condition.

But whichever method a rider or trainer chooses to use, his basic responsibility to the horse is to see that it is in a condition capable of negotiating a three-day event. It is also the rider's responsibility to himself to see that he is fit for eventing also. For some, merely the amount of riding they are having to do to get the horse fit is enough to knock them into shape. Running is an invaluable exercise, while swimming and skipping both help. Lucinda Prior-Palmer says that she is 'very, very lazy. I just can't stand running and thinking I've got another mile to go, so I skip and think that I've got another 299 to go which only takes five minutes, so it's better that way.' However, each individual person has different requirements in the programme of physical fitness and each rider must work out for himself what he needs to do in preparation for the competition.

An advocate of personal fitness . . . Jane Holderness-Roddam and Warrior go over the rails at the bottom of the Slide – minus a stirrup! . . .

. . . but regain it to take the next fence, the Faggot Pile (1978).

One rider remarkable for her dedication both to her riding and her work is Jane Holderness-Roddam, who trains down in the New Forest with her sister, Jennie Loriston-Clarke. Described by the popular dailies as 'the galloping nurse' when she won Badminton at the age of twenty on Our Nobby, Jane has not neglected her nursing and does 'quite a lot of night duty in the spring, when I'm getting horses fit, at the local hospital at Lymington. I probably do one or two nights a week which doesn't interfere with riding during the day. I'm lucky because I don't need very much sleep once I get fit and used to it.' She is a great advocate of personal fitness: 'My brother [Michael Bullen] was always very strict about that and was a great inspiration to me. He always used to make sure that I got myself fit in the early days.' In his capacity as both radio and television commentator at Badminton for twenty years, Raymond Brooks-Ward has been able to observe that it is in their basic preparation that many people, and girls in particular, fall down. 'Coming from one-day eventing to three-day eventing they fail totally to appreciate how fit a horse, and they themselves, have to be to go in for that type of competition. They have coasted round in a one-day event and suddenly they're in a three-day event and the horses are cooked and they're cooked . . . it's a different ball game.' Hopefully this type of sight is becoming rarer as people become more knowledgeable and qualifications tighten.

As the spring horse trial season gets underway and Badminton competitors are in the last stages of preparing their horses for the great event, so the Park is slowly transformed; not only by the fence building which has been going on for some months already and is described in Chapter Seven, but also by the tentage contractors, the telephone engineers, the electricians and the grandstand builders. Four weeks before the Event the trade stand area is pegged out to accommodate 150 exhibitors and the shedding begins to go up. Miles of cable are laid, linking the excellent and long-standing public addresss system with the familiar blue- and buff-liveried bus, Control HQ. The grandstands appear like monolithic giants from the flat parkland and telephone lines link the Event with the outside world. The steeplechase course has been accurately measured, the pegs are in the ground and it takes the Willis Bros. about a week to set up the prefabricated fences, flag the course and erect the running rails. The Park breathes anticipation as each person goes about his duty. At this stage, while not actually resorting to 'worry beads', Col. Weldon has been heard to admit to waking at night, still anxious over the smooth running of the Event, although, of course, it usually runs like clockwork.

Badminton week arrives with everyone turning a 'weather-eye', so to speak. The skies frequently open with April showers and, while 1959 was the notoriously wet year, 1966 and 1975 actually had to be cancelled, the former before the Event itself got underway, although all the preparations were complete, and the Irish and French teams had already arrived (having left before the news could reach them); and the latter, sadly, at the end of the second day's dressage, by which

Michael Bullen, here on Young Pretender in 1964, is very strict about personal fitness.

Above: *'The familiar Blue and Buff liveried bus . . .'*

Left: *The course is ready! The Duke of Beaufort makes his traditional 'inspection' of the course with Col. Frank Weldon who is here seen explaining the intricacies of the Dog Kennel . . .*

. . . while His Grace's dogs try it out for size!

time the Park had been reduced to a quagmire.

All being well, however, competitors arrive in force on the Wednesday morning prior to the Event in time for the 10 am competitors' briefing. Some riders will have arrived on the Tuesday if the anticipation of an impending competition does not adversely affect their horses; some horses will go completely off their feed, something no one wants to go on for too long before such a gruelling event. The final lead-in to the event is best described by Lucinda Prior-Palmer, whose enthusiasm for Badminton is infectious.

Badminton is the most exciting week of the horse-year for me. I really love the place and I have such a soft spot in my heart for it. It's wonderful packing up at home and loading up, getting the last rug on, etc. We arrive at Badminton on the Tuesday in time for the Wednesday briefing, so it's nearly a seven-day event. Chugging up the motorway and seeing the first RAC notice for 'Badminton Horse Trials' is all most exciting and off the motorway, as you draw near to the village on the little lanes, you look to see if a flag is going to appear above the next wall. Eventually, above the trees you just see the flag-pole on top of Badminton House and almost simultaneously the string along the verges to stop people parking, so you know you're nearly there. The bit I really love is unloading the horses and just jumping on them bareback or whatever, and just going out for a walk in the park to stretch their legs after the drive. All the trade stands are showing signs of occupation but without the real excitement of the day because there's no crowd, but there's a marvellous anticipation – a silent, waiting feeling. I know the horses feel it too because they just grow another foot; their ears are pricked and they look at everything. They see a red and white flag marking a fence as quickly as I can; it's marvellous. I remember in 1975 when it was rained-off, I had three horses to ride, which

wasn't quite so peaceful, but I'll never forget that awful sinking feeling as we walked on the grass, of the hooves going right in and I knew Be Fair wouldn't get round because he hated mud. That whole lovely feeling I get at Badminton was totally ruined because (a) I didn't know if I would have enough energy to complete the course on three horses, and (b) that feeling of everything sinking, sinking, sinking under you. It was probably just as well that it never happened. But the rest of them have always been filled with that same sort of anticipation; there is something magic about that place. It means more to me than anywhere; it is the birthplace and breathes out the history of the three-day event.

On the second day we have the briefing, which is great fun because you meet all your friends again. Frank Weldon chalks little pictures of his fences on the blackboard: I think he's worried that he might have been too clever building the course and he wants to make sure that none of us gets too caught out so he tells us some of the answers! It's very useful actually because a lot of eventing is mixed up in penalty zones and unless you're sharp on some of those difficult combinations he builds, you can get yourself a refusal or an elimination just by crossing your tracks inside the zone. Col. Weldon is very good in that way as he doesn't want to cause too much misery.

One of the best bits of all is getting off on the start of Phase A, roads and tracks walk-round. This always sees a fight to get behind Frank Weldon's Land Rover! There's not really much you can do about it if you don't win pride of place on Phase A but when you can really fight for your place is when you've got to the steeplechase and have walked round there and get back to start driving around Phase C in a long convoy. That's when the motor rallying begins to try to get first place before the first gate! You can imagine the sort of pranks that go on! Everyone is then peaceful for the next five or six kilometres until we hit Worcester Avenue when the track opens right out again and vrrrrm . . . everybody goes up there

Above: *At the Wednesday evening vets inspection (l to r) Mr Michael Naylor-Leyland, Major Derrick Dyson and Col. Frank Weldon.*

Left: *His Grace and Col. Weldon look out over the Footbridge of the 1979 course.*

Right: *Col. Weldon gives the 1979 competitors a few clues on the Lexington Dog Kennel fence at the Wednesday morning briefing. With Col. Weldon are two members of the Ground Jury, Monsieur A. Bühler from Switzerland and Monsieur F. Lucas of France.*

sideways, vying for a better position. It's extremely amusing as you come across by the Lake to look back along Worcester Avenue and see all these Land Rovers, Range Rovers and the odd car which is trying to make its way around, all of which are filled with competitors!

On returning to the 'box', Col. Weldon explains to riders where they must weigh in and out – extremely useful for competitors anxious at the prospect of their first Badminton, and some may then go on to inspect the course for the first time. Many people will choose not to walk the course at this time, preferring to leave it until later when they can be alone to make their own decisions. It is the last stage of preparation which calls for complete concentration and judgement: a mistake made here will mean a mistake on the cross-country phase itself, which could be disastrous. The rider must decide on the walk-round how he is going to jump each fence; more than that, he must decide which are going to be his alternative routes if circumstances on the day prevent him from taking his first choice. Of course, on the day, anything might happen and a rider may be forced to take some completely unpremeditated action, which is why a quick brain and reactions are two of the most important natural gifts which a rider can possess.

All now lies in waiting for the horse trials public. With the logistics completed of getting them in and out, of feeding and amusing them, and, on a down-to-earth note, of providing them with sufficient lavatory facilities, all is ready for the opening day of the Event. One last formality for the competitors before the competition gets underway is the veterinary inspection on the Wednesday afternoon. It is an anxious

moment for the riders for, after the weeks of preparation, to be failed at the first vet's inspection at Badminton would be nothing short of tragedy. Obviously, to stop allegations of cruelty the inspection must be stringent and examination panels are tightening up: it is by no means a mere formality. The worry is that by the time a horse gets to Badminton standard – or indeed beyond – it's no longer young. It's had drops and jars during its career, and it is bound to be a little stiff, which makes it extremely difficult to trot up completely sound – in hand. The horse will be walked around for ten minutes or so prior to the inspection and then trotted up in hand before the vets. Lucinda Prior-Palmer always likes to run her own horses up as there is a particular knack to trotting a horse up well if he is a little stiff. If he can be encouraged to move forwards freely, not leaning in towards the runner, he will trot up sound enough to pass, unless, of course, he really is lame, in which case he should be withdrawn anyway. Surprisingly, the second vet's inspection on the Sunday morning causes less problems as the cross-country will have loosened up all the stiff muscles and, unless any real injury has been sustained, these horses will trot up much sounder then.

With the veterinary inspection over successfully, the competition is really underway. 'The hum and the buzz has begun,' says Lucinda, '. . . and the butterflies begin!'

Drops and jars. Janet Hodgson on Larkspur jump into the Quarry (1976).

6

THE THREE DAYS

The three-day event is the ultimate in combined training competitions. Each competitor completes each of the three major sections on three separate days although, where entries dictate, major events – Badminton included – now run over four days, with the dressage phase covering the first two and the whole competition from the competitors' briefing to the presentation of awards lasting nearly a week. The two phases of roads and tracks, a steeplechase and cross-country phase develop into the speed, endurance and cross-country test on the third day with the object of the final day's show-jumping being to demonstrate that, after the rigours of the previous day, the horse is still supple and obedient, with enough energy necessary for him to continue to serve his rider, in the time-tested traditions of the Military.

The first riders begin their dressage tests on the Thursday morning at Badminton, in the purpose-built show arena in the Park; a far cry from the wonderfully informal arena of earlier days, laid out in front of Badminton House with straw bales for 'grandstand' seats.

Despite the mistrust with which our foxhunters regarded dressage, it is, after all, only training; training which must be an integral part of a horse's and rider's education if they are to be a balanced combination capable of negotiating all three sections of the Event in perfect harmony. Despite what the dressage purists say, the three-day event horse should not be expected to show the perfection of the solely dressage horse, but he must be level and calm, fluently responsive to his rider's aids but showing that degree of brilliance or sparkle without which the test would be accurate but dull. The problem which faces eventers is that, corned-up as their horses must be to face the gruelling test before them, they are apt to show rather too much sparkle. HM the Queen's Goodwill was one such horse while Chris Collins found it a constant problem with his brilliant cross-country horse, Smokey VI, who actually 'blew up in the dressage and did the most appalling test' in 1976, but nevertheless came through to finish tenth. Another problem in this respect which is often overlooked is that a horse which is three-day eventing fit has simply not developed the same set of muscles as the purely dressage horse. He is the athlete performing gymnastics: thoroughly capable but not perfect.

The standard of dressage test performed at Badminton is to medium level on the British Horse Society's scale but the actual test is that laid down for three-day events by the FEI. At this level the horse is required to collect and extend his paces while maintaining the same regular rhythm throughout. He should not appear to be running or rushing his movements and the rider must keep a mental metronome ticking all the time to ensure that the rhythm remains absolutely constant whatever the movement. In terms of pure dressage the rider is the conductor, the horse his orchestra and the test the symphony: if conductor or orchestra lose sight of the timing, the full beauty of the music is lost. The two should move as one unit, and the rider is under as close a scrutiny as the horse. In 1952, Mr Henry Wynmalen, who judged at that year's Badminton, wrote about a virtually unknown event rider and his observations indicate just what the judges are looking for:

Right: *Mary Gordon-Watson on Speculator leaving the stables on her way to the dressage arena.*

Above: *Jane Holderness-Roddam awaits her turn in the dressage.*

Right: *The first riders begin their dressage tests on the Thursday . . . Chris Collins on Gamble halts to salute the judges.*

Left: *Exercises on two tracks. Princess Anne and Goodwill half-pass right.*

Below: *Extended trot. Carawich and James Wofford of the USA.*

Extending the paces: Lucinda and Killaire at medium trot.

THE SCALE OF MARKS IS AS FOLLOWS:
6. VERY GOOD
5. GOOD
4. FAIRLY GOOD
3. PASSABLE
2. BAD
1. VERY BAD
0. MOVEMENT NOT EXECUTED

THE F.E.I.
THREE-DAY EVENT DRESSAGE TEST (1975)

To be ridden in a snaffle or double bridle
Arena 60m. x 20m.

Time allowed 7½ minutes
For every second exceeding the time allowed a penalty of half a mark will be deducted from the score sheet
Errors over the course are penalised
FIRST TIME - - 2 points
SECOND TIME - - 4 "
THIRD TIME - - 8 "
FOURTH TIME - - Elimination

No. 69 HORSE George RIDER Miss L. Prior-Palmer

		Test	*Max Marks* 1	*Marks Allotted* 2	*Observations*
1.	A X	Enter at working canter Halt – Immobility – Salute Proceed at working trot	10	8	
2.	C S EBE EV	Track to the left Medium trot Circle to the left 20 meters diameter Medium trot	10	6	
3.	V A L	Working trot Down centre line Circle to the left 10 meters diameter	10	8	
4.	LS	Half-pass (left)	10	8	
5.	C	Halt – Rein back 5 steps – Proceed at working trot without halting	10	7	
6.	R BEB BP	Medium trot Circle to the right 20 meters diameter Medium trot	10	8	
7.	P A L	Working trot Down centre line Circle to the right 10 meters diameter	10	8	
8	LR	Half-pass (right)	10	9	
9.	C	Halt – Immobility 5 seconds – Proceed at working trot	10	5 4	[illegible]
10.	HXF F	Change rein at extended trot (rising) Working trot	10	6	running a bit
11.	KXM M	Change rein at extended trot Working trot	10	6	
12.	C HSXPF F	Medium walk Change rein at extended walk Medium walk	10	4	not over stepping
13.	A	Working canter – Circle to the right 10 meters diameter	10	7	
14.	AC	Serpentine 3 loops, the first and the third true canter, the second counter canter	10	8	
15.	MXK K	Change rein at extended canter Working trot	10	7 6	
16.	A	Working Canter – Circle to the left 10 meters diameter	10	9	
17.	AC	Serpentine 3 loops, the first and the third true canter, the second counter canter	10	8	
18.	HXF F	Change rein at extended canter Working trot	10	5	
19.	A L	Down centre line Working canter to the right	10	5	Crooked
20.	G	Halt – Immobility – Salute	10	5	[illegible] Halt not square
	A	Leave arena at walk on a long rein			
Collective Marks					
1.		Paces (freedom and regularity)	10	6	
2.		Impulsion (desire to move forward, elasticity of the steps and engagement of the hind quarters)	10	6	
3.		Submission (attention and obedience, lightness and ease of movements, acceptance of the bridle)	10	7	
4.		Position, seat of the rider, correct use of the aids	10	7	
		MAX. TOTAL MARKS	240	161	

Total of column 2 .. .. .. ——
Faults to be deducted: *(see top right hand corner of sheet)* Time .. —— Wrong course —— Total Faults ——
Total points to count .. .. ——
Judge's Signature

NOTE The working, medium and extended trots must be executed "sitting" unless the term "rising" is used in the test.

Lucinda Prior-Palmer's dressage sheets.

'I had never seen A. E. (Bertie) Hill before. I was most favourably impressed. A very nice position on the horse, nice sensitive hands and very delicate legs and, what is so seldom seen, aids timed in unfailing sympathy with the horse's rhythm.'

The horse is also asked to perform exercises on two tracks (not, as someone once thought, repeating the same movement twice on a different line) or lateral movements in which the hind legs follow a separate track from that made by the forelegs. Thus in the half-pass, which is executed at the trot to the left and to the right, the horse moves diagonally forwards and sideways on two tracks, the head inclined in the direction of the movement and the forehand leading the quarters. Throughout the test, the horse should be attentive and obedient, with acceptance of the bit and the rider's hands.

In the early 1930s, the FEI ruled that competitors must ride their dressage tests from memory: hitherto it had been permissible to have each movement called, but in international competition, the problem, among others, of having to have an interpreter, outweighed the advantages of commanded tests. This ruling obviously increases the burden upon the rider, for not only must he be working to obtain the best possible performance from his horse, but he must also be concentrating on the next movement, as errors of course are penalized on a rising scale of two, four and eight penalties for up to three mistakes, with a fourth resulting in elimination. There is also a time limit on the twenty movements of the test, of seven and a half minutes, although a horse moving forward freely and easily, as it most certainly should at this level, will have no difficulty in complet-

THE SCALE OF MARKS IS AS FOLLOWS:
6. VERY GOOD
5. GOOD
4. FAIRLY GOOD
3. PASSABLE
2. BAD
1. VERY BAD
0. MOVEMENT NOT EXECUTED

THE F.E.I.
THREE-DAY EVENT DRESSAGE TEST (1975)

To be ridden in a snaffle or double bridle
Arena 60m. x 20m.

Time allowed 7½ minutes
For every second exceeding the time allowed a penalty of half a mark will be deducted from the score sheet
Errors over the course are penalised
FIRST TIME - - 2 points
SECOND TIME - - 4 "
THIRD TIME - - 8 "
FOURTH TIME - - Elimination

No. 69 HORSE George RIDER Miss L. Prior Palmer

	Test	Max Marks 1	Marks Allotted 2	Observations
1. A X	Enter at working canter; Halt – Immobility – Salute; Proceed at working trot	10	8	
2. C S EBE EV	Track to the left; Medium trot; Circle to the left 20 meters diameter; Medium trot	10	7	
3. V A L	Working trot; Down centre line; Circle to the left 10 meters diameter	10	8	
4. LS	Half-pass (left)	10	8	Rather lacking impulsion
5. C	Halt – Rein back 5 steps – Proceed at working trot without halting	10	7	Off hind left behind
6. R BEB BP	Medium trot; Circle to the right 20 meters diameter; Medium trot	10	7	
7. P A L	Working trot; Down centre line; Circle to the right 10 meters diameter	10	8	
8 LR	Half-pass (right)	10	8	
9. C	Halt – Immobility 5 seconds – Proceed at working trot	10	6	Halted early not □
10. HXF F	Change rein at extended trot (rising); Working trot	10	8	[illegible]
11. KXM M	Change rein at extended trot; Working trot	10	9	
12. C HSXPF F	Medium walk; Change rein at extended walk; Medium walk	10	6	Not a great deal of extension
13. A	Working canter – Circle to the right 10 meters diameter	10	8	
14. AC	Serpentine 3 loops, the first and the third true canter, the second counter canter	10	9	
15. MXK K	Change rein at extended canter; Working trot	10	8	Head slightly unsteady
16. A	Working Canter – Circle to the left 10 meters diameter	10	8	
17. AC	Serpentine 3 loops, the first and the third true canter, the second counter canter	10	8	
18. HXF F	Change rein at extended canter; Working trot	10	8	Quarters swinging
19. A L	Down centre line; Working canter to the right	10	6	
20. G	Halt – Immobility – Salute	10	6	
A	Leave arena at walk on a long rein			
Collective Marks				
1.	**Paces** (freedom and regularity)	10	7	
2.	**Impulsion** (desire to move forward, elasticity of the steps and engagement of the hind quarters)	10	7	
3.	**Submission** (attention and obedience, lightness and ease of movements, acceptance of the bridle)	10	8	
4.	**Position**, seat of the rider, correct use of the aids	10	8	
	MAX. TOTAL MARKS	240	181	

Faults to be deducted: *(see top right hand corner of sheet)*
Total of column 2 ....
Time ....
Wrong course .... Total Faults ....
Total points to count ....

37.4

Judge's Signature ....

181
161
191
533

NOTE The working, medium and extended trots must be executed "sitting" unless the term "rising" is used in the test.

THE SCALE OF MARKS IS AS FOLLOWS:
6. VERY GOOD
5. GOOD
4. FAIRLY GOOD
3. PASSABLE
2. BAD
1. VERY BAD
0. MOVEMENT NOT EXECUTED

THE F.E.I.
THREE-DAY EVENT DRESSAGE TEST (1975)

To be ridden in a snaffle or double bridle
Arena 60m. x 20m.

Time allowed 7½ minutes
For every second exceeding the time allowed a penalty of half a mark will be deducted from the score sheet
Errors over the course are penalised
FIRST TIME - - 2 points
SECOND TIME - - 4 "
THIRD TIME - - 8 "
FOURTH TIME - - Elimination

No. 69 HORSE George RIDER Miss L. Prior Pal

	Test	Max Marks 1	Marks Allotted 2	Observations
1. A X	Enter at working canter; Halt – Immobility – Salute; Proceed at working trot	10	8	
2. C S EBE EV	Track to the left; Medium trot; Circle to the left 20 meters diameter; Medium trot	10	8	
3. V A L	Working trot; Down centre line; Circle to the left 10 meters diameter	10	8	
4. LS	Half-pass (left)	10	8	
5. C	Halt – Rein back 5 steps – Proceed at working trot without halting	10	9	
6. R BEB BP	Medium trot; Circle to the right 20 meters diameter; Medium trot	10	9	[illegible]
7. P A L	Working trot; Down centre line; Circle to the right 10 meters diameter	10	9	
8 LR	Half-pass (right)	10	8	
9. C	Halt – Immobility 5 seconds – Proceed at working trot	10	7	
10. HXF F	Change rein at extended trot (rising); Working trot	10	8	
11. KXM M	Change rein at extended trot; Working trot	10	8	
12. C HSXPF F	Medium walk; Change rein at extended walk; Medium walk	10	6	Not regular behind
13. A	Working canter – Circle to the right 10 meters diameter	10	8	
14. AC	Serpentine 3 loops, the first and the third true canter, the second counter canter	10	8	
15. MXK K	Change rein at extended canter; Working trot	10	8	
16. A	Working Canter – Circle to the left 10 meters diameter	10	9	
17. AC	Serpentine 3 loops, the first and the third true canter, the second counter canter	10	8	
18. HXF F	Change rein at extended canter; Working trot	10	8	
19. A L	Down centre line; Working canter to the right	10	5	Crooked canter, hind legs to side
20. G	Halt – Immobility – Salute	10	8	
A	Leave arena at walk on a long rein			
Collective Marks				
1.	**Paces** (freedom and regularity)	10	7	
2.	**Impulsion** (desire to move forward, elasticity of the steps and engagement of the hind quarters)	10	8	
3.	**Submission** (attention and obedience, lightness and ease of movements, acceptance of the bridle)	10	9	
4.	**Position**, seat of the rider, correct use of the aids	10	9	
	MAX. TOTAL MARKS	240	191	

Faults to be deducted: *(see top right hand corner of sheet)*
Total of column 2 ....
Time ....
Wrong course .... Total Faults ....
Total points to count ....

Judge's Signature ....

NOTE The working, medium and extended trots must be executed "sitting" unless the term "rising" is used in the test.

ing the test within the time allowed.

Each movement in the test (which is performed in an arena measuring 60 m by 20 m) is marked out of ten good marks – until 1977 it had been six – and, with the forty collective marks for paces, impulsion, submission, and position and seat of rider and the correct use of aids, the total number of possible good marks is 240. Each rider is judged by a jury of three judges who sit at the short end of the arena, one at the centre line and one each at the quarter lines, opposite the rider as he makes his entrance. As each movement is completed, each judge's score is shown electronically on a numbered column alongside each position, each having observed the movement from a different view. The 'electric scoreboard' was invented at Badminton. It is now also used at Burghley, but nowhere else in the world. There is no doubt that it increases spectator interest, but unfortunately – human nature being what it is – it is impossible to guarantee that *every* mark shown on the 'board' is a true representation from each judge. If a judge hesitates, or changes his mind, an incorrect mark is sometimes shown on the indicator, but of course the written record is accurate. The three scoring sheets are collected on completion of each test, calculated during the next competitor's test, and announced directly that has finished.

The scoring of the three-day event has become something of an enigma, and not even some competitors would pretend to understand it. It has undergone several changes but, without confusing the issue more than necessary, the whole competition is scored on a penalty basis. Penalties incurred for each test, to the nearest whole number, are added together, the winner being the competitor with the lowest total of penalties. In order that the dressage scores should not

Princess Anne takes Goodwill for a walk – and a graze! – in the Park.

exert too strong an influence on the final results – they should, in theory, have a quarter of the influence of the cross-country and four times the influence of the show-jumping – the dressage penalties may be multiplied by a factor between 0.5 and 1.5. The Ground Jury make the decision on the exact figure of the Multiplying Factor which depends upon the severity of the cross-country. The harder the cross-country, the higher the Multiplying Factor and this will widen the range of scores between the best and worst dressage performances which will mean that the best cross-country horses come out on top. The exact factor to be used is decided prior to the commencement of the dressage. Since 1977, when the total dressage marks were increased from 144 to 240, all dressage penalties are further multiplied by 0.6, thus scaling down the new marks to the old level. If all this seems a trifle bewildering, suffice it to say

Below: *Columbus and Capt. Mark Phillips enjoy a relaxing canter.*

that, by this method, penalties from each section are kept within the same range.

The whole system of dressage marking is best illustrated by looking at the three sheets of Lucinda Prior-Palmer's test on George when they won in 1977 (see pp. 82–3). First the three total scores are added:

$$181+161+191=533$$

The sum is averaged:

$$\frac{533}{3} = 177.7$$

and the average subtracted from 240 = 62.3. The Multiplying Factor of 1 leaves the figure the same and the penalties are then multiplied by 0.6, giving the result, 37.4 (rounded up to the nearest whole number).

The judges on this occasion were Col. the Hon. C. G. Cubitt, Lt. A. Bühler from Switzerland and Mr A. Orlos from Poland, who, together with veterinary surgeon Mr W. J. B. Watson, formed that year's Ground Jury, whose task is explained in another chapter.

First in the dressage arena on the Thursday morning is the 'guinea pig': a non-competitor who performs the test for the judges in order that they may then confer on the marks given and agree on similar standards for the competition proper. As for competitors, on whichever day they are drawn to complete the dressage section, it is obviously necessary for the horse to be exercised on the other day. A horse doing dressage on the Friday will probably be hacked out quietly on the Thursday, to get him accustomed to the people already arriving, and, after completing the dressage, will be given a short, sharp, pipe-opening gallop up Worcester Avenue leaving him feeling on top of the world. If he is competing on the Thursday, he will probably be given just the gallop on the Friday. Obviously, exactly what riders decide to do is dictated by the temperament of their horse. Lucinda Prior-Palmer usually likes to sit on her horse watching other people doing their dressage if she is not competing until day two, 'so he gets the

Richard Walker adds a final shine to his boots before the dressage but . . .

. . . is interrupted by autograph hunters!

Watching other competitors perform their dressage tests . . .

feel of it all', but she avoids doing any more schooling for fear of boring her horses – 'If they're fit and if they're highly-couraged, they aren't going to put up with a lot of discipline . . . you've got to teach them to put up with discipline for as long as you want it, and when you want it, but don't tempt providence by flogging and flogging. I might well be wrong, but I've always felt that way.' Jane Holderness-Roddam has found boredom a problem with her Badminton winner, Warrior, who 'loathes dressage' and is 'terribly difficult because he needs a certain amount of work just to get the buck and kick out of him when he's eventing fit, but he gets into the arena and then just goes absolutely dead . . . he just says "Ugh! This is such a bore"!' As for Smokey VI (referred to earlier), Chris Collins has 'wanted to give him the impression that he's not really doing anything and to get him to do the dressage before he knows where he is'! Once the dressage is over, riders will walk the cross-country course for the final time. In Lucinda Prior-Palmer's words: 'You just walk up and down between each fence, inspecting every nettle, every dock leaf, and decide what route you're going to take, at the same time having a very good idea of what your second escape route is going to be: not just saying "Oh, over there", but actually walking the line so that you've got about eighty lines covering the thirty-five or so obstacles in your head.' While both Lucinda and Jane Roddam are amongst those riders who prefer to be absolutely alone on their preliminary walks around the course, again to quote the former, 'by the time it gets to the evening when you're still unsure of the Lake and you're still absolutely unsure of how to get across the Vicarage "V"', older, more experienced advice is sought: 'maybe Dick Stillwell' for Lucinda or, for Jane, her equally well-known brother and sister, Michael Bullen and Jennie Loriston-Clarke, the former an Olympic event rider himself. Jane stresses, however, that ultimately it is only the rider who knows how his or her horse jumps and 'you really must stick to your decision once you've made

The spectators are in! Jane Holderness-Roddam (centre) takes a last look at the Sunken Footpath with (on her right) Warrior's joint owner, Mrs Suzy Howard.

it. The people who dash from person to person seeking advice must get in such a muddle.'

It is, by this stage, a very serious business for competitors, who should not underestimate the value of walking the course – just as important as actually riding it. By this time, however, the public is in, and spectators walking the course can make life extremely difficult for competitors trying to get a good view of a fence in order to go to bed that night with a very clear idea of how to tackle the problems which Col. Frank Weldon has set them on the speed and endurance section.

Speed and endurance day is the most spectacular and thrilling of the three-day event and it is the section above all which, in Richard Meade's words, is 'close to the heart of the English rider because we have such a tradition for racing and hunting ... the excitement of riding across country is quite exceptional.'

The object of this test has been explained in many places and in many different ways, but when eventing was new to Britain in 1949, the Badminton programme described it as 'an endeavour to prove the degree of endurance of a really good horse which has been well-trained and brought to a state of excellent condition. At the same time it is a test of the rider's knowledge of pace and the use of his horse across country.'

While most of the 200,000 or so people who pack Badminton Park on 'cross-country' day know that riders have to cover a total distance of some sixteen miles, many believe that this is all over the massive fences about which the crowds polarize. In fact the actual cross-country phase – Phase D – is just over a quarter of the total distance and when the first competitors walk up to the start of Phase A to weigh in and check their watches with the master clock just before noon on the Saturday, it is just over 3¼ miles of roads and tracks which form the first test. This phase is undemanding of the horse but may present problems for a rider trying to restrain a fresh horse from exceeding the average 9 m.p.h.,

'The excitement of riding across country is quite exceptional . . .' Richard Meade.

which will mean a steady trot or mixture of walk and canter. This very thing happened one year when a soldier's horse bolted with him on Phase A and they were eliminated.

All phases are measured in metres, and kilometre markers along the route enable riders to pace themselves while check points ensure that no short cuts are taken! The Optimum Time for this phase is twenty-two minutes and competitors are penalized one point for each second over this, up to a time limit of 26 min. 26 sec. – one-fifth over Optimum Time, and over which incurs elimination.

From the first roads and tracks phase, competitors move directly on to Phase B where they are for the first time required to extend themselves. This is the steeplechase course, which, at Badminton, is just over two miles and must be completed, ideally, in exactly five minutes, which means averaging 26 m.p.h. The ten fences here are regulation steeplechase-type fences, of not over 4ft. 7in., and here again the rider's judgement of pace is tested to the full. It is in this section that Olympic gold medallist and now successful trainer, Bertie Hill, finds that riders fall down 'more than anywhere else. There are not many three-day event riders who give a horse a good ride on the steeplechase for the simple reason that it's thought to be something and nothing – a steeplechase fence is nothing to ride over – but in fact . . . you see some very bad riding. They ride them like cross-country fences, kicking and pulling and pushing, whereas I maintain that that's where an event is won and lost.' A former amateur jockey, like Bertie Hill, Chris Collins has the attitude: 'With the steeplechase way of jumping fences . . . I'm happy to let the fence arrive rather than making terrific adjustments before.' Noted as one of the fastest riders across country, Chris believes that this philosophy saves him precious seconds even though he will take some fences 'faster, probably, than some people think is sensible!' While some of our most successful riders admit that the steeplechase is the phase they like least of all, results show that they have the determination to ride on, over whatever faces them. It is the part of the competition, however, for which many ill-prepare themselves and disagreement with the distances involved in the steeplechase, particularly at Olympic and World Championship level, is heard. Experience at the 1978 World Championships at Lexington, Kentucky, showed that under such conditions of heat and humidity, the FEI's Technical Delegate might use his discretion to reduce the severity of the speed and endurance section. But at Badminton, the most perfect setting for a three-day event, in the temperate English spring, it is unlikely that any fit horse will be unduly taxed by completing the second day: it is, in fact, rare to see a horse finish distressed at Badminton as the parkland rides so well. Olympic three-day event rider, Michael Bullen, recalls the strict regime of training with the late Col. V. D. S. Williams, on whose horses, Cottage Romance and Sea Breeze, he was regularly placed at Badminton, which involved running 'in the odd point-to-point not to race them but just to get them used to galloping over fences, which is very good and stops horses looking at ditches, etc.'. He is fierce in his condemnation of the 'moaners and groaners' and believes totally in the original concept of the Military, 'that was set up and has run for many years. I don't see why it should change just because some of the modern generation don't think they can ride around a steeplechase course of two miles; it's only because they're too bone idle to get their horses fit!' Strong words indeed, but words which clearly newcomers to eventing should heed.

Lucinda Prior-Palmer underlines the importance of riding a good steeplechase: 'There is an awful lot that can go wrong so easily and if you make a mistake on the steeplechase, as far as doing well goes, you might as well forget it, because you don't need those sixty penalties for a fall.' A second fall of horse and/or rider in the steeplechase will mean elimination. Penalties on the steeplechase are incurred at a rate of 0.8 of a point for each second over Optimum Time, up to a time limit of ten minutes. With this in mind, it is here that the three-day event rider must use his skill and judgement to gauge the fitness and performance of his horse in the conditions on the day.

John Shedden, winner of the first Badmin-

Above: *A large crowd gathers around the start of Phase A at noon on the Saturday.*

ton and successful trainer under rules, says, 'This is the whole art of winning a three-day event: you have to adjust. Do you get round the steeplechase dead on time – five minutes – and, if you do, will you have enough steam to get across country? It's a test not only of horsemanship but of horse*master*ship: of being able to get your horse to the end of a long course and complete it in the best possible time, without one phase wrecking the others.'

Richard Meade, regarded by many as our top event rider, recalls an error of judgement he made in this respect on his own horse, Barberry, in 1964, the year of their Olympic début. The horse was not as fit as Richard had thought him: 'I went too fast on the steeplechase course and blew him up. He was a very tired horse on the cross-country. The interesting thing is that this happened to

Phase A: Mr. Bruno Goyens de Heusch of Belgium sets out on the start of the Speed and Endurance.

Above: *'In the box' – the horse is refreshed before the start of Phase D.*

some people at the World Championships of 1978 in Kentucky. One learns by one's mistakes.'

So, one by one, competitors leave the steeplechase course and proceed straightaway on Phase C, six miles of roads and tracks to be completed in an Optimum Time of forty-one minutes. The purpose of this second roads and tracks is to allow the horses to relax and wind down after the gallop on the steeplechase and it is at this stage that, as Lucinda Prior-Palmer says, 'the whole thing becomes a joy . . . as you come back up Worcester Avenue, you start to see the House and pin-heads of people round the Lake in a thick black mass, and it hits you that in about fifteen minutes you'll be flying round that course and they'll all be watching you – fall in the Lake or whatever – and you start getting a little bit nervous and think about something else quickly!'

Miss Bridget Clarke loosens Harper's Bazaar's girth as they commence the 10 minute compulsory halt.

Horses will normally recover very quickly from the steeplechase on Phase C, but to allow them extra relaxation, some riders will dismount and run alongside – emphasizing how fit the rider himself needs to be. This, in fact, was perhaps more commonplace in the past, and Col. Frank Weldon, for one, always ran until he decided that the running stiffened him up more than the riding! Another more serious hazard was illustrated at the 1968 Olympic Games when Jane Bullen, as she then was, tripped and fell, only maintaining contact with her horse, Our Nobby, by grabbing hold of his tail! Any inclination to stop, however, for even a short time, must be curbed as the clock moves on relentlessly and penalties will be incurred as for Phase A. Richard Meade ensures that his horse is back and breathing right before he canters on in Phase C. Very often the rider behind will start to catch up but if the horse is not allowed to settle then trouble could be on the way.

In order that she may have a little extra time at the compulsory halt before Phase D, Jane Holderness-Roddam paces herself at four minutes to the kilometre which is easier to work out and gives her twelve minutes in the 'box' as opposed to the statutory ten minutes. This compulsory halt was introduced in 1969, its purpose being that any horse deemed unfit to continue on the cross-country by the horse examination committee be eliminated then, thus preventing any distress to the animal. It is a busy but useful interval for riders and their grooms to refresh their horses, perhaps take the saddle off and give the horse a sponge down, check all bandages are secure and have any shoeing problems attended to, the emphasis being on speed but thoroughness. Riders can gather information from their 'ground crew' of helpers on how others have coped with a particular problem on the course while the horse will be walked around quietly to prevent it from stiffening up. Most riders, because they are human (though one might be forgiven for thinking them superhuman) now feel some nerves. The ebullient Lucinda admits that, on doing all that is required of her in the 'box', she then 'hurries off to the loo because that's the only place one can go – there's nothing else to do. It's all rather

Tension usually disappears when one's actually on the horse: Hugh Thomas on Playamar, runners-up in 1976.

unnerving because there's still another five minutes, which is one heck of a long time when you're waiting. I normally have to be dragged out because I go into a sort of trance. I sit there rather like Rodin's The Thinker, just running through each fence, wondering how I'm going to ride it and asking for help from the Good Lord every now and again when I don't think I'll ever manage it. Then, more often than not, somebody knocks at the tent flap or whatever, shouting "Come on, three minutes before you have to go".... I must say at that point I do wonder rather why I do it: I always feel extremely nervous.... I have that terrible sinking feeling of doing something wrong, of letting the horse and myself down by making a hash of something.' Jane Holderness-Roddam echoes the sentiment: 'I always go through a slight moment of panic if I can't quite remember which fence comes after which.' So does Olympic rider, Hugh Thomas: 'One's frightened of getting it wrong, doing silly things, full of tension which one hopes, when

'Caution and safety' are the watchwords says Chris Collins, seen here completing the 1974 course on Smokey VI.

one's actually on the horse, will disappear: it usually does.' But it is once they are on their way that these riders know exactly why they do it. Lucinda is 'absolutely thrilled as each fence goes underneath' and any rider one cares to talk to will say the same thing, with the added, unique, sensation that they are riding at Badminton, the event above all other national, and for some, international, events they want to do well at or, for the few, win. The 1978 winner, Warrior, 'just loves Badminton,' says Jane Roddam, 'it's the greatest competition ever.'

Riders are set off on the cross-country at not less than four-minute intervals – at Badminton it is often five depending on the number of starters – and they have before them 4½ miles of galloping parkland with approximately thirty-five fences to negotiate, constructed, according to the schedule, of timber, stone or brush and including banks. The design and construction of these is dealt with in the next chapter. The Optimum Time is a little over twelve minutes and they are penalized at 0.4 of a penalty for each second over that, up to a time limit of approximately thirty-one minutes. Here again the rider must know his horse, and know from the feel it gives him how fast he dare go. It is no use a rider blazing off with his foot hard down, as he may find he has run out of petrol before the end! 'Caution and safety' are the watchwords according to Chris Collins, who, because of his racing legacy is always 'conscious of the shortest route and where to turn quickly. In all fast riding you've got to have the right philosophy and then all the little things add up. If there are thirty fences and you save a second at each one, that's thirty seconds, which is twelve time faults: one's got to do everything to save time, get the horse away quickly, turning, etc., there's a lot in it ... so you've got to deliver the fast round, but you've also got to deliver the clear round. One has to weigh up and get it right: it's no use the horse being exhausted over the last six fences and falling, and it's no good going too slowly and not making the time. You've got to have judgement and think ahead the whole time in your riding.'

The crowd around the competitors' video in the 'box'.

Riders who have drawn late numbers will possibly use the extra time to advantage by watching the earlier numbers go on the cross-country on the competitors' television monitor in the 'box'. By so doing they can see how the course is riding and, if a rider makes an error, those watching will hope to learn by the mistake, and not make it themselves. Although she loves to watch others go, Lucinda recalls the first time she was first on the course, in 1977 on Killaire, on which she finished third: 'I don't think I've ever felt so sick because there was a bounce into the Lake which had never been done before and I knew that there were forty-five competitors at least standing in front of the television, watching to see if the jump was possible. It was a horrible feeling but being wonderful and like a cat as he is, Killaire just put in a stride where you would not have thought it possible and popped into the Lake. As it turned out, in fact, anybody who didn't put in a stride that year fell into the Lake!'

It is at this level of competition that any defects in the preparation of horse or rider will display themselves as glaring faults. A competitor is on the speed and endurance for a minimum of one hour and a half and it is no place for the weak and faint-hearted. A tiring horse can do without a floppy rider on its back at the end of the course, and such a combination spells disaster. Michael Bullen, a great advocate of fitness, is self-critical of a performance at Burghley when he knew he was not in eventing condition and subsequently fell. He decided it was time to stop competing. Qualifications are forever tightening for our two championship three-day events, Badminton and Burghley, and are due to become even stricter from 1980 onwards. However, even at Badminton one occasionally sees riders who are just not fit enough, which is a mere squandering of months of work and no small amount of money.

The supreme achievements at Badminton as far as both stamina and skill go were by Bill Roycroft in 1965 and Lorna Sutherland (now

Above: *One of Badminton's greatest achievements. Lorna Sutherland parades her three mounts in 1970: The Dark Horse, Gypsy Flame and Popadom.*

HRH Princess Anne prepares to dismount and weigh-out after an exhilarating, penalty-free cross-country on Goodwill.

Clarke) five years later. Each performed the remarkable feat of riding three horses at one Badminton: a total distance of nearly fifty miles in one afternoon and four-and-a-half hours around one of the most demanding three-day events in the world. And they each completed their performances with considerable success: Roycroft finished second and sixth, and second in the Little Badminton, on Eldorado, Stoney Crossing and Avatar, while Lorna Sutherland was placed on her two distinctive skewbalds, Gypsy Flame and Popadom, with the Dark Horse just out of the money.

The timing, scoring and results 'service' at Badminton has been reduced to a fine art over the thirty years. A later chapter fills in the details, but suffice it to say for the present that provisional scores can be announced within minutes of a horse finishing. The large

Top: *Jane Cooper, and her father Bert await their turn to run up before the vet.*

Above: *Jennie Loriston-Clarke and Tom Smith at the veterinary inspection.*

Right: *Capt. Mark Phillips and HRH Princess Anne make their way through the big crowd in the stable yard . . .*

His Grace the Duke of Beaufort.

Captain Mark Phillips on Columbus, 1979.

Left: Jane Holderness-Roddam and Warrior take a bold leap over the Keeper's Rails

Overleaf: Lucinda Prior-Palmer and Village Gossip at the Woodpile. The old Tree Trunk can be seen through the core of the fence.

Clarissa Strachan and Merry Sovereign go into the Lake.

Left: H.R.H. Princess Anne and Goodwill airborne over the 1979 Footbridge Fence.

The Royal party, accompanied by their hosts, are introduced to the Duke of Beaufort's hounds.

Top: *Officials at the Sunday vets inspection (l to r): Mr Michael Naylor-Leyland, Mrs Robert Hall, M. François Lucas, Major Lawrence Rook, Mr W. J. B. Watson, Mr David Somerset and Major Derrick Dyson.*

Above: *Sunday morning (l to r): Col. Frank Weldon, Major Lawrence Rook, Major Derrick Dyson, Mr Michael Naylor-Leyland, Miss Anne Spiller and Miss Joanna Boswell. . . .*

Left: *. . . while Lucinda gives the TV camera a characteristic smile!*

Poised to take her fourth victory, Lucinda Prior-Palmer prepares to take Village Gossip and Killaire into the arena for the parade of three-day event competitors.

scoreboard in the trade stands' area heralds the overnight leaders at the end of each day and nowadays mistakes at Badminton are the very remote exception to the smoothly run rule.

On completing Phase D, riders have one, important last duty to perform and must proceed immediately to 'weigh-out'. Throughout the speed and endurance, as in the following day's show-jumping, each horse must carry a minimum of 11 st. 11 lb., which means that many of the girls have to carry a good deal of lead in their saddle cloths.

With two-thirds of the Event completed – for those who remain in the competition – or, in terms of the relative influence of the tests, one-seventeenth to go, competitors can perhaps relax a little at the three-day event invitation dance at Westonbirt. However, they are required to be 'on parade' again at 10 am on the Sunday for the final veterinary inspection, held in the stable yard at Badminton. This has become almost as much a spectacle as the Event itself, with the presence of HM the Queen attracting some visitors perhaps rather more than watching the thirty or so horses being trotted up before the Ground Jury. It is indicative of the ever-widening interest in horse trials that BBC outside broadcasts' producer, Fred Viner, decided to televise part of Sunday's inspection for the first time in 1978.

After the veterinary inspection comes the traditional church service in Badminton's St Michael and All Angels Church, set in the Park and adjoined to the House by a passage which leads directly into the Library. In her book* Lucinda Prior-Palmer recalls the time when, poised for victory for the first time, she went to the church service with 'gratitude to give and one final favour to ask'.

The final jumping test over show-jumps takes place on Sunday afternoon, commencing at noon if those remaining in the competition number more than twenty. In practice, this rule is flexible and just a few over that number will share the added prestige of jumping before the Royal Family and a capacity crowd watching with rapt attention as the final pages of the thriller unfold to reveal who will actually 'do it'!

The afternoon performance is preceded by the parade of three-day event competitors, after which riders jump in reverse order to decide their final placings. The purpose of the three-day event jumping test is to prove the suppleness of the horse, not how high or wide it can jump, and how he performs will depend on how he's done the day before. The track of the course should be, according to the FEI rules, 'irregular and winding, with changes of direction, so as to constitute a test of hardiness. It will be related to the condition in which a well-trained, fit horse may be expected to be at this stage of the competition.' The course includes ten to twelve obstacles, including at least one double, as solid and as imposing in appearance as available materials allow. No jump exceeds 3 ft 11 in. in height or 5 ft 11 in. in spread. Despite the fact that it is an easy course by pure show-jumping standards, it nevertheless provides a cliffhanger finish. A horse whose

**Up, up and away* (Pelham Books).

Walking the show-jumping course.

WHITBREAD
Basil Brush

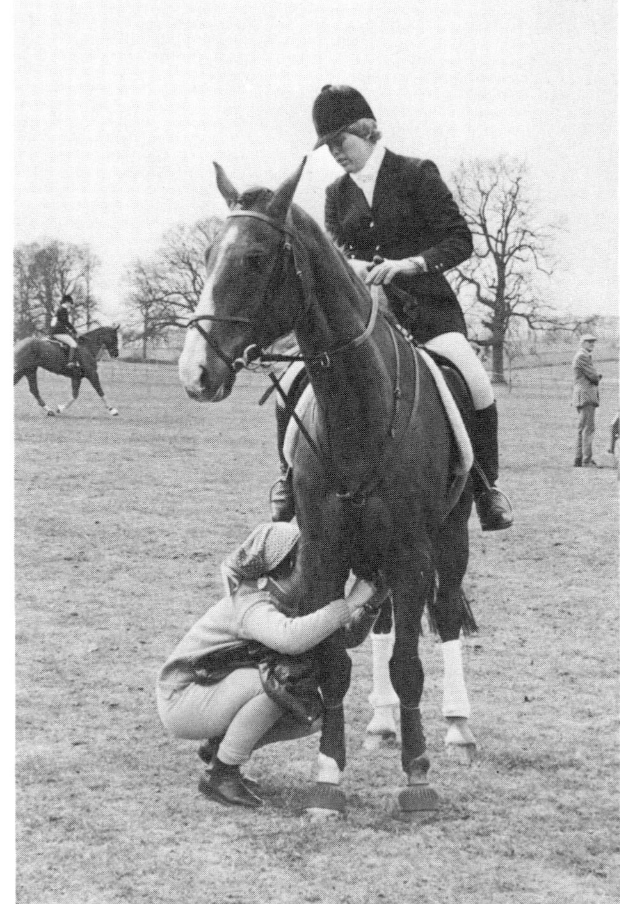

Waiting their turns . . . competitors in the show-jumping collecting ring.

show-jumping is sticky can throw away a competition time and again. On the other hand, riders must be conscious that they are still riding to a time limit, and not, as Richard Meade did in 1972, lose the competition to time penalties. The show-jumping test is still the weakest section of the three-day event but, as in everything, riders are paying more attention to it and are improving. 'Obviously a great deal hinges on it,' says Lucinda Prior-Palmer, 'and it's a rum way to lose a competition, especially Badminton.'

Suspense in the arena can be electric if the difference between the top two competitors is less than five penalties for one show-jump down. Such was the case in 1979 when the margin existed between the first three riders and Lucinda Prior-Palmer had to jump clear to score her fourth Badminton championship.

Sue Hatherly on Monacle during their clear round into second place in 1979.

And at the end of the three days? In 1979 the Badminton Horse Trials remained the richest three-day event in the world, with a total of 4,000 sovereigns added by Whitbread and Co. Ltd. £1,500 and the Whitbread Trophy go to the owner of the winning horse, and other monetary prizes go down in stages to £50 for twelfth place. Replicas of the Whitbread Trophy are awarded to all riders of prize-winning horses, and remaining awards make an impressive list right down to £10 for the groom in charge of each horse completing the competition.

So what does it mean, in personal values, to do well at Britain's oldest, most established three-day event which, to all intents and purposes, has become our national championship?

'If you ask any British rider which three-day event in the British Isles does he want to win,' says Martin Whiteley, 'absolutely 100 per cent would say Badminton.' More than this, most will say that it is *the* event in the world they want to win apart from Olympic, World or European Championships.

As Col. Bill Lithgow says: 'Badminton is like the Lord's Test Match against the Australians: the one that everybody wants to make a 100 in!'

24
25
47

7

ACROSS COUNTRY AT BADMINTON

'The art is to make the obstacles look far more dangerous and alarming or difficult, than in fact they are,' says Col. Frank Weldon. And, from the outset, the section of the three-day event which has attracted, thrilled and fired the imagination of the British rider and spectator, is the cross-country. It is a progression of our national heritage to race and hunt and, in 1949, when eventing first came to Britain via Badminton, it was the strong attraction of cross-country which swayed many riders in that first year to have a go.

Because, rightly or wrongly, we British, by tradition, are so preoccupied with riding across country, this chapter deals specifically with that phase of the three-day event as it appears at Badminton today under the hand of Col. Frank Weldon.

Badminton, says Col. Bill Lithgow, 'is the daddy of them all', and public and riders alike have come to expect certain standards of severity at our premier national event. All horses and riders must earn the attention of the international team selectors by doing well at Badminton which, each spring, sets a subtle test of equestrian skill over the sophisticated course. Badminton is still the international selection trial, and Frank Weldon will try to produce a course over which the most suitable horses and riders will display themselves to good advantage before the Selection Committee. While many people, Col. Lithgow included, would not want to see Badminton any more severe than at present, others feel most strongly that it is not necessary, nowadays, to produce an 'Olympic-standard' course as a mere test. There can obviously be some sympathy with this view: a horse's physical ability and soundness can be tested over lesser courses than Badminton. What Badminton proves is a horse's *mental* attitude to the really big courses; and if a question has been posed as to a horse's continued mental capacity, as was the case at Lexington in 1978, it will only be answered by seeing the horse perform over a championship-trial course, which Badminton is. Moreover, Badminton brings to the fore those who ride with intelligence – those who are psychologically, as well as physically, able to cope with the demands of international competition. In 1979, the foreign entry was one of the biggest ever, proving the international importance of the Event, while Badminton has always been a 'second home' for Australian riders, who regard it as highly as do our own.

The chairman of the Badminton Horse Trials Committee, and the man who insisted that Col. Frank Weldon came in as director of the Event against the wishes of some is Mr David Somerset. He echoes the sentiment of many in believing that, as a course builder, Col. Weldon 'is probably the greatest in the world, and regarded as such by both the riders and spectators'. Hugh Thomas sees in

Terrifying the riders without hurting the horses! A foreshortened view of the Quarry with Miss F. M. Lochore and The Young Laird successfully negotiating the combination.

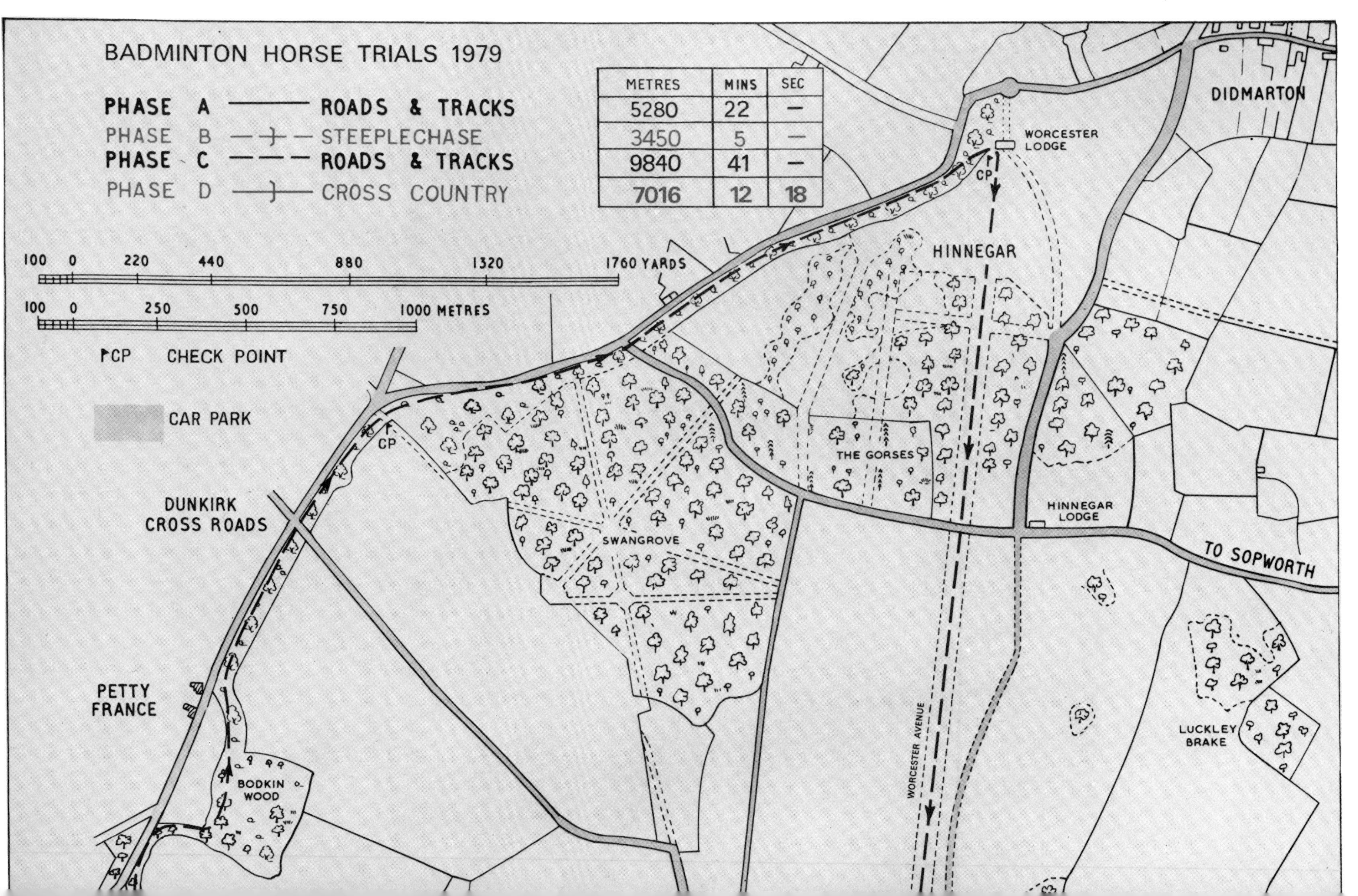

METRES	MINS	SEC
5280	22	—
3450	5	—
9840	41	—
7016	12	18

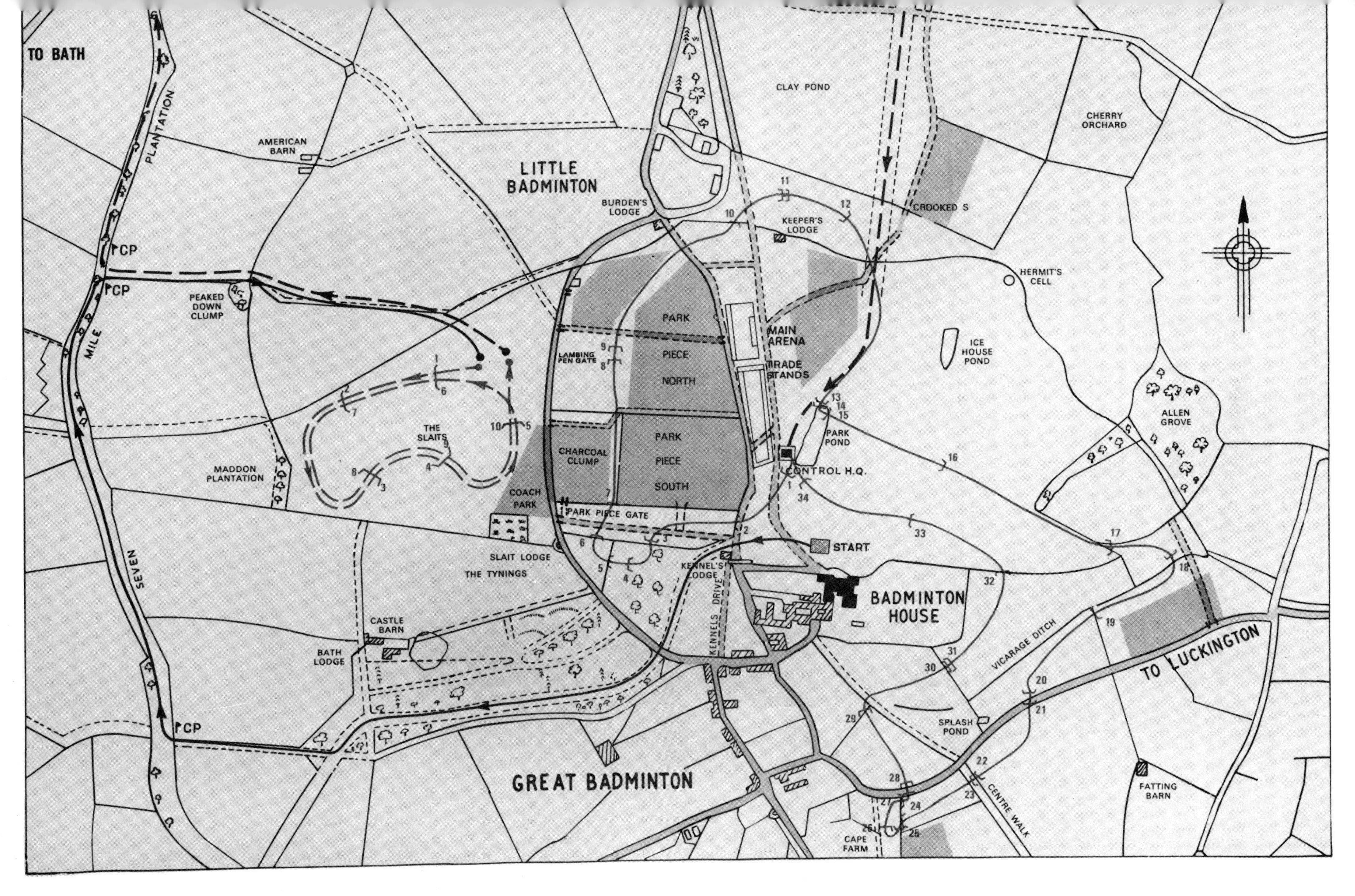
TO BATH
PLANTATION
MILE
SEVEN
CP
CP
CP
AMERICAN BARN
LITTLE BADMINTON
BURDEN'S LODGE
CLAY POND
CHERRY ORCHARD
KEEPER'S LODGE
CROOKED S
HERMIT'S CELL
ICE HOUSE POND
ALLEN GROVE
MAIN ARENA
TRADE STANDS
PARK POND
CONTROL H.Q.
PARK PIECE NORTH
PARK PIECE SOUTH
LAMBING PEN GATE
CHARCOAL CLUMP
PARK PIECE GATE
COACH PARK
PEAKED DOWN CLUMP
THE SLAITS
MADDON PLANTATION
SLAIT LODGE
THE TYNINGS
CASTLE BARN
BATH LODGE
KENNEL'S LODGE
KENNELS DRIVE
START
BADMINTON HOUSE
VICARAGE DITCH
SPLASH POND
CENTRE WALK
CAPE FARM
FATTING BARN
TO LUCKINGTON
GREAT BADMINTON

Frank Weldon 'the talent for confounding the competitors and armchair critics, who look at the course the day before and say either, that "this is easy" and it proves not to be, or "this is very difficult" and it equally proves not to be. That, I think, is the great talent of a course builder – to do something which the horses jump well (and he's always keen on something that makes the horses jump well) and frighten the riders silly!' He inspires a unique confidence in riders: 'You somehow feel,' says Lucinda Prior-Palmer, 'that when Frank produces an impossible-looking fence, that nobody has seen before in their lives, because *he's* built it, it's possible.'

But what happens in the months of preparation leading up to the Badminton Horse Trials in April (weather permitting) each year, when the ropes, the flags and the foliage – or 'eye-wash' as Col. Weldon describes it – appear around those great fences like festive decorations? What goes into designing and building such a course which, year in and year out, must live up to its long-standing, well-earned and closely guarded reputation? The same natural features, with those emotive names – Vicarage Ditch, Luckington Lane, The Lake, Tom Smith's Walls – appear time and again, but each time, because they are Col. Weldon's 'prestige and pride', with variations on the theme. Apart from the tradition that the course at Badminton is run one year clockwise and the next anti-clockwise, the planning of it causes Col. Weldon to 'think all the year round. Worry all the year round'. Regular visitor as he is, in one capacity or another, to most of the world's significant international three-day events, he is a firm believer in borrowing other people's ideas, if they are good. With his feel for what a horse can jump, and flair for design, he always tries to improve upon the original. Inevitably, however, 'most have to be dreamt up at home'.

'You somehow feel . . . that when Frank produces an impossible-looking fence . . . because he's built it, it's possible.'

To start at the end, so to speak, when Badminton is over for the year, the crowds gone and the Park empty of canvas and cars, work begins on dismantling the entire course. This is done, obviously, a good deal more quickly than putting it all up again, but nevertheless keeps the two course builders busy for a month. All the timber is then put into storage for the next time around. Despite the fact that the materials are bought from the Badminton Estate at less than the market price, timber is still an expensive commodity, and extravagance is both unwanted and unnecessary.

So the praise and congratulation, the agony and the hot air abate for another year and the deer return to graze at liberty in the Park and drink from that famous Lake. But in the autumn, as surely as the season will see the leaves turn slowly golden, so other changes will be afoot in Badminton Park. Perhaps about as subtle as an elephant walking over a tray of eggs, compared with Nature's gentle ways, so the bulldozers and the diggers come in like gigantic moles to make banks where there were no banks before, dig ditches and clear streams, all in the process of preparation for the spring. But, like the popular slogan 'the impossible we perform immediately, miracles take a little longer', by the time the trees are thinking of performing their own particular miracle, those banks, ditches and

Three studies at the open water:
Debbie West on Baccarat.
Major Derek Allhusen on Lochinvar.
HRH Princess Anne on Doublet.

steps are themselves a part of the landscape.

So the hard graft begins in the autumn. The huge growth in the popularity of Badminton as a spectator attraction, coupled with the economic need to farm more intensively and profitably, means that Col. Weldon has available to him much less land than his predecessors had twenty or so years ago. Indeed, in earlier days, no attempt was made to confine the speed and endurance phases into a 'circuit', so to speak. Phase A started out on the Sopworth road, running up to the steeplechase on the point-to-point course. Phase C came back to the Park via the Seven Mile Plantation and the cross-country started at the back of the House, literally in the Duke's back garden. Phase D meandered on through the Park while the final Phase E run-in finished halfway along Worcester Avenue! Nowadays the whole course must be confined to the same area each year and, although the change of direction helps to alter the character of some fences, any major change, or any enterprising new idea, must be wrought by mechanical means to alter the nature of the ground. October and November are the best months for this work which can be completed with turves laid, with any luck before the hard weather comes.

A small, but (thanks to the good account they give of themselves at Badminton), now highly successful firm of fencing contractors have constructed the course under Col. Weldon's supervision since 1966. Alan Willis, of Willis Bros., who served his 'apprenticeship' as a Badminton course builder under George Stoneham, took over when the older man retired after many years' service to the Event. In earlier years, the course was constructed by Charlie Chappell, whose work was much admired and helped to promote Badminton as the prestige event. Alan Willis is now assisted by Gilbert Thornbury and, working as a two-man team, they construct the course 'double-handed', so to speak. Col. Weldon and Alan Willis form a unique 'indispensable' duo. David Somerset says of the former, 'They always say that nobody's irreplaceable but I'm not sure that he may be the exception,' while Frank Weldon, in turn, speaks equally highly of Alan Willis. Willis, says Col. Weldon, 'has a great feel for materials

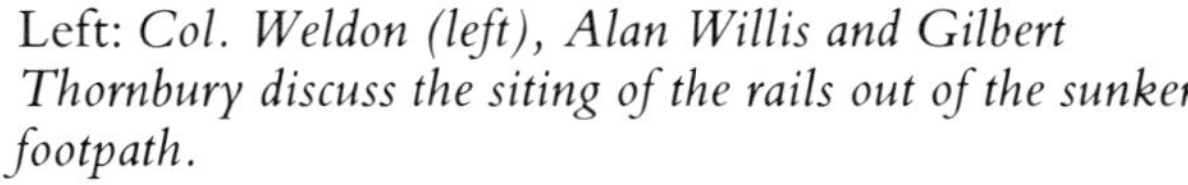

Left: *Col. Weldon (left), Alan Willis and Gilbert Thornbury discuss the siting of the rails out of the sunken footpath.*

Below: *The tractor makes easy work of sinking a post into the frozen February ground.*

Above: *Measuring up for the 'bounce' into the Lake.*

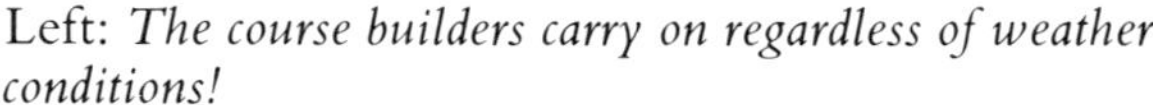

Left: *The course builders carry on regardless of weather conditions!*

Discussing where the upturned punt will go. Badminton House appears ghostly in the wintry mist!

A post goes into the frozen lake two months before the Event.

Over the impressive Whitbread Dray go Sue Hatherly and Monacle.

and an eye for what will look right'. He takes as much pride in his work as Col. Weldon does in his: each turf on each bank is laid with precision – indeed, he makes an art of it.

Art as it may be, however, both Weldon and Willis will use mechanical aid wherever necessary. Until Alan Willis took over, everything was done by hand, right down to digging-in the hundreds of posts which each took many man-hours. Now with the aid of a tractor and tackle, a post can be 'bumped' into position in a matter of minutes. Depending upon the nature of the fence, the time taken to build each one varies between two days to two weeks, including the time it takes Willis's to fell the timber they require; at the outset they will estimate and order from the Badminton estate the amount of new timber they need and they will then be told from where they may select and take their supplies. The felling and cutting timber to size may often take as long as the fence building itself, but it is important to select suitable material.

Although Col. Weldon will commit a new, complicated design to squared graph paper at home, 'most of the planning has to be done looking at the ground'. His expertise is borne from experience and an innate feel for a fence. With his builders, he will work from fence to fence, armed only with his measuring tape and stick (invented and made by the Colonel on the lines of a horse-measuring stick) deciding on the spot, the striding and heights of his famous combination fences. This, he believes, is the only way – an entire course cannot be consigned to the drawing board, despite anything people with less knowledge have tried to tell him.

With the major earthworks completed, the course is left to rest and settle for six weeks or so. In the middle of January the work recommences in earnest, continuing through to the Event itself. Big, solid timber fences, like the ones at Badminton, are now commonplace at any event, but that is what

Fences from the 1979 course as depicted by Reginald Bass

Post and Rails

Whitbread Barrels

Elephant Trap

Keeper's rails

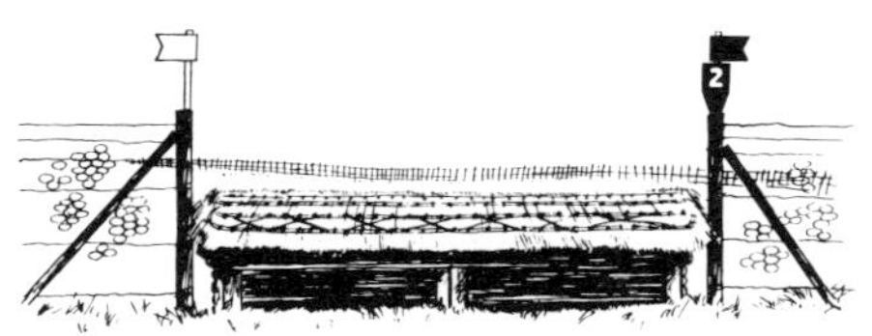

Lamb Creep

Water trough

Sunken footpath

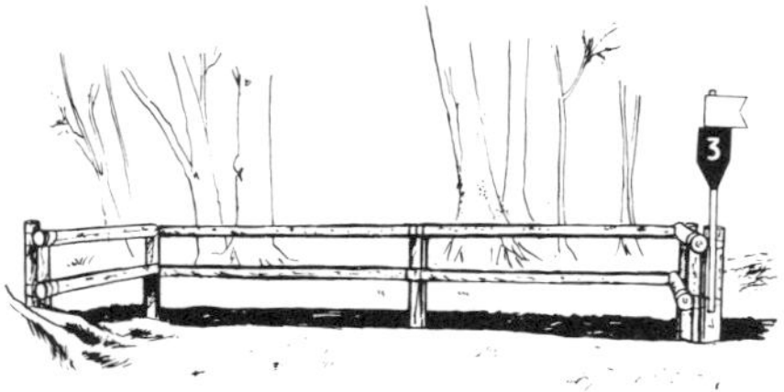

Arrowhead

Quarry

Canal turn

Huntsman's Leap

Quarry

The Lake

Whitbread Dray

Luckington Lare

Pardubice Taxis

Park Wall

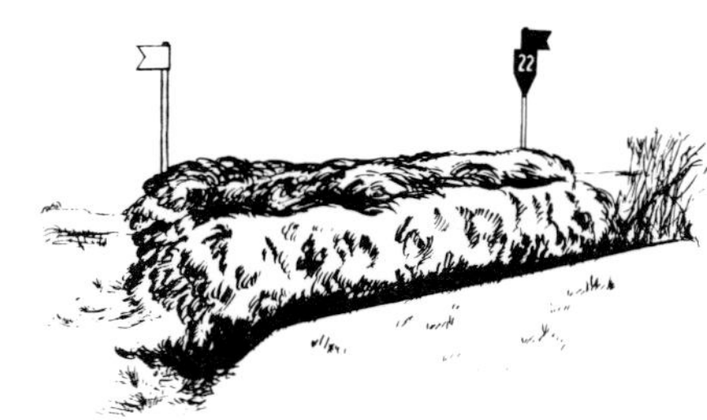

Aintree chair

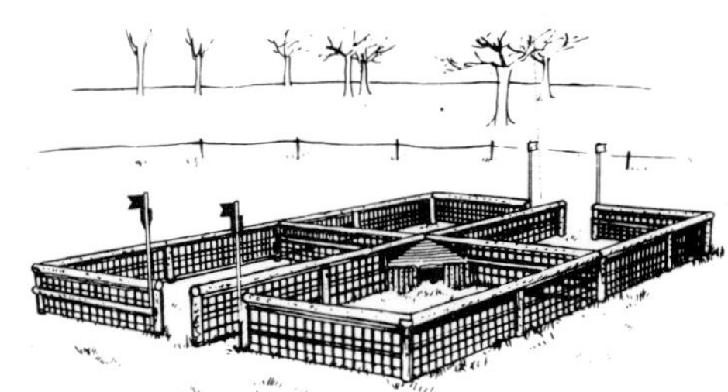

Lexington Dog Kennels

Footbridge

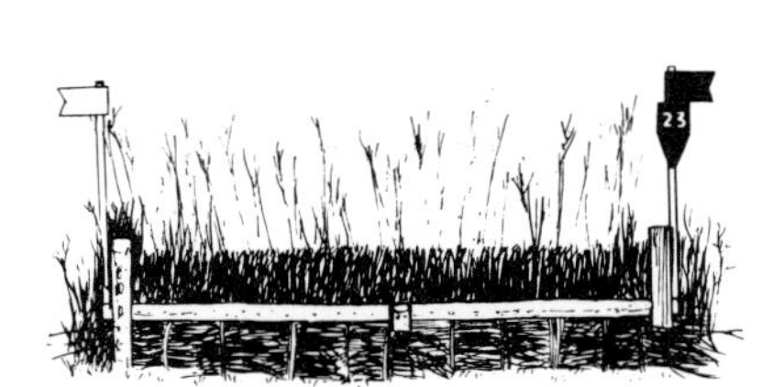

Bullfinch

Zig-zag

Trakehner

Tom Smith's Walls

Woodpile

Huntsman's Leap

Tom Smith's Walls

Whitbread bar

has revolutionized the design of courses and Col. Weldon stresses the need for them to be fixed very firmly. He has learnt the amount of damage that a horse can do to a fence without causing itself too much inconvenience. Despite what has been said by some vociferous critics in the past, the idea is to preserve horses rather than injure them. Although the obstacles are more difficult and sophisticated than twenty years ago, 'every possible precaution is taken to avoid hurting the horses and some of the most imaginative ideas have to be discarded if they conflict with that principle,' Col. Weldon points out. He continues, 'I like to think that Badminton has led the way in producing courses where the best trained, best ridden horses are successful, rather than just those with the most guts and determination – although both those qualities are still required.'

What, then, makes a good course designer? Col. Weldon believes that 'you certainly don't have to have been an Olympic rider to produce a good course, but you must know what a horse is capable of doing, and how both horse and rider are likely to react in certain circumstances. That can probably be learnt by practice and experience but it must help if you have done it yourself. You are then more likely to know instinctively what is going to make riders sit up and take notice, as well as the sort of situation where, provided the rider is skilful or enterprising enough, the horse will have less difficulty than might be expected. Of course there are rules to be obeyed which are laid down in the FEI's International Regulations. The actual construction can be learnt from books or by watching others, but the design of obstacles is more art than science.' Working within that framework, Col. Weldon displays his undoubted qualities of showmanship. He saw Badminton out of the doldrums, when interest in eventing was waning, and through to the success it is today. His courses are very much his stage, on which his character is indelibly printed. 'By now I have quite a selection of obstacles up my sleeve, some of

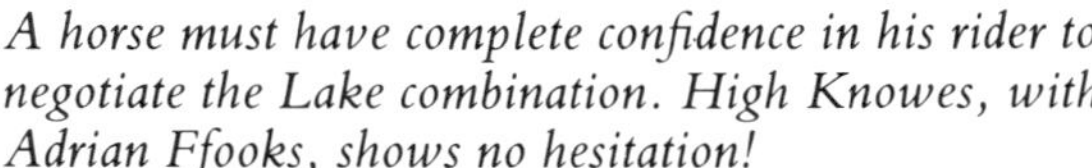

A horse must have complete confidence in his rider to negotiate the Lake combination. High Knowes, with Adrian Ffooks, shows no hesitation!

which have not been used for several years. So, from the riders' point of view, they would be a new problem. In fact, the riders would probably be quite happy if they were always the same, but spectators have long memories. It is partly for their benefit that I try to bring something new and enterprising each time because, after all, they pay to make it all possible!' In actual fact, the riders are just as keen to see different fences and, while some are slightly unnerved by Col. Weldon's slightly tongue in cheek attitude, the older, more experienced competitors have come to appreciate his dry humour.

Another aspect of this showmanship, though perhaps not quite so obvious, is the design of the course with an eye for television coverage. Early in the year, the B B C outside broadcast's producer, Fred Viner, will visit Col. Weldon to decide which fences the TV cameras will cover. In reality, at Badminton, there are very few that have to be missed as a result of this judicious planning and the consideration given to this aspect by Col. Weldon when siting a fence. The only real limiting factor is the number of cameras available and the expense.

As the Event approaches, the final touches have to be put to the course. The entire four-and-a-half miles of cross-country have to be roped to keep back the enormous crowds while chestnut paling has to be provided for the 'box'. All this goes into the debit account of the cross-country phase but, when all the sums have been done and the books balanced, the cost of actually constructing the entire course, taking 1978 as an example, was approximately £7,000. A lot of money? At the World Championships in Lexington, Kentucky, in the same year, two fences cost £9,000 apiece.

Although the character of the Badminton courses has changed greatly over the last thirty years, the rules regarding actual dimensions have not altered much, and any changes which have been made are to safeguard the horses. The maximum height for a fence on the cross-country section must not exceed 3 ft 11 in., measured from the point from which an average horse would normally take off. Obstacles with both height and spread should not exceed a width

Above: *'My heart does something at Badminton it doesn't do anywhere else' . . . Lucinda Prior-Palmer on Killaire in 1977.*

Right: *Andy Brake and Bampton Fair enter the Lake: it is about a foot deep.*

of 5 ft 11 in. at the highest point and 9 ft 2 in. at the base. Only half the total number of fences may be of maximum height, but brush fences and bullfinches, through the tops of which horses may jump, may exceed 3 ft 11 in. provided the solid part of such fences falls within that limit. The fence which perhaps provides the greatest spectacle at Badminton, the Lake, is in fact only about a foot deep where horses enter the water and the floor is absolutely dead level: the horse has not had the benefit of a walk-round, however, and he must have confidence in his rider to take the plunge.

Around each fence is a rectangular penalty zone, extending roughly eleven yards before and to each side of the fence, and twenty-two yards beyond it. Leaving the penalty zone without having negotiated the fence incurs twenty penalties: 'a maddening sort of fault' as Jane Holderness-Roddam once found to her cost. It is only within this zone that faults can be penalized: twenty penalties, forty

penalties and elimination for first, second and third refusal, run-out or circle respectively, at the same fence; the fall of horse and/or rider at an obstacle incurs sixty penalties, and the third such fall in the cross-country results in elimination, as does the omission of a fence, the retaking of an obstacle already jumped or jumping a fence in the wrong order. The only circumstances in which a rider may receive outside assistance while he is competing are the catching of a loose horse by a third party, helping the rider to remount after a fall, or helping to adjust saddlery at any time, provided the rider dismounts to receive such assistance: any other assistance results in elimination.

The pitfalls are obviously many but to complete a Badminton course successfully brings greater personal, if not so tangible, rewards. 'My heart,' says Lucinda Prior-Palmer, one of Badminton's greatest supporters, 'does something at Badminton that it doesn't do anywhere else. Of course, I haven't won a World Championship or the Olympics, but I enjoyed winning Badminton eminently more than winning either European championship.* You can never tell whether the World or Olympic championships are going to be fair competitions because they're never held in the same place. Badminton is the barometer – the stabilized middle-line through – and as near as I can imagine to perfection as a competition. I would prefer to do well there than anywhere else.' A fitting tribute to the Event by Lucinda, whose name will be for ever linked with Badminton for her remarkable and well-deserved record. Will anyone ever repeat her incredible four wins on four different horses? As she is still only in her twenties, it is more than likely that she will add to her own record.

While the products of Col. Weldon's inventive mind present riders with a tough

*Lumuhlen, 1975, on Be Fair; Burghley, 1977, on George.

Capt. Mark Phillips and Columbus tackle the Normandy Bank. Columbus has his hocks well underneath him . . .

Mark collects him up again . . .

. . . and they take the rails and ditch . . .

. and leaves his rider a little behind as he springs onto the Bank.

. perfectly!

Safely down and on to the next.

set of questions to answer, the vast crowds add to the problem by distracting the inattentive horse and rider. The need to contain over-enthusiastic spectators behind rope barriers means that the whole course is effectively cordoned-off for the riders, sometimes making an approach to a fence tricky. In earlier days, before the need for the roping-off, competitors could take their own line into a fence – even take a short cut; now they are channelled along, probably having to make vast last minute adjustments as they enter the 'bubble' around the fence. From the competitor's view, the whole course looks totally different on the day than it did during the walk-round, with some 100,000 people lining the route. Jane Holderness-Roddam describes the feeling:

You can't see half the fences as you come towards them, nor can the horse. Horses are a bit startled by all the crowds, especially if they're all rushing towards the fence. It can be very awkward nowadays when you come round a corner and suddenly there's a massive fence and the whole perspective of it has changed when it's surrounded by people, either because it looks much smaller or it's got lost in the crowd. You've really got to make your horse concentrate. It's all right on an experienced horse but on a horse that you're taking round for the first time, nowhere before will it have seen the crowds that it's going to see at Badminton, and it's going to come as a bit of a shock. For this reason they must be fully confident about their jumping, so that you can concentrate on making them concentrate on what they're doing. For the horse that may be looking around – and Warrior loves to think that there may be people looking at him – you just have to make sure that they're attentive and let them know there's more to do than just having everybody looking at them. The only thing I don't like about the enormous crowds is that people can be so stupid: they've no idea there's a horse coming or they'll see you galloping towards them and just stand there! I've certainly jumped over dogs and things before now, which so easily could cause a horrid accident. In some ways, though, the crowds are nice because they're so responsive and give a huge cheer if you jump something well which is a great boost to the morale. But the main thing is that you must be able to concentrate, apart from the crowd, because some horses do get rather stage-struck and there are a lot of people and there's a tremendous atmosphere that you never get anywhere else.

Jane Holderness-Roddam has never jumped a course so consistently big as Badminton. Here she clears the Elephant Trap on Warrior.

Chris Collins also sees the positive aspect of the crowds: 'I think these bigger fences are rather better ringed by a crowd and the horses play to the gallery a bit.'

Since the inception of Badminton, the whole concept of the building of a cross-country course, right down to the smallest hunter trials has altered. Huge timbers and imposing-looking obstacles are now the norm; with well-defined outlines they invite a horse to jump them well whereas, in earlier days, although the courses were more straightforward, they were less well built using flimsy timber, the result being that any mistake by horse or rider was catastrophic. A debate on which type of course presents the rider with most problems could, in itself, fill a book, but perhaps Richard Meade's observation is relevant: 'Your whole approach to the event is entirely dependent on the horse you're riding. That's why the courses look so small to some spectators! And they look particularly small to the people who used to event and have given up – you see the course through the eyes of the best horse you've ever ridden.' Bearing in mind that Richard Meade's eventing career extends back to 1963, and he is now regarded as Britain's top rider, he is probably one of the best equipped to answer questions on how courses have altered. He continues: 'Courses have got much more complex in that there are fewer fences where you can just get going and gallop. Somebody once said to me there was a time at Badminton when after the sixth fence you could light a cigarette and just kick on, for ten fences, but that doesn't happen now! More and more problems are set for the riders and it requires a higher degree of precision.' All are agreed that, technically, today's riders are better prepared in each section of the competition although Badminton's first winner, John Shedden, bemoans the fact that few people nowadays have the opportunity

Richard Meade's eventing career goes back to 1963. Here he is seen at his first Badminton three-day event in 1964.

to ride, unhindered, across a good hunting country, which is the best schooling ground for this type of riding, for both horse and jockey.

Even with all her experience, Jane Holderness-Roddam says that she has never jumped a course as consistently big as Badminton. So what qualities does an event rider need to possess, not only to continue to face these huge obstacles, but also to be successful in the process? 'Don't ask me, I've no idea!' says Richard Meade but he continues with a maxim which lesser mortals would do well to heed if they ever dream of aspiring to his heights: 'I think you've always got to be trying to improve, and prepared to learn to improve every aspect of your performance. I think the other thing is, as in any sport, when things go wrong you've got to fight back. Things do go wrong in sport; you've got to be *resilient.*' Lucinda Prior-Palmer, our top lady rider, has much the same attitude: 'I've often asked myself what particular attributes an event rider must possess and, I think, perhaps pig-headedness, to help you get through those moments when you just might want to give up, coupled with a humbleness; if you're not willing always to learn and admit to yourself that you were wrong when everyone expects you to be right, that is going to be your downfall. The more you learn the more there is to learn.' To quote the late Henry Wynmalen in his 1952 Badminton commentary: 'However natural the gifts may be, no person will ever become a fine horseman without unending practice, experience and work. Further, he must be prepared to acknowledge how little he knows.'

Other people are unanimous in believing that a rider must have a very quick brain; things can go wrong very suddenly during a three-day event and only the person on top of the horse can sort them out. Underneath her calm composure, Jane Holderness-Roddam is an extremely competitive, determined rider and she modestly admits that 'you've got to be slightly brave'. Col. Bill Lithgow is perhaps more explicit: 'They've got to have tremendous guts!' Badminton, for many, is the ultimate; to get round and finish the event is an achievement of which they are justly proud. Those riders who win and do well consistently have an added quality, perhaps more an instinct, the absolute desire and determination, the will to *win*. Determination, dedication and confidence in the horse are all essential qualities which, ideally, should be combined with natural ability and an eye for a stride into a fence: especially the combination fences which, because they are more technical, must be ridden, one might say, almost like a show-jump. It is people who are endowed with these qualities who will rise to the top. Former competitor, and now Chairman of the Horse Trials Support Group, Martin Whiteley believes that this natural ability is plainly the greatest asset to start with. 'If you haven't got it, you've just got to work that much harder and train that much more. You have to have enormous enthusiasm and determination and you've got to keep going.' Like Richard Meade, he says, 'things go wrong frequently and you've got to pick yourself up and start again. Temperament is tremendously important. You've got a competition spread over many days, and at the top level there is considerable strain. I think you have got to have someone with the temperament who isn't going to lose sleep, go off his food and get in a desperate state. This is Richard Meade's greatest quality, quite apart from his natural ability. Jane

Racing is at the background of eventing, an influence reflected in . . . the Pardubice Taxis fence – here looking deceptively small, negotiated by Miranda Frank on Touch and Go.

... Bechers, with (left) Nick Straker on Ruan and Jane Thorne on Spartan Boy ...

... the Canal Turn, with Princess Anne on Goodwill

... and the Aintree Chair, negotiated here by Capt. Mark Phillips on Columbus.

Holderness-Roddam is another with a marvellous temperament which I am sure shows with her nursing and shows very much with her riding.' A colourful description of temperament is left by Thomas de Grey, a 17th-century horsemaster: 'The exquisite horseman must not be of a life dissolute or debauched, nor of a nature harsh, furious, choleric or hare-brained. For the least of these vices is unbecoming to a person of this profession, but he must be of a life sober, and in his functions laborious and diligent, of complexion phlegmatic and patient. He must indeed be the master of his passions.'

Complete confidence in the horse is an over-riding necessity: 'One's got to trust the other absolutely and entirely,' says John Shedden, and into this comes the need for the rider to be a good horsemaster, a quality which will reveal itself in the performance of the horse on the day. A good horsemaster will have prepared his horse to the peak of fitness for the event and will know how to save his horse's energy over the speed and

Diana Thorne (now Mrs Henderson) on The Kingmaker flies out over the Normandy Bank.

A promising young combination, Sandy Brookes and Weldon Playboy, seen at the Park Wall.

endurance phase, so that by the end of Phase D, the horse is not only *not* showing signs of distress, but finishes at a positive gallop with stamina in reserve. The Australian rider, Laurie Morgan, Gold Medal winner at the Rome Olympics and winner at Badminton a year later, sums up on horsemastership.* 'A rider must know the maximum speed and endurance of the horse from his experiences of preparing the horse for the competition, and providing his horse is correctly prepared, it is there for the tapping. In the cross-country phase of most competitions I feel as happy as a puppy released from his chain, and providing my horse is fit I feel he has the same attitude.'

Laurie Morgan continued: 'The Mecca of all horse-trial riders in England is Badminton'; few would dispute that this remains the case. The preceding paragraphs give an impression of the type of rider likely to succeed at top level competition but it is appropriate to return to the reaction of competitors and others in the sport to the courses set by Col. Weldon, whom most people recognize as amongst the best, if not *the* best, course designer in the world. Although each year there are gasps of incredulity as the wraps come off each new fence, most people will acknowledge Col. Weldon's own rule which opens this chapter. Some are concerned that Badminton should be such a consistently large course and would like to see a reduction in the severity of the cross-country. But as Col. Lithgow says, Col. Weldon believes in Badminton. 'From the word go,' summarizes Martin Whiteley, 'Frank Weldon set himself a standard which, on the whole, has been admirably maintained.' It is generally agreed that if there was one year in which the Badminton course was not good, it was 1973, when horses were continually punished for being bold, by landing in a six foot drop or in the face of a bank. Raymond Brooks-Ward, MFH, and television commentator, has reason to remember 1973, as there were so many eliminations that they began to wonder whether they would get any horses on the

**The Horseman's Year*, 1962, edited by Dorian Williams (Collins).

Gill Watson on Shaitan, the reserve horse for the Mexico Olympics and 1969 Burghley winners, confidently over the 1970 double oxer.

course for television at all, but, he says, 'Frank Weldon is a big enough man to admit that it did happen and it was the only time in all the years he's been building there that he fell down. Apart from that, his courses are always fair; they don't over-test the horses but they make the riders think, think, think all the way round. He really is the most creative man in combined training in the world.' Col. Bill Lithgow adds, 'I've got the most enormous respect for Col. Frank Weldon's judgement but I think he would say himself that when you're operating on the margin, it's very easy to go just that little bit too far.' Apart from that one year, Jane Holderness-Roddam has always found Col. Weldon's courses 'fantastic – always so beautifully built and proportioned and the take-offs and landings so good'. This last aspect is something which course builders, even at top level, often neglect, a point in case being at Kentucky, in 1978, for the World Championships. But having been an Olympic three-day event rider himself, Col. Weldon knows all the pitfalls and, over the years, he has reduced his course designing and building to a fine art. It is rare indeed to see a 'bad' fence at Badminton. There are stops and falls but these are spread over the course as a whole rather than many people coming to grief at one or two bogey fences. This again is a mark of a great course builder.

As director of the biggest three-day event in the world, Col. Weldon is also responsible for the smoothly run organization, but his flair for this is described in the next chapter.

8

BACKGROUND TO BADMINTON

When an event runs as smoothly and efficiently as Badminton Horse Trials, one is apt to become complacent about the vast amount of time and effort which goes in to making it all possible. One is even more likely to forget about those many people who busily work behind the scenes: some for months in advance and others perhaps just at the Event itself; but all of whom are important cogs in the well-oiled machinery. This book would not be complete without paying tribute to the organization of this classic event in the horse trials calendar.

To repeat all the praise one hears for Col. Frank Weldon and his 'army' of assistants and helpers would complete this chapter. It would also, perhaps, bring accusations of sycophancy from cynics. Michael Bullen goes a long way to summarizing the general feeling:

I don't think there is any event in the world that is run as well as Badminton. Nowhere: without exception. Badminton is *the* premier event. People talk about how well Lexington was run. It was, for somebody who's never done it: it was run very well, but Badminton knocks them all into a cocked hat. Everybody knows what to do and how to do it; there's no fuss or bother. As well as getting how ever many? – 50,000 cars? – in and out, it's a masterpiece of organization. OK, they've had thirty years to do it and perfect it every year, whereas other people haven't. There isn't a big event anywhere in the world that isn't basically modelled on Badminton, because that's where it all really started, in a big way, and it's where everybody, basically, wants to come to. It's absolutely brilliantly run!

Alan Willis and Gilbert Thornbury still at work on the Friday morning making steps for spectators at the Luckington Lane.

Certainly, Badminton is the 'model' event and people come from the world over to witness the phenomenon and go home with a clearer idea of how to run their own events. Jane Holderness-Roddam, who was a member of our World Championship team in 1978, echoes her brother's view in saying that the organization at Lexington was obviously based on our own system.

Badminton's first winner, John Shedden, while praising the organization throughout the history of the Event – despite the little things that often went wrong in the early days – 'would go even further to say that I shouldn't think there's any organization better today, if as good!' And from the modern competitor's point of view: 'Everything is done for you,' says Lucinda Prior-Palmer. 'The timing is so good. I have nothing but praise.' In spite of Frank Weldon's classic remark that the spectators come first, they pay to come in, Chris Collins acknowledges the 'very good deal' the competitors get: 'I think it's because Frank Weldon is a former competitor he still sees things from the competitors' viewpoint.' Hugh Thomas adds, 'His bark is always worse than his bite and he knows as well as anyone that if it weren't for the competitors you wouldn't get the public in anyway. Although sometimes I think you would get people to go to Badminton to watch a donkey because it's the place it is!'

The huge scoreboard, a Badminton innovation, which records the scores as they happen.

The whole operation is masterminded from the permanent Badminton Horse Trials office. Formerly the village forge, it lies back off the road in the centre of the village, literally a stone's throw from the main stable yard. The main office, which is shared by Col. Weldon and his assistant director, Major Derrick Dyson, is festooned with plans and charts of where trade stands and grandstands will go; how the traffic will flow; how grooms will be accommodated and how horses will be stabled. It is the nerve centre which, clearly and methodically, organizes the movements of, literally, thousands. Major Dyson, who competed at Badminton in the 1950s and was second in command to Col. Weldon in the King's Troop, is described by the latter as 'a first-class administrator'. Chairman of the Event, David Somerset, says of Major Dyson: 'He is a very remarkable chap and, luckily for us, an accountant!' He needs to be, for an amateur could easily get into an expensive muddle with the income from all sources, which in 1979 approached £¼m., out of which such a

Major Derrick Dyson on Water Gypsy in 1954.

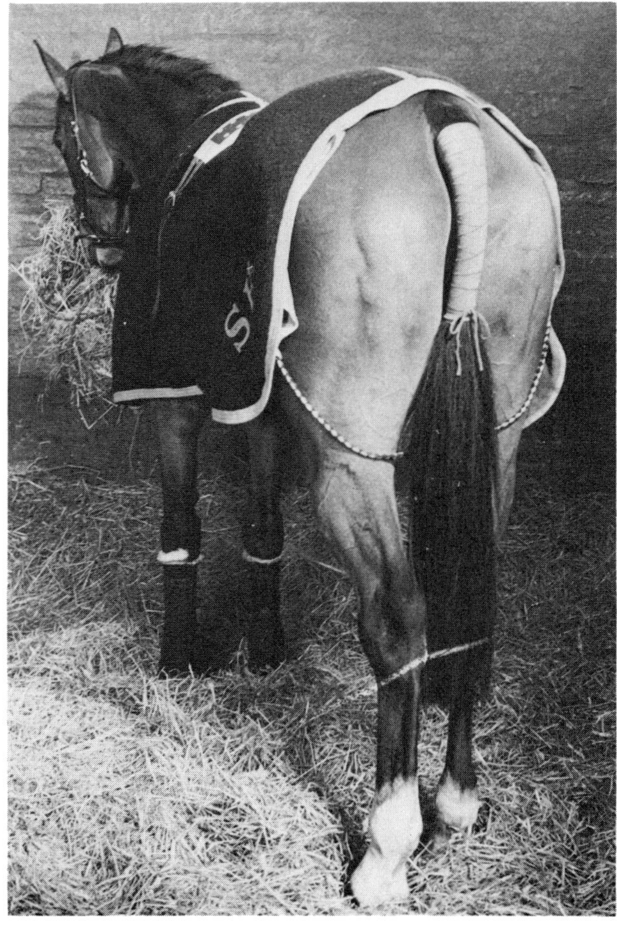

Competitors get a very good deal . . . 1978 winner Warrior relaxes in his box at Badminton . . . while his stable mate, Just So, has his plaits taken out for the day.

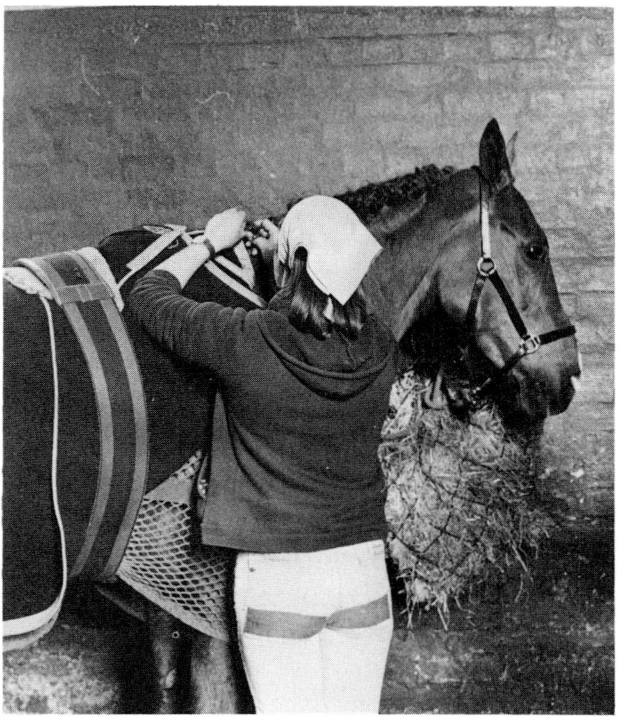

wide variety of payments have to be made. Major Dyson also looks after the allocation of trade-stand space, marking out the position for the stands along with the many other tents and grandstands. He has the onerous task of dealing with the many contractors, organizing the programme sellers, arranging the insurance, estimating the number and position of the lavatories and generally taking charge of the tented village which springs up each year in Badminton Park.

The 'queen pin' of the office, as Col. Weldon calls her, is Victoria Sanford who is employed permanently by the Horse Trials but who, in fact, works full-time only for the few months leading up to the Event. She is, however, 'on-call' throughout the year and, as well as running the day-to-day administration of the office, she is also responsible for producing the Event programme. Victoria's 'bible' is one of the keys to the smooth-running of the Event. It is a methodically-kept check list against which she can record whether the large number of voluntary officials have received the right number of passes and tickets to which they are entitled. Clearly an area in which accuracy and tact are paramount.

Working with Victoria on a part-time basis is Jane Gundry, daughter of Major Gerald Gundry, Joint Master of the Duke of Beaufort's Hunt. She is a great asset in that knowing, as she does, the many sporting people in the district, she can organize stabling for the visiting show-jumpers, whose competition entries she also handles. Also because of her local connections she organizes the dozens of Land Rovers which are needed during the competition to ferry the twenty or so doctors and vets, plus a clamouring press, around the course and she is also responsible for some of the publicity of the Event. Suitable local shops, and those a little farther afield in Bath, Bristol and Cheltenham, are approached and will generally produce, for nothing, window displays around the Badminton theme. Col. Weldon's publicity policy is grounded on the belief that if something is good enough it will publicize itself and he restricts the advertising budget to £750, some of which is spent in advertising in the local press and *Horse and Hound*, but the remainder produces car stickers and little publicity cards which can easily be distributed far and wide without any heavy financial burden upon the Badminton purse-strings.

Joan Petre is another of the unsung heroes on the permanent staff who has run the box office for fifteen years and made herself indispensable. She handles all the advanced ticket applications in respect of car parking, dressage and show-jumping grandstand seats, and visitors' caravans, not just from this country but all over the world, accounting for over £65,000 each time. Working chiefly from her home, Mrs Petre starts to worry in earnest in the autumn, when the committee meets to decide entrance prices for the following year. The different sorts of tickets must then be printed in their thousands, corresponding exactly with the grandstand plans. Application forms are sent out to nearly 4,000 regular customers and a steady trickle of these will come in until the general advertisement appears in *Horse and Hound*: then the flood gates open and Mrs Petre works flat-out until the Event itself. This work demands not only meticulous accuracy but the tact and patience of Job, not to mention keeping an eagle-eye on those who try to get something for nothing.

While, obviously many people who attend the Event recognize the great contribution made to the sport by the Duke of Beaufort, it is easy to forget the great sacrifice he makes by allowing his Park to be used – and by some, regrettably, abused – for the Trials. But David Somerset explains, 'The Duke is a man of tremendous enthusiasm – it was his inspiration which set the whole eventing story in motion. And for years he's gone on with his enthusiasm for it. It's quite an inconvenience for him to have the whole place mucked up year after year with thousands of people trampling about, not just from the unsightliness of it but from the farming point of view. It holds up everything. Many of the people working on the Estate are suddenly called in to do all sorts of other jobs, so if he didn't enjoy it and feel very strongly about it, he wouldn't need any excuses to say he didn't want it!'

The most obvious disruption to the day-to-day running of the Badminton estate is in the stable yard. Ever since the inception of the Event, the Duke of Beaufort has given over his magnificent yard for the accommodation of the event horses. While, by the time of the Event, some of his hunters will have been turned away for the summer, others will have to be found stabling elsewhere in the village. Major Ronnie Dallas, secretary to the Duke of Beaufort's Hunt, takes charge of the stable management officially, as a committee member, but the yard is run during the Event, as it is for the rest of the year, by the Duke of Beaufort's stud groom, Brian Higham. A dedicated professional, in the old-fashioned sense, one cannot help but get the impression, that for Brian Higham, the sudden influx of forty of the world's most valuable event horses, causes no more disruption to the running of his yard than preparing the Duke's hunters for a normal day with hounds. He even enjoys it all, not only for meeting old friends again, but for the pride he

Above: '*. . . thousands of people trampling about*'.

Right: *Major Ronnie Dallas competing at Badminton in 1951 on Most Valiant.*

takes in preparing the yard for the onslaught. Indeed it is a showpiece but no less a very efficient working model. After twenty-one years at Badminton, Brian Higham is known and respected by all; top riders will telephone him for advice, and he, delighted that they should ask him, is all too willing to oblige. Nowadays, owing to more stringent qualifications, the entry at Badminton will not usually number more than forty or fifty, but actual numbers are not known until a few days before the Event, and up to a 100 horses could be accommodated without causing any inconvenience.

A list is made up of which competitors want what type of bedding for their horses, and each entry is allocated a box, either in the main yard, the Portcullis yard, or the Brassey yard, a short walk away. The day before the Event, Brian Higham, assisted by Tom Smith (a tenant farmer who is just as well-known as his famous Walls), who helps out in the yard for the week of the Event, attach cards to each stable door proclaiming the incoming occupant. All the boxes are scrubbed out before the bed of a competitor's choice is laid fair. Brian Higham is meticulous: 'I wouldn't want people to think I hadn't inspected the boxes myself.' Nothing is left undone – right down to polishing the brass fittings – and then Brian's only worry is that he has no absolute control over the visiting grooms and owners. He and his staff keep a close eye on the visiting horses, however, and he himself comes down to the yard for a late night check before he can return home happy. If he has a motto, it is to 'keep the customers satisfied'. If a competitor has asked for a peat bed, but arrives at the event wanting straw, it will be changed immediately and without fuss; kettles of hot water will be supplied for poultices and linseed is prepared on the Saturday for horses after the speed and endurance phase. All the feed is supplied and even this is a product of Badminton – even the linseed is grown on the Estate.

Competitors' grooms are accommodated free of charge, thanks to the Whitbread sponsorship, and live in, either with the Badminton grooms or in caravans provided by the organizers. All their meals are provided in the palatial servants' hall in Badminton House, the high walls heavy with antlers, the trophies of an earlier sporting era, and copper pans, all kept in pristine condition, and equally a reminder of a past era. The groom's job at any event, and perhaps even more so at Badminton, is more than just looking after the horse. He or she must work to a timetable, for each competitor has deadlines to meet and the groom must be able to work quickly, but thoroughly, under pressure. For many, the facilities at Badminton, and the conditions in which, for one week of the year, they have the privilege to work, give a unique opportunity to sample what is, possibly, the last of the great establishments in the old-fashioned tradition. There is a special unit for washing-down and drying-off the horses – a great bonus – and a new indoor riding school will be available to competitors to exercise and school their horses in future events.

The atmosphere in the stable yard at Badminton breathes history and excellence, and no doubt both competitors and grooms alike can learn from the experience of living and working there. Brian Higham adds: 'I probably learn things myself.' Indeed all the Duke's employees are involved in one way or another in the production of the Event and take just as much pride in its success.

Although Charlie Chappell, the head forester who has worked on the Estate for sixty years, no longer builds the fences himself, his advice and assistance is still invaluable. He knows every inch of the woodlands, and most of the timber now being used was planted by himself fifty years ago; he not only says which trees can be felled but, from his expert knowledge, can suggest where the most suitable ones can be found for any particular purpose. John Davis unselfishly assists whenever he can with the hire of tractors and trailers. He is also, incidentally, a skilful

Tom Smith surveys his walls!

signwriter and in his spare time produces the lettering on the hundreds of notices.

In quite a different sphere, Leslie Vacher, the butler, cheerfully puts up with the annual invasion of the grooms' canteen into his domain, even though his resources are already stretched to the limit looking after the Royal party.

Yet if there is one man without whom the Event could hardly take place, it is Desmond Staines, the Clerk of Works. A skilled carpenter, he works throughout the year in his spare time, constructing and maintaining the vast amount of equipment required such as the scoreboard, arena fencing, litter baskets, dressage boards, signs and white stakes. He also acts as quartermaster, looking after the sheets and blankets for the grooms' quarters, the white coats for the stewards and what's left of the thousands of toilet rolls ordered each year! Nearer the Event, he and his small gang do all the annual work not done by the contractors, like erecting the chestnut paling around the 'box', putting up the arena fence and distributing the litter baskets. During the Event itself he organizes the collection of tons of rubbish and, immediately it is over, when everything is being removed as quickly as possible from the Park, he arranges for local children to pick up the loose paper at 50p a bag.

Undoubtedly the most important visiting officials are the members of the Ground Jury, invited, and with expenses paid for, by the organizers. FEI rules insist that for an international competition like Badminton, one member at least of the Ground Jury and one member of the Committee of Appeal must be foreign judges in order to avoid undue bias. At Badminton there are always at least two foreign judges on the Ground Jury and sometimes three when, for instance, it is possible to invite the judges at an important forthcoming championship, like the Olympic Games, in order to give competitors the benefit of experiencing their likes and dislikes. Furthermore, by a recent change in the rules, the FEI emphasize that the Ground Jury is

One of the last great establishments . . .

. . . breathing history and excellence . . .

responsible for the whole conduct of the competition at this level of international events. They have to approve the course and the dimensions of the fences on both the steeplechase and cross-country before the competitors arrive and, in some circumstances such as difficult ground or weather conditions, they must decide on any changes to be made. Theoretically this means that the Technical Delegate, who is such an important figure at open international championships, is redundant; but although he no longer has any official status, he still has a useful part to play. For instance, in this country all three-day event courses are approved by a three-man course inspection panel, of which the Technical Delegate is one, who pay at least two visits during the con-

The Red Cross stand by to retrieve people from the Lake – waders at the ready!

struction of the course. During the competition, although the Ground Jury is the authority, the Technical Delegate can be particularly useful in the event of any protest or objection, in co-ordinating the evidence and summoning witnesses.

The Ground Jury will usually consist of three internationally approved judges, mentioned earlier, who judge the dressage, and a veterinary surgeon – now Mr W. J. B. Watson, formerly Joint Master of the Berkeley Foxhounds, whose great practical experience helps him to know instinctively, for instance, how an exhausted horse behaves, and what minor lameness it is safe to overlook. The Ground Jury is entirely responsible for the judging and conduct of the competition and officiates at the two main veterinary inspections. Any decision of the Ground Jury can be appealed against by the competitor to the Committee of Appeal, on which His Grace the Duke of Beaufort sits; a veterinary decision is, however, final.

The majority of the stewards and other officials is made up of local people, many of whom established links with the Event in 1949. Mr David Somerset is appreciative: 'We are very lucky in having, during the Event, a tremendous amount of voluntary help – all the fence judges and ground stewards: these people just give up their time for us.' Badminton is not, however, still the 'happy-go-lucky' amateur event of the early days, and Col. Weldon now insists on having professionals at key places and people dedicated to the job in hand everywhere else.

The steeplechase and cross-country phases are timed by totally impartial, professional timekeepers; the 'trick cyclists' as Col. Weldon nicknames them, as they usually operate at cycling events. He is particularly sensitive about this point. 'Timekeeping is not nearly so difficult as, for instance, in athletics, as we are thinking only in terms of commenced seconds, rather than tenths or hundredths, but it is still quite possible to make mistakes. For instance, on a conventional stop-watch (which has now been superseded by digital timers) it is easy to read tenths of a second but equally easy to get it wrong by a whole minute – as I found in my second year at Badminton when I was mistimed by a whole minute on the steeplechase, which meant the difference of finishing second instead of first.'

While the timekeepers see riders on and off each phase, the job of seeing them around the steeplechase and cross-country is of course that of the fence judges. The steeplechase fences are judged by soldiers recruited by Major J. Turner from the School of Artillery, Larkhill, while Lt.-Col. E. G. V. Northey organizes the voluntary helpers around the cross-country course. The speedy collection of information from both timekeepers and fence judges is vital to producing fast, accurate results. 'Scoring', says Col. Weldon, 'is largely a matter of organization and communication' and it is another area where 'professionals' are involved. Two girls from the Horse Trials Office at British Horse Society headquarters, who spend the season travelling the country to score at official events, are responsible for the quick processing of information. Col. Weldon comments: 'Scoring is not nearly so complicated as one might think. To the public, and even to those connected with the sport, who have never done it, the whole business of scoring is wrapped in mystery, but any intelligent girl, who doesn't flap, picks it up in a remarkably short time. All that is needed is plenty of practice.'

One of Badminton's most well-known past scorers is Miss Jane Pontifex, now a journalist on *Horse and Hound*, while Miss Nichola Gibb, who 'retired' in 1978, unravels the jumbled thread, the wrong end of which most of the uninitiated seem to pull.

Scoring falls into a very straightforward pattern and, providing all the necessary information is fed into the scorer, and that *she knows what to do with it*, there should be no problem. She must, of course, be very much aware of anything that should have been fed in, but has not, in order that it is chased up rightaway to avoid delay. For these reasons, the scoring team is situated very close to the action on each day.

For the dressage there are just two people in the scoring team – everything is very carefully checked at all stages. Judge's score sheets are collected as each horse leaves the arena and the score calculated as the next horse is performing its test. On completion of the next test, the score is announced and marked up on the main scoreboard. After each movement of a test, each

Top: *'Providing she knows what to do with it . . .' Anne Spiller and Joanna Boswell, the BHS scorers.*

Above: *The score columns beside each dressage judge's box: a Badminton innovation.*

Right: *An eager team of runners from the Beaufort Pony Club.*

judge's score lights up on the tall column by each box and this acts as an interesting guide for spectators as to how the different judges are marking. In each judge's box there is a person switching on the appropriate number as the judge says it, and in the centre box is a master switch; when all three judges have given a score for a movement, the marks are displayed.

For the speed and endurance the scoring team move down to the 'box' area – at the start and finish of the cross-country. There are specially-designed time cards for timekeepers to fill in and these are passed in to the scorer. As the steeplechase is some distance from the 'box', communications between the two are vitally important if scores are going to be announced over the public address. There is an excellent telephone system at Badminton supplied by the Wessex Yeomanry and as soon as a horse completes the steeplechase, its starting and finishing times are passed to the scorer who calculates the time penalties, by simply reading from a prepared table, and passes them, firstly, to the commentator, who straightaway can announce them over the public address, and secondly by telephone to the scoreboard. Confirmation of the steeplechase times comes down in batches of cards after every six horses – purely as a double check again. Similarly, sheets come down from each steeplechase fence judge, as written proof that each horse did jump each fence without penalty. As each horse finishes Phase C (roads and tracks), a card is brought immediately with the finishing time recorded and this can then be married up with its starting time which has already been telephoned over with the steeplechase times. Finally, in the cross-country phase, a time card is brought across immediately the horse finishes, and the interrogator – at Badminton this is Col. Weldon's son, George – discovers from the rider, as he weighs in, what sort of round he has had. This means that a provisional score can be announced immediately a horse has finished.

For the dressage and the speed and endurance, score sheets are typed as each horse finishes. The only delay in this comes at the end of the cross-country when the actual jumping score has to be confirmed by the sheets which are brought in from the individual judges by Pony Club runners. This is becoming quite a problem at Badminton where the children have to fight their way through crowds of people, particularly at the end of the day when the crowds are heading the same way as the runners, and there can be some delay. On the whole the provisional scores remain unchanged but obviously the result sheet cannot be duplicated until these scores have been confirmed.

On the final day, the scorer is beside the show-jumping judge and commentator giving the total and final placing as each horse finishes. Final results sheets are then typed as soon as the jumping is finished and are usually available by the time the prize giving is over.

However clear Miss Gibb's explanation, it does not detract from the responsibility of the scorer, and the fast production of results is yet another indication of the efficiency with which Badminton is run. In the earliest days, when Badminton first started, the first erroneous results were not available until 10 o'clock the next morning, but now they are

on the score board within minutes of a competitor finishing.

The public address system at Badminton has always been a feature of note. In 1952, W. E. Lyon wrote: 'The Gloucester Hussars (Armoured Cars) did splendid work in feeding the loud-speaker unit with information by wireless, so that wherever you were walking you knew just what was going on at various points . . .' Nowadays, the system is just as efficiently run by the Wessex Yeomanry, while the commentator now also has the advantage of a TV monitor set fed by cameras covering practically every jump.

With the interest shown in eventing, and Badminton in particular, by HM the Queen and the Royal Family, there has been an attendant interest among members of the popular press. Wherever Her Majesty goes on the course, she is bound to be shadowed by a body of fevered photographers, jostling and pushing one another to get *the* picture. A competitor may come and go, but the motor-drives whirr away with only one subject in focus! The control of this element gives press officer Jim Gilmore the greatest headaches. In charge of the 250 or so press for eight years, Jim Gilmore is efficient and effective in his role, and it must be as much due to him, as perhaps to the fact that the novelty is wearing off a little now, that HRH Princess Anne is comparatively little worried by the

Above: *Still carrying a worried look is Press Officer Jim Gilmore in the centre of the Sunday morning crowd.*

Below: *Eventing's 'Golden Girl'! Lucinda attracts quite a following as she makes her way to the dressage.*

Acting as mounted stewards on the cross-country are the Duke of Beaufort's huntsman, Brian Gupwell, and Stud Groom, Brian Higham.

press at Badminton. Indeed, Lucinda Prior-Palmer appears to have become an equally popular target.

The press has always been well looked after at Badminton: a factor show organizations often neglect. As early as 1952 Land Rovers were supplied to ferry press-men around the course and main-line phones were installed for their use.

If Badminton is the home of eventing, it is an even greater stronghold of foxhunting and, apart from the occasional blue and buff collar worn by a competitor entitled to wear the colours of the 'home team', the Duke of Beaufort's Hunt, other links are never far away. Visitors to the Trials may well catch a glimpse of hounds out at exercise, while on the Saturday, mounted stewards wearing the green livery of the Beaufort, the yellow of the Berkeley and the more traditional red of the Avon Vale and the VWH Hunts take up their positions around the course, giving a fitting reminder of our great heritage from which stems our excellence in the sport of eventing: the real 'background' to Badminton.

9

TRIALS AND TRIBULATIONS

There is plenty that can go wrong at a horse trial. Incidents related in the previous eight chapters have illustrated the point: the hasty rebuilding of the course in 1951, the disaster for our team in the 1952 Olympics, the cancelled 'Badmintons'. Personal disasters have been legion; horses failing veterinary inspections; 'blow-ups' in the dressage; falls on the cross-country – some, tragically, fatal. In the first category one could not help but feel sympathy for the Belgian rider, Mr Hillaire Tielemans and his beautiful stallion, Nelson, who perhaps unwisely had enjoyed a day's hunting with the Duke of Beaufort's only days before the 1979 Event but had sustained a knock on a wall and were spun at the first veterinary inspection.

Badminton weather is always capricious and its unpredictability has, from the very first year, been the greatest trial for the organizers. The 1949 Event was wet, but 1959 far exceeded all the worst expectations! With storms raging around the coast, preventing the Irish from embarking for Badminton and killing a French horse on the Channel crossing, Badminton remained remarkably serene on the day before the Event. The forecast was for slight rain, but the ever-hopeful 'becoming brighter later' was promised, and all remained optimistic. After two hours' continuous rain on the morning of the dressage, the prospects looked about as gloomy as the weather, and by the time the last horse of the morning entered the arena to perform his test, it had become 'so churned up that people were wondering how on earth the next fourteen would fare. X, the centre-point, was almost hock-deep: the corners appeared to have been ploughed and at E, half-way down one side, the horses had to splash through three inches of water.'*

By the end of the day, during which the rain never ceased, the Park was a quagmire. Should the event continue, was the question on everyone's lips. 'We hunt in such weather, so why not this?† was the cheerful answer of Douglas Nicholson, and the official response was much the same. The course would be altered accordingly, but the show would go on. And go on it did. Sheila Willcox, riding her comparatively novice horse, Airs and Graces, told Dorian Williams in a television interview that she was 'scared stiff'‡ about the problems the cross-country course would present: in the event, she coped admirably. The sun actually shone on the third day, and 'straw tracks were laid across the acres of mud (1,000 bales were given to Badminton by local farmers – a compliment to the reputation and high regard enjoyed both by Badminton and the Duke of Beaufort).§

Although the 1959 event ended 'in a blaze of glory', with Sheila Willcox marking up her third consecutive win, it was a great personal

Argonaut and Mason Phelps nose dive at the Vicarage 'V'.

**The Horseman's Year,* 1960.
†Ibid.
‡Ibid.
§Ibid.

Lorna Sutherland (now Clarke) on Peer Gynt comes back over the Luckington Lane.

They jump the first element well . . .

. . . but the horse begins to have a look at the bank. Lorna drives him on . . .

. . . and gets him on to the bank, but . . .

Peer Gynt never really takes off.

He leaves a front leg behind . . .

and they somersault . . .

. . . over the rails . . .

Happily both horse and rider emerge unscathed.

thousands who were hoping that he and Countryman would win the Badminton Championship. Leading at the commencement of the show-jumping, they had one fence down (which they could not afford) and were beaten into second place.

In *The Horseman's Year* of 1960, Dorian Williams doubted whether, after the 1959 experience, conditions could 'ever now be bad enough to justify such an event being abandoned'. Four years later, after the severe winter of 1962–3, Badminton just held out against the elements by going 'one-day', and this proved one of the 'wettest days of a very wet spring', but in 1966 and 1975, conditions most certainly proved bad enough to justify cancellation. In 1977, gale force winds ripped the canvas off the grandstand on the Friday morning and delayed the start of the dressage. Against such disasters the Badminton organization is completely insured; in earlier days, the British Horse Society underwrote the Event against cancellation, now Badminton arranges its own insurance.

As for personal 'trials and tribulations', Frank Weldon recalls his first disastrous attempt at eventing as his major trial. However, 'the most embarrassing occasion as an organizer occurred at Badminton about ten years ago when all but one of the first fifteen competitors were eliminated at a fence near the Keeper's Cottage. It was a tree trunk barely three feet high, located close beyond the natural ditch, which proved to be a good deal more sophisticated than it looked. It was not until the later competitors, their trainers and supporters having profited by the early mistakes and worked out a different approach, that anyone got any further. After that most people cleared it effortlessly but in the meantime there was near mutiny amongst the spectators waiting impatiently at what they thought were far more imposing obstacles at the Luckington Lane.'

Golden Willow, Badminton's first winning horse, was a fiery character sired by an American racehorse and 'he was bred to be wild'. His rider, John Shedden, who describes himself as a physically strong rider, had to restrain Golden Willow's over-exuberance across country by riding him in a gag snaffle and tight standing martingale.

M. Jurg Zindel and Range Warden, uncollected in the Lake . . .

Even this did not curb Golden Willow's great spirit and they became the first and last combination actually to fly the Irish Bank without putting a foot on it – a spread of 37 ft! 'Golden Willow and I understood one another,' says John Shedden, 'I knew the form rather! He had a remarkable sense of self-preservation and when he hit the parallel rails at Badminton with his chest, at full gallop, he scrambled over to land vertically, his tail over my back and galloped for five strides on his forelegs before we regained equilibrium! There are enough trials and tribulations at this game,' agrees John Shedden. 'Three days before Badminton, Golden Willow was let loose by one of my girls in the yard. He galloped round, slipped up on the concrete, fell against the cement walls and cut all four legs to smithereens. That night all four legs were swollen. Of course he was full of corn and if you get an injury then, everything blows up. My only chance was to give him a dose of physic that night in order to keep him cool and get those wounds right.'

More memories of mishaps in the 1950s come from Col. Bill Lithgow. 'I rode at Badminton three times and the best I ever did was to be eliminated at the last fence. It was

. . . and disconnected out of it!

Near drama for Bill Roycroft on Warrathoola.

terrible! On television – the lot! It was the jump into the Lake, which in those days was only a tiny little tree trunk which you could have walked over – but my horse would *not* go! The Event was all terribly well organized but they were the early days and things could go wrong. I remember the first time I rode at Badminton, in 1953, I hardly knew what the word "Dressage" meant. The best you could say was that I got "round", but then I was given quite a good mark. A number of people came up to me in the collecting ring to congratulate me but I said "I think you'll find they've got it wrong by 100". Sure enough, after the next competitor they announced the correction.'

Similar, but more crucial mistakes in scoring were not rectified when they befell Frank Weldon, who was over-timed by a minute on the steeplechase in 1953, and John Shedden who was held up on the cross-country course in 1950, but the time was never deducted from his final score. 'There have always been odd sad stories about Badminton,' says the latter, 'the famous fence judges who go home with the last scoring sheets so the scores can't be announced!'

Martin Whiteley recalls a rider error which, although humorous, has a serious lesson to teach.

In the early days, Phase A, which nowadays is very nice through the woods, covered about a mile-and-a-half along a road; it couldn't conceivably now, because the road is covered in cars. But we had to trot along the road which was hard and had no proper verge to it, and the questions were whether it would hurt the horses and should one have studs in? So I thought I'd been frightfully clever and found a short-cut to the steeplechase course. It was perfectly legal as it didn't miss out any flags, but it did cut off a corner of the road by cantering through the fields and jumping over a couple of little walls. I'd looked at this carefully; but there was one field of kale and one had to jump into it, canter across and jump out. I'd looked at the walls and they were very jumpable but I had not – and this is the lesson – actually walked through the kale. Anyway, the moment came and I was on Phase A, lolloping along

Martin Whiteley on Happy Talk in the 1964 Little Badminton, at the Open Water. A moment later they turned a somersault!

Merlin Meakin and Lynette take a tumble at the Bullfinch.

through this kale, very relaxed, and I cantered straight into an electric fence which I hadn't realized was there. Of course the horse stopped absolutely dead and went backwards, and I went straight on and landed on my head in the kale, totally unhurt, but of course I arrived at the steeplechase course with mud on my back and I was never allowed to forget that incident. But it was 100 per cent my own fault.

Sadly, at any horse trial, there are bound to be isolated cases of a horse being killed or having to be destroyed, and Badminton, of course, is no exception. Dorian Williams recalls the very first year Badminton was televised which demonstrated the nightmare of live television. 'The first horse we picked up on the cross-country was a grey, which I can see to this day. He fell at the Vicarage Ditch and broke his leg. There was no other horse on the course; there was nothing else we could turn the cameras to. So the cameras looked at the crowd and suddenly there was a sickening report as the horse was shot. That was appalling.' The most widely publicized tragedy was obviously that which was the most dramatic when, in 1976, Lucinda Prior-Palmer's mount, Wideawake, dropped dead minutes after receiving the Whitbread Trophy. Lucinda remains philosophical:

Wideawake's death was indeed a tragedy but I felt that if a horse was going to die, and obviously his cards were up, then to die in his moment of victory was, in a way, quite beautiful. That was the only thing I could think of. There was no use saying what a shame, because obviously it was *the* most awful shame. I felt that it was so much my luck that he should have died then and not just before he entered the show-jumping arena which would have meant his elimination. But he won, and got his prize, got his gallop round, and he died; and for that reason it wasn't the most awful experience that I think it appears to be because you have to find the good side of these things. But if you look at Wideawake's death from a 'what a pity' point of view then that was worse than anything will ever be again. But you mustn't look at it from that way.

As far as riding is concerned, Lucinda has had sticky moments on her Badminton rides.

I think there are tricky moments in every ride round and you always wonder how you got away with XYZ and then every now and again you hit Z and it doesn't come off and you go wrong. I had a very nasty moment at the Coffin when Be Fair won in 1973. He nearly stopped at it then slithered over the side of the first rail and missed the ditch out, so I had to come back in and travel along the ditch instead of going over it to get round the flags. The worst moment for me was having a crashing fall on Be Fair at the 'S' fence a year later. He was expected to win because we had won the year before. That really was awful from a competitive point of view.

Jane Holderness-Roddam was another rider to have a near stop, in 1978 when she won on Warrior. A momentary hesitation on top of the Quarry had spectators' hearts in mouths. A point of some debate on television commentaries, it was described by Jane as a slight 'stall'. She explains what happened:

Warrior is always so intelligent he would never take off on anything that he thought had no landing. And I think that's what he thought. He jumped on to the top and just stopped, dead! It felt like only a second – it was only a second or two. But he's so clever that the moment he could see the landing he was all right. But as you approached that fence it did look as though you were jumping straight into mid-air. He would never do anything that he thought might hurt himself and I think he gave everybody else much more of a fright than he did me. The only problem I've really had at Badminton was with a horse called Troijoy. She was so star-struck by all the

Opposite:

Top: *Michael Tucker in trouble at the water!*

Bottom: *Miss Rosemary Prout on her (appropriately named?) Farewell!*

crowds and goings on that I had a disastrous time at the double bounce fence: we should have gone jump-jump-jump, but we didn't and I landed in the middle of the fence. That shook her up completely. She wouldn't jump the next fence, which was the Trakhaner, and we both ended upside down in the ditch, which was a very nasty experience.

Badminton has 'always been a little unlucky' for Chris Collins, who says:

I could catalogue my problems! The first two years, 1970 and 1971, which were my entry into the sport, I was nearly last. In 1970, I fell off when the horse refused at a bounce fence on the cross-country and in 1971 I fell off in the steeplechase; the horse I had then was slow and I was about fifth last. In 1972, I was twelfth but with a very expensive refusal in so much as the horse went over the side of the fence and went outside the penalty zone, so I had to come back in again, and that took a lot of time, which prevented me from being second or third. The Selectors rang up to ask for the horse without me for the Olympics! In 1973 the horse coughed during Phase C so I withdrew him and in 1974 Smokey was lying fourth after the cross-country and I knocked down one show-jump which pushed him down to ninth, but Centurion went well and was tenth. In 1975 the Event was cancelled, and in 1976, Smokey blew up in the dressage and then had a refusal at the Chevrons, but still did the fastest round and was in the money. In 1977, I had a silly refusal at the zig-zag fence but still had the fastest time and my dressage was better and we were sixth.

In 1978, Chris did not compete owing to a broken ankle and, in 1979, Radway gave him a bad fall on the steeplechase which landed him in hospital for a couple of days.

Our top rider, Richard Meade, has often found himself piloting comparatively inexperienced horses around Badminton and recalls:

Of two horses which have given me tricky rides, the trickiest was Laurieston. He took a lot of chances with his jumping and you never quite knew whether he was going to take a fence by the roots or not. He used to stay on his feet but he would hit the fences all ends up in the early days. At Badminton, however, I had a good ride on him; he hit a couple of fences fairly hard but apart from that he went brilliantly. That really was the turning point in his career as far as I was concerned, and in our career together. Bleak Hills

Troijoy gave Jane Holderness-Roddam a 'disastrous time'!

Above: *Mr David Somerset and Countryman come to grief in the show-jumping phase of 1957.*

Right: *Brig. Darling on Trinity Point in the 1961 Event. Incredibly they got over this fence. Brig. Darling was tragically killed in a hunting accident in 1978.*

Laurieston – Richard Meade's trickiest ride.

was not at all an easy horse, but again, Badminton brought him on a lot as far as I was concerned. As a result of Badminton, he was an easier horse to control and direct in the World Championships at Kentucky. Of course, the more difficult the horse, the more exciting it is if he goes well.

Michael Bullen remembers many close shaves: 'There's a very good photograph of me with my horse perpendicular to a gate at Badminton. I can remember thinking it was time I got off and the picture shows me in a very good position.'

During the early 1960s, Bertie Hill concentrated on National Hunt racing but when a horse called Chicago arrived on the scene, he turned his attention back to eventing. 'He was a grand horse to ride, and although we won a lot of events, the Badminton trophy always eluded me. Having led in the dressage at his first Badminton, he was very unlucky to injure himself when he slipped on landing over a steeplechase fence, and he had to be withdrawn. I rode him at Badminton again the following year, 1970, and this time I made the stupid mistake of taking the wrong show-jumping course when we were there with a winning chance. He was second after the dressage and had given me a superb ride in the steeplechase and cross-country phases and I felt I had cheated the horse. It was the best ride I ever had and it was the last time I rode there.'

Some of the most amusing stories – which at the time of their making were something of a trial – come from the world of television commentating. As Raymond Brooks-Ward says:

Obviously all sorts of things go wrong for us in television . . . I think the worst was when we were actually doing the Sunday afternoon pull-together programme and a fly crossed the head of the tape machine and broke the tape. Because it was two hours after the Event was over, there was only one cameraman and me left. That's all. I had to talk for what seemed like an age, but was about a minute, until he repaired the tape.

On the amusing side, one year at Burghley, Barbara Hammond, unfortunately, had a fall in the trout hatchery going out and another coming back. I suppose, editorially, the decision was taken that this was very, very photogenic and they showed it at the opening and the closing titles. Christopher Hammond was naturally quite indignant about this and when we came to Badminton the next year, without my knowledge, they put up Ba Hammond at the trout hatchery at the start of the programme on Grandstand. Chris Hammond came flying up the stairs of the commentary box to take me to task, thinking it was all my fault! Fortunately we had a big stage manager who stood at the top of the stairs and managed to calm him down.

Dorian Williams has the story to finish them all!

On one very wet year – 1959 – the BBC couldn't get its equipment on to the ground and eventually I finished up commentating on some Post Office vehicle which was very high and narrow with just room for me to stand, with a little ledge in front of me for my notes and a monitor set down by my side. Just as we went on the air, I heard the producer say through my earphones, 'I'm terribly sorry old boy, but we've lost your picture.' He then added, 'but go on speaking because the viewers have a picture. The cameramen will tell you what you're seeing.'

So for the next seventeen minutes, which may not sound very long, something like this happened: I would hear through my earphones:

'Camera No. 5; number 3 approaching the Lake' ... look through my sodden programme, 'And here is Frank Weldon going at a great gallop ...'

'Sorry old boy, he's gone.'

'Oh!'

'Camera No. 9 at the Quarry; number 7 coming up the hill,' quickly finding number 7.

'And number 7, Mr Jeremy Beale on Fulmer Folly coming very fast ...'

'Sorry old boy, it's a girl!'

'Oh!'

Well this went on for seventeen minutes and eventually, to my enormous relief, I heard the producer say, 'It's all right old boy, we've got your picture back.' So I took a step backwards to look at my monitor set: but of course there was nothing to take a step backwards on to. So I went out. Head over heels and there I was, strung up like a trussed chicken, by my earphones! Somebody came and pushed me back in but of course by that time I had been so used to talking about what I couldn't see that I just went on talking

Chicago and Bertie Hill – they might have won the 1970 Event 'but for a stupid mistake in the show-jumping'.

"Lady, you don't happen to have one about horses being unfair to riders?"

Badminton has had its share of critics: this picture, courtesy of Giles, hangs in the Trials office.

To 'Badminton',
With deepest sympathy,
from Giles.
'74

throughout and nobody really noticed it.

But there was rather a funny sequence to that, the next day. I was going up to the show-jumping and I heard an announcement over the loud-speaker asking me to meet the director of the horse trials in front of Badminton House. It had been pouring with rain and I thought they were going to cancel it, so I struggled down like Capt. Oates himself through the blizzard, absolutely plastered with the straw which they had laid on the tracks. Well, of course, the director wasn't there, but I thought he might be in the house, so I opened the first set of the double doors, but as I did so the second doors blasted open and the sudden draft whipped my hat off my head and whizzed it right across the baronial hall to land on a mantelshelf, my hair desperately trying to join it! I heard a titter. So I looked round by the side of the door and there were five people in the hall, four of whom I recognized immediately. One was the Queen, one was Princess Margaret, one was the Queen Mother and one was Lord Snowdon. I stood there feeling a bit of a Charley. However, Princess Margaret stepped forward and said, 'You're the very person we wanted to see. When you were televising the cross-country yesterday, did you fall out of your commentary box?' So I said, 'As a matter of fact, Ma'am, I did.' She turned to the Queen and from what she said I gather they'd had a bet on it!

Frank Weldon summarizes and offers some sound advice: 'You are very lucky if things always go smoothly, and I have had my fair share of trials and tribulations, both as a rider and as an organizer. But if you have any sense, you try to profit from your mistakes.'

10

A ROYAL EVENT

While the success of Badminton is due directly to the Duke of Beaufort and the hard-working directors and committees, no one would deny the very special role that HM the Queen has played in her unfailing support for the Event.

It was with great significance that, in 1949, King George VI and Princess Elizabeth became Patron and Vice-Patron respectively of this new equestrian event, but it was not until 1952, the year of her accession, that the Queen attended Badminton for the first time. 'Her Majesty the Queen, the Duke of Edinburgh and Princess Margaret plan to pay a private visit to the Olympic Horse Trials, as guests of the Duke of Beaufort. The Royal Party will thus have the opportunity of seeing our prospective Olympic horses in action.'* It was a gesture most loyally appreciated by the Duke of Beaufort: 'As far as I am personally concerned, of course, we have been extremely fortunate in having the support of the Royal Family throughout.'

In the 1950s, no one had coined the word 'walkabout' and the fact that HM the Queen was attending the horse trial at Badminton, and literally rubbing shoulders with her subjects was indeed a novelty. Dorian Williams recalls: 'When the Queen started attending very regularly, and could be seen driving around the Park with the Duke of Beaufort, and the Duke of Edinburgh driving the children, in Land Rovers, it was a very attractive thing for the public. People thought "Well, I might be standing next to the Queen", and there neither was, nor is, anywhere else you can do that to be perfectly honest. So the very fact that the Queen was making a little holiday of it got enormous publicity; you could say that, through Badminton, eventing was the sport that the Royal Family adopted. Because the Queen and her family like to be associated with Badminton, largely through their great affection for the Duke of Beaufort, it got tremendous publicity and the more people wanted to come.'

And come the people did. 'I think lots of people come entirely to see the Queen and not to see the competition so much,' says the Duke of Beaufort, and surely, in no other country in the world would the reigning monarch be found wandering amongst the crowds as HM the Queen and her family do at Badminton. They have helped to make it a household word. 'At no other sporting event,' says Col. Frank Weldon, 'does the Queen mix with her subjects as a spectator or is unselfish enough to present the prizes down to the last rosette – and the public naturally appreciate it.'

However, Her Majesty has played a much more personal part in the success of Badminton, and in the sport in general, than just as a spectator. Her first gesture to the British eventing effort was to invite the international teams to train at Windsor, using the stables of the Royal Mews and the wide expanse of the Great Park, for six weeks prior to any major competition, and of course in 1955 the European Championships were held there. Now she is host to an annual event in the Great Park which, in 1979, became one of our five annual three-day events.

In 1956, Bertie Hill had to make the heart-breaking decision to sell his brilliant Countryman. Their success had greatly increased the value of the horse, and capital

**Horse and Hound*, 1952.

HRH Princess Anne and Doublet clear a show-jump in fine style at the end of their first Badminton. They finished fifth.

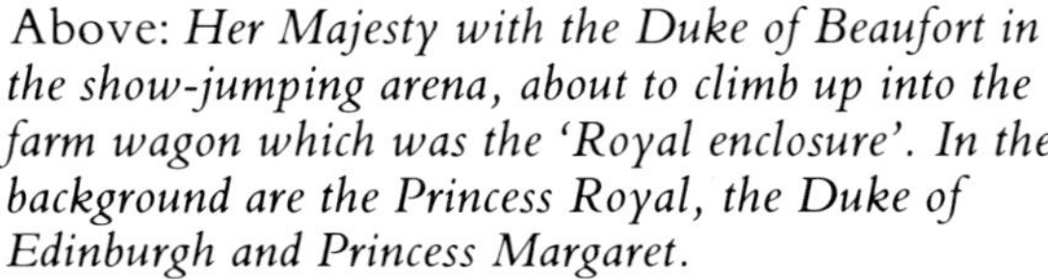

Above: *Her Majesty with the Duke of Beaufort in the show-jumping arena, about to climb up into the farm wagon which was the 'Royal enclosure'. In the background are the Princess Royal, the Duke of Edinburgh and Princess Margaret.*

Above centre: *1960: HM the Queen and Princess Anne arrive at the arena with the Duke and Duchess of Beaufort.*

Above right: *'... I might be standing next to the Queen! ...'*

Right: *HM the Queen Mother presents Richard Meade with his winner's awards in 1970.*

Far right: *At the end of the 1974 Event Her Majesty presented the Whitbread Trophy to the winner Capt. Mark Phillips. He promptly gave it back to her as the owner of the winning horse, Columbus. Amusedly looking on are (l to r) Mr Michael Whitbread, the Duke of Beaufort, and the Duke of Edinburgh.*

CONTROL

Right: *Prince Philip discusses an amusing point with Col. Bill Lithgow.*

Below: *Her Majesty the Queen with Col. Gordon Cox-Cox, trials director from 1954–64.*

Above: *The Royal Box on the last day of the 1956 Event.*
Left: *HRH Prince Charles leaves the Dressage arena in 1960.*
Facing: *Her Majesty the Queen looks on as her horse trots up for the vet.*

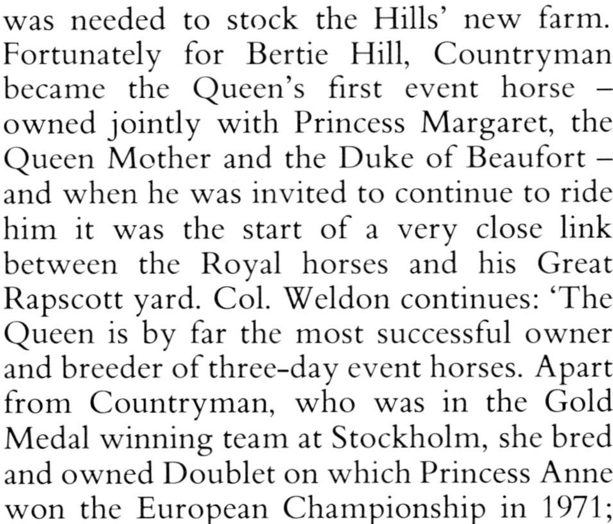

was needed to stock the Hills' new farm. Fortunately for Bertie Hill, Countryman became the Queen's first event horse – owned jointly with Princess Margaret, the Queen Mother and the Duke of Beaufort – and when he was invited to continue to ride him it was the start of a very close link between the Royal horses and his Great Rapscott yard. Col. Weldon continues: 'The Queen is by far the most successful owner and breeder of three-day event horses. Apart from Countryman, who was in the Gold Medal winning team at Stockholm, she bred and owned Doublet on which Princess Anne won the European Championship in 1971; and Columbus, on which Capt. Mark Phillips won at Badminton and was so cruelly robbed of the World Championship at Burghley; and she also owns Goodwill on which Princess Anne was second in the European Championship of 1975.'

While the Royal patronage of Badminton attracted spectators, HRH Princess Anne's personal competitive involvement – and success – has undoubtedly given to the sport an image which people would like to emulate; and they try in their thousands. Whether many will ever have her single-minded dedication and determination is very doubtful. To insist on completing an Olympic course

after a concussing fall and to return to compete at Badminton mere months after having a child are two examples of extraordinary resilience, while the very fact that she finds *time* to event with a diary full of official engagements is, if anything, an exaggeration of the qualities an event rider must possess and her own capacity for sheer hard work. At an event, she is a competitor first and a princess second; who can blame her occasional abrasiveness when thoughtless photographers rob her of precious concentration so vital to the job in hand? It is not *because* she is a Princess of the Realm that Princess Anne is a successful eventer, but *in spite* of it!

Since 1952 Her Majesty has attended Badminton on all but one occasion, when she was on a State Visit to Australia. In 1977, her Jubilee year, on behalf of everyone present at the Event, the Duke of Beaufort presented Her Majesty with a fine bound volume of Elizabethan manuscript. The gift was a token of the thanks owed to the Queen for her presence at Badminton and for the interest and support which she has always given, since the commencement of the Trials in 1949. The presence of her family lends to Badminton a unique paradox: it is an *informal* Royal event which contributes to the spirit of the great occasion embodied by Badminton.

11

BADMINTON YEAR BY YEAR

1949

Twenty-two of the original forty-three entrants started in the first Badminton Horse Trials on Wednesday, 20 April, when in blazing sunshine, well over 1,000 spectators gathered around the dressage arena laid out on the lawn in front of the House, their cars standing six deep. Dressage performances were far from perfect: there was a lack of straightness throughout, especially revealing in the rein-back, and it was noticeable that most horses were not on the bit. Competitors had had relatively little time to prepare their horses for the test which was, by Olympic standards, fairly easy and many horses were clearly not ready for a double bridle – then obligatory. Capt. Tony Collings on Mrs G. Chrystal's Remus gave a performance such as was expected of him; smooth, polished and accurate and, dropping only fifty-six points from a possible 350, they moved into the lead after the first day, thirty-three ahead of their nearest rival, Lt.-Col. P. Leech on Lucky Chance. In third place lay John Shedden and Golden Willow, whose temperament made him unreliable in the dressage arena.

Fortunes changed drastically on the second day when, in pouring rain, Golden Willow's devouring stride put John Shedden into the lead, while Remus showed that he had not the speed required for such a competition and, despite a faultless performance, they lost their lead. One jump down on the last day was not enough to topple John Shedden, while almost thirty points behind was Mr Ian Dudgeon, on Sea Lark, who had put up a great performance around the course and was to become a regular visitor to Badminton. Brig. Lyndon Bolton, who had represented Britain in the Olympic Three-Day Event a year earlier, filled third position. Setting the pattern for the future, in fifth position was Miss Vivien Machin-Goodall (the late Mrs Boon) who showed that here was a sport at which men and women could compete on equal terms.

Making his first visit to Badminton was Lt. E. A. Boylan, who finished 10th, while Mr Reg Hindley who became one of the 1952 Olympic team, was 11th. In 12th position

Ian Dudgeon on Sea Lark put up a great performance and became a regular visitor to Badminton.

John Shedden on Golden Willow.

was Lt.-Col. C. Legard who started the speed and endurance section in a mackintosh but, obviously feeling over-dressed for the occasion, completed the course in a steeplechase jersey!

Golden Willow

Described by his rider as 'the most lovable, the greatest, and most terrifying horse I have ever ridden', Golden Willow was by Cloth of Gold by Sir Galahad II, a top-class American race horse, out of Pussy Willow, and was owned by Mrs Eleanor Home Kidston who had kept his dam with John Shedden prior to the war. Golden Willow was foaled in 1943 in the States but returned after the war to stand in the same box as had his dam, and was earmarked by John Shedden as his Badminton mount. 'His was a sad story,' recalls John Shedden.

After his second Badminton, in which we finished fifth and were desperately unlucky not to win, Mrs Home Kidston's friends persuaded her that it was a waste of time eventing him and he must go racing; he would win the Grand National! My opinion was that the horse was raving mad and that no one would ever train it for racing; I could only just hold him across country with gadgets on and I knew that no jockey on this earth would hold him in a snaffle. In training for Badminton he had stood so far off a steeplechase fence that we landed and then took off again to jump it beautifully! I had hoped to make an international show-jumper of him, but he was taken into training and on his first gallop, I understand, he ran away for fourteen miles and broke down. It broke my heart. It took a year and a half to get him right and I desperately wanted him back but he went back into training, ran away at exercise one morning, broke down again and was shot. It was an absolute tragedy.

1950

In beautiful spring weather a phenomenal number of people visited Badminton for the second three-day event in the series leading up to the Helsinki Olympics. Again Capt. Tony Collings and Remus produced a performance of suppleness and grace to take a convincing lead in the dressage over Miss Patsy Hildebrand on Mr P. McCann's Lily, a formidable combination in combined training, despite the fact that the standard generally had improved. This time however he took no chances with the cross-country which, although not fast, was sufficient to keep him in the race. John Shedden, the first competitor to ride two horses – Golden Willow and Mrs Fanshawe's Kingpin – was hot on Capt. Collings's heels at the end of day two, but two fences down by the inexperienced Kingpin let the Olympic team trainer through to win by two and three-quarter points. Mr Reg Hindley and Stealaway, who gave a good consistent dressage display to be in fourth position after day one, had three fences down on the show-jumping to drop them down to sixth. Major R. Hern, on Millfield Public School's King Willow, gave an outstanding display of horsemanship: completing the cross-country in astonishing time, King Willow fell at the penultimate fence and dislodged his bridle; undeterred, Major Hern remounted, completed the course with two reins on one side of the horse's neck, and still incurred no time faults. The bank, by its construction, proved something of a bogey and many horses came to grief in trying to fly it. Golden Willow was the only one to manage it, incredibly enough, as John Shedden had steadied him right back hoping that he would know what was expected of him!

Of the thirty starters, eighteen completed the three days.

Remus

When Miss G. Chrystal was recommended to look at a six-year-old 16 hh bay Irish

Capt. Tony Collings and Remus.

hunter gelding at the Mill Hill Riding Establishment, she immediately took a half-day off from her war-time nursing to inspect and, subsequently, buy a potential Badminton winner. His breeding unknown, Remus was a kind horse with enormous character and sense of humour. A great 'show-off', he loved the dressage arena when he could be the centre of attention and, indeed, under the expert guidance of Capt. Tony Collings, he finished top in dressage in both his Badmintons. His two passions in life were ice cream and a Corgi called Mr Tod, who had been trained to lead his friend around with a halter-rope! Remus ended his career, as befitted his breeding, with several seasons hunting, then retired at grass where he would playfully spend his time ducking his head under water in the stream which ran through his meadow.

Major John Miller and Stella; seventh in 1951.

1951

Badminton was 'open to the world' as host to the first international event in Britain and visitors came from Ireland, Switzerland and Holland: a team from the latter made their own way over to England – with no Government support it was a costly exercise with each horse costing £30 on the ferry and currency difficulties to hamper them – as they felt so strongly about the international importance of the Event. The Swiss fielded a strong team of horses which, although fat and unfit, were sufficiently supple and obedient to be able to tackle the second day. And so it proved, for the hopeful British were fairly trounced by the continental opposition when both our teams were eliminated. Our weakness in dressage was glaringly apparent against the Swiss, our leading scorer being Reg Hindley on Stealaway with 114·75 penalties against the leading score of 48·75 by Capt. A. Blaser on Mahmud. The Coffin proved the downfall of the British, with refusals and falls, but the obedient Swiss horses made little of it, and it was no surprise at the end of the competition to find that they had taken first, fourth, sixth and ninth individual placings with their A and B teams first and second. Britain's face-saver was a young girl just out of Pony Club – Miss Jane Drummond-Hay (now Mrs Timmy Whiteley) on Happy Knight – who made valuable ground by jumping one of the only clear rounds on day three to finish second. That competitions can be won and lost on the show-jumping was more than adequately demonstrated here: Mr E. Van Loon of Holland on Nerantsoula was in contention for first place before four show-jumping fences down pushed him back into third, to allow Capt. Hans Schwarzenbach through to win on Vae Victis. S. C. M. 'Tommy' Thompson on Capt. Naylor Leyland's Torloisk jumped the fastest cross-country to bring him up to fourth overnight but dropped behind Lt. Tony Bühler from Switzerland to finish fifth. Some horses were beginning to make their mark as potential Olympic mounts; Major Miller's Stella was seventh, Mrs Baker's Starlight, ridden by Lt.-Col. D. N. Stewart was eleventh and Mr Reg Hindley's Stealaway finished thirteenth. (See also Chapter Two.)

Capt. Hans Schwarzenbach on Vae Victis receives his award from the Duchess of Beaufort. Jane Drummond-Hay looks on.

Vae Victis

A French horse of no known breeding, Vae Victis' career was as chequered as any horse to have appeared at Badminton before or since. His association with Capt. Schwarzenbach began at the St Gallen horse show when a Swiss officer tried to sell him to the Captain. He was not impressed with the animal and refused him, but on returning home late the same night, was bemused to find the horse in his stables.

The Swiss officer had delivered the horse with a message saying that it had been sold to Capt. Schwarzenbach! The ensuing saga was indeed mysterious as, despite telegrams and strongly worded letters, the horse remained. Capt. and Mrs Schwarzenbach began to exercise him as he could not stay in all the time, but problems arose when Vae Victis stumbled, breaking both knees. To forestall further complications, the Captain telephoned the owner and finally bought Vae Victis for a low sum.

After the months of silence from the previous owner, Capt. Schwarzenbach had not heard the last of him when the sale was completed. Through his studied approach to the horse, the Captain conjured the best out of him and his value increased many-fold when he competed successfully at Lucerne. The Italians were keen to buy, but they were very firmly turned down. However, reappearing on the scene, the previous owner claimed that Vae Victis was still his and sold him to the Italians for a substantial sum. The horse had been installed in the Italian stable before his rightful owner discovered him missing, but happily, through the intervention of the President of the Swiss Federation for Riding, the horse was restored to the Schwarzenbachs.

At nine years old, Vae Victis carried his owner to victory at Badminton, the only Continental combination ever to have done so, and they returned two years later to take third (Individual) at the first official European championships.

1952

With the top horses and riders *hors concours* in the run-up to Helsinki, the 1952 Badminton was anyone's race. Twenty-six started from an entry of forty-four and Jane Drummond-Hay, who had saved British face the previous year, came back on a different horse, Abbeyfeale, to take a twenty points lead after the dressage. However, a ducking in the Lake on the cross-country, which caused the removal of Abbeyfeale's bridle, put them right out of contention. The only rider to return the same position after both days was Penny Moreton from Ireland on Vigilante, while the overnight leader was Brig. Lyndon Bolton who had represented Great Britain at Aldershot in 1948. In third position by a narrow margin was Capt. Mark Darley on Emily Little, while Brian Young on Dandy filled fourth place.

Once again the Coffin took its toll as did a drop fence of hazelwood bundles where Liza Mandy gave her rider Frank Weldon a 'heavy toss' and he was taken off unconscious to hospital.

Everything again hung on the last day. Both Brig. Bolton and Penny Moreton lost their chances with three fences down apiece, moving them down to third and fifth respectively, while Brian Young moved up to second with two fences down and Mark Darley jumped one of the few clear rounds to win. It was a consistent Badminton for the Irish who finished first with Mark Darley, fourth with Penny Moreton and fifth with Harry Freeman-Jackson on Cuchulain.

Second in 1952, Brian Young and Dandy.

In the year of her accession, H M the Queen visited Badminton on the first of what has become an annual visit.

Emily Little

This15·3 hh flaxen-maned chestnut mare had more in common with her owner, Capt. Mark Darley, than at first meets the eye. An Anglo-Arab, she was a descendant of the famous Darley Arabian which was brought to this country by a forebear of her owner.

Capt. M. A. Q. Darley riding Emily Little.

Capt. Darley bought the mare, in 1950, from her breeder, Miss Smith of Shilton, Warwickshire and took her to Germany where he was serving. He took time to school her properly under expert guidance and proceeded to compete with her in the show-jumping ring. This was her forte and she knew nothing of cross-country or dressage prior to a combined training event at Beaminster, a week before Badminton, where she finished in reserve position. She spent four days at Porlock prior to Badminton, but it was her show-jumping experience which won the Event. Capt. (later Col.) Darley went on to concentrate on her obviously most talented side and twice rode her to victory in the King's Cup at the Royal Tournament.

Emily Little spent her retirement with Major and Mrs Lawrence Rook where she produced a number of good foals.

1953

Badminton was host to the European Championships, the first CCIO of the FEI, and Britain more than vindicated their trouncing of 1951. At the last minute Starlight was withdrawn from the team because of his tendency to 'blow-up' in the dressage and in came Frank Weldon on his comparatively new horse Kilbarry. Individuals from Sweden and Holland entered the championships as well as teams from Ireland and Switzerland.

Ironically, Starlight was on his best behaviour and produced his very best to take equal second after the dressage with Mr H. Horngreen's Raton. Both the latter and the leading dressage horse, Capt. L. Meyer's Aphrodite were eliminated later for jumping faults, to leave the path clear for Major Rook, whose brilliant performance was by far and away the best on the cross-country, and who had only one down of the three fences in hand on the third day. He thus became the first British rider, and the first person since 1948, to finish a three-day event with bonus marks. Of the British team, Kilbarry finished seventh in the dressage and went on to jump a steady clear cross-country into second place, the position he retained after one fence down

Major Lawrence Rook on Starlight.

in the show-jumping. With Reg Hindley and Speculation in sixth place and Bertie Hill on Bambi V in seventeenth place Britain took the team as well as the individual title. Capt. Schwarzenbach returned to finish third on Vae Victis while Brig. Lyndon Bolton was ninth on Flanagan, which later became a well-known successful show-jumper for Pat Smythe.

Phase C of roads and tracks surprisingly caused many horses to tire unnecessarily, as their riders had not taken into account the following wind which did not refresh and cool the horses as they proceeded on an abnormally warm day.

Starlight XV

Bought as a potential race horse by Mrs J. R. Baker, Starlight, like Golden Willow, was another temperamental star and this tendency dogged him throughout his subsequent eventing career. One of the original number of horses to go into special training under Capt. Tony Collings at Porlock, Starlight was initially ridden by Dick Hern, nowadays better known as a flat race trainer, but was taken over by Major Lawrence Rook as his ride for the 1952 Olympics. So near to individual and team victory, a fall in a blind irrigation gutter near the end of the cross-country led, somewhat indirectly, to the elimination of the pair and consequently the team. (See Chapter Three.)

Always an unknown quantity in the dressage arena, where he had rather a short fuse, Starlight was excluded from the British team at Badminton the following year but confounded everyone by winning. Returning to grace, he was a member of the winning European Championship teams of 1954 and 1955 but in the Olympic year he exploded during his Badminton test and was no more considered for international competition.

1954

In the second Badminton to be won by a mare, the first six places in the dressage were held by mares. Leading after the first day was Miss Margaret Hough on her own Bambi V, which had previously been ridden by Bertie Hill. In second place was another well-known mare, Tramella, owned and ridden by Miss Diana Mason, now very well-known as a top-class dressage rider.

The speed and endurance section was marred by errors in timekeeping which affected several competitors but none more than Frank Weldon on Kilbarry, who was mistimed on the steeplechase and only twelve of the maximum thirty-six bonus points were credited to him. He went on to a fast clear cross-country which put him into overnight lead ahead of Margaret Hough but then lost it by having two show-jumps down. Margaret Hough jumped clear to win, by 1·6 points – becoming the first lady rider so to do, while Diana Mason came a close third to Frank Weldon – just 3·7 points behind his 65·90.

Twenty-four competitors finished the sixth Badminton Horse Trials – more than ever before – among them, in ninth position, the British team's great benefactor Ted Marsh on Crispin, which had been at Porlock and which he generously lent to Bertie Hill for the European Championships at Basle, which he subsequently won.

Bambi V

Irish bred, Bambi V came into Miss Margaret Hough's possession in 1951 as the result of an exchange with a show pony. Miss Hough

Diana Mason on Tramella, a close third to Frank Weldon in 1954.

In trouble in the show-jumping section, Ted Marsh on Crispin finished ninth in 1954 and the horse was then lent to Bertie Hill for the European championships.

The first lady winner, Margaret Hough on Bambi V.

immediately lent her mare to the British team and she went into training at Porlock for the 1952 Olympics, where she attacked her work vigorously (see Chapter Three). She was not chosen for the 1952 team, but in 1953 Bertie Hill rode her to team victory in the European Championships at Badminton.

She was retired from eventing, after an illustrious career, at the age of fifteen and produced a foal regularly each year for many years of happy retirement.

1955

'Badminton' moved, lock, stock and barrel in May, to Windsor where the European Championships were held by kind invitation of HM the Queen. Despite the later date, weather conditions were appalling and the subsequent effect upon the severity of the course was marked.

With four in each team (the best three to count), representing Britain were Diana Mason on Tramella, Bertie Hill on Countryman, Lawrence Rook on Starlight and Frank Weldon on Kilbarry. The total number of starters was a record fifty-four, necessitating the dressage to be split over two days.

Diana Mason showed her superiority in the dressage to finish first in that section while to tremendous applause Frank Weldon on Kilbarry came into second place. The severe cross-country took its toll with many falls: Tramella fell twice, could not recover after the second time and was eliminated at the Irish bank. Kilbarry, however, put in a faultless cross-country and, with maximum bonus on the steeplechase he could not be caught, thus winning his first Badminton. Bertie Hill had one refusal on Countryman at the notorious sandpit fence but his very quick time helped him into third position while Starlight, who had suffered a fall, finished fifteenth. However, the British team won easily with all others but the Swiss eliminated. Thirty-four riders completed the event, but the last placed was 435 marks behind the winner.

Kilbarry

Bought originally as a potential racehorse, capable of carrying his owner, Frank Wel-

Maj. F. W. C. Weldon on his way to winning his second Badminton. The old tree trunk now forms the core of the wood pile.

don, to victory in the Gunners' Gold Cup at Sandown, Kilbarry showed great promise by winning his first point-to-point. It was to be his only race, however, as a virus infection affected his wind and he was Hobdayed. The operation was not a complete success and you could hear him coming half a mile away, so plans for racing had to be shelved. Kilbarry and Frank Weldon went on to become one of the most popular and well-known combinations ever in eventing. Kilbarry played bridesmaid to Starlight and Bambi in 1953–4 but determined not to make it an ignominious third time, took full honours and the European Championship at Windsor in 1955, and when Badminton returned home in 1956 he cemented his greatness by winning a second time, going on in the same year to be a member of the Olympic Gold Medal team at Stockholm.

Standing an impressive 17 hh, Kilbarry was thought the world of by his owner, and his untimely end was tragic. An insignificant fence at a one-day event took its toll of one of Britain's greatest event horses, and Kilbarry's career came to an abrupt end at just ten years of age, the most brilliant horse his owner has ever ridden.

The Australians made the first of many visits. Laurie Morgan on Gold Ross in 1956.

1956

In this, the Olympic year, Badminton provided, in the time-honoured tradition, the most important trial. It also saw the end of Starlight's international career as he behaved so badly in the dressage that he was withdrawn from the competition and the selectors had to look for a new Olympic horse.

The Australians made the first of many visits to what has become almost their own national event and the Irish were there, as ever, to make their own final Olympic selection.

A young rider called Sheila Willcox, in her first event at Badminton (although she had finished thirteenth at Windsor the previous year), set the standard in the dressage with an incredibly low penalty of 57·78. The cards were down and, when Kilbarry entered the arena, an expectant hush fell over the crowd. Their anticipation was rewarded: he produced the best test of his life to score 1·56 penalties under High and Mighty's total! Each could ill afford to give an inch and neither slipped. Each gained maximum bonus on the steeplechase – which had moved to the Slaits from Didmarton – and likewise on the cross-country. Everything then rested on the show-jumping and when each pulled a clear round out of the bag Kil-

Anneli Drummond-Hay made her first appearance on Trident.

Penny Moreton and Red Sea came through to finish second.

barry and Frank Weldon took the honours with a bonus of 51·78 (under the present scoring system both Weldon and Willcox would have finished with just their dressage scores; the first time this had happened).

Laurie Morgan from Australia finished third on his own Gold Ross, giving an extremely promising performance, and behind him was Bertie Hill on Her Majesty's Countryman whose dressage had been slightly disappointing and kept him down. Jane Drummond-Hay's sister, Anneli, made her first Badminton appearance, finishing sixth and, although she was one of the three British girls to finish in the first ten, lady riders were still debarred from the Olympics. Once again Mr Ted Marsh came to the rescue by offering his very good novice horse, Wild Venture, on which he finished tenth, and this became Lawrence Rook's Olympic ride in place of the deposed Starlight.

1957

With Kilbarry's brilliant career cut so tragically short, this year's event was something of a one-horse race; Sheila Willcox and High and Mighty knew no equals and led throughout, to finish with an impressive bonus of 79·37: indeed her dressage penalty had been an unbelievable 24·33. With his owner, Ted Marsh back in the saddle, Wild Venture produced a creditable dressage and went on to achieve a double maximum which placed him second after two days. However, two fences down in the show-jumping was too expensive a mistake and Penny Moreton from Ireland came through to take his place on Col. Hume-Dudgeon's Red Sea.

High and Mighty

With success in innumerable one-day events, High and Mighty achieved recognition well before his first Badminton win, but his early career had been dogged by misfortune: a severe cough had delayed commencement of training while in a cross-country ride some time after, he fell into a hidden bog and stayed there, embedded, for some forty-five minutes before he could be extricated by tractor.

Irish bred out of a Arab × Highland pony mare, High and Mighty stood 16 hh. His success was due in no small way to hard and dedicated work by both horse and rider which led to two consecutive Badminton wins – by 1958 it was a question of Sheila Willcox first and the rest 'somewhere' – and the individual European Championship in 1957.

On her marriage, Sheila Willcox gave

Sheila Willcox on High and Mighty over the Vicarage Ditch.

Anneli Drummond-Hay and Pluto dropped a place in the show-jumping to finish third in 1958.

High and Mighty to Ted Marsh who had many seasons' hunting on him with the Heythrop before he was finally put out to grass and died at the age of twenty-two.

1958

As predicted, no one could touch High and Mighty, and Sheila Willcox opened her account with easily the best test, while double maximums on the speed and endurance put her so far ahead that not even the ten penalties for a show-jump down could alter her position. Indeed she won by the widest margin in the history of the event.

The fairly new combination of Laurien and Major Derek Allhusen came second after a critical clear round, gaining a place on Anneli Drummond-Hay whose twenty jumping penalties were an expensive mistake. There was much change of fortune in the show-jumping and most positions in the first ten altered. David Somerset, competing at his first Badminton on Countryman, which he had bought, slipped a place in Ted Marsh and Wild Venture's favour, but still finished a commendable seventh.

David Somerset competing in his first Badminton in 1957, finished seventh.

1959

Competition was again wide open and the unforgettable rain storms which deluged vir-

Frank Weldon on Samuel Johnson in 1959; he finished with two horses in the first ten.

Sheila Willcox on Airs and Graces won her third consecutive Badminton.

Shelagh Kesler on Double Diamond won the first Little Badminton.

tually the whole event made the outcome even more indistinct. With traditional British phlegm, however, the show went on, despite the fact that the ground was reduced to a quagmire; there was not a piece of dry clothing in sight, cars – and Land Rovers – became bogged and still it rained torrents.

Competitors had to perform their dressage in appalling weather and beneath them the arena was reduced to a cart track. Despite the fact that Sheila Willcox's new novice, Airs and Graces, disliked such conditions they took the lead at the end of day one. The decision was taken to press on regardless, and the cross-country course was altered accordingly, with five fences omitted and a further four lowered. Although the rain stopped, the atrocious ground conditions remained and the accent was on careful riding for the biggest entry ever, which had necessitated the instigation of the Little Badminton event. David Somerset, however, knew the capabilities of his great Countryman who had coped with such conditions in Stockholm, and pressed him as fast as he dare to make up fifteen places and take the lead from Sheila Willcox on Airs and Graces, Ted Marsh on Wild Venture, Derek Allhusen on Laurien and Frank Weldon on Samuel Johnson.

The narrow margin between David Somerset and Sheila Willcox produced one of the most nail-biting show-jumping tests in the history of the event. Countryman went first and toppled one fence; Sheila Willcox jumped clear to win, thus becoming the first and, still, only rider to achieve three consecutive Badminton wins. The order to fifth remained the same after the jumping and Ted Marsh also took sixth place with Blue Jeans. Frank Weldon also appeared twice in the first ten, rising to ninth on his own Fermoy despite two falls on the cross-country.

In the Little Badminton Mrs J. O. McMillen on Robinwood lost her commanding lead by having four of the last five fences down in favour of Shelagh Kesler on Double Diamond.

1960

In Olympic year, Badminton provided a delightful contrast to the mud of 1959 when all three days took place in glorious spring weather. In the first year of the valuable Whitbread sponsorship, the handsome new trophy was carried off to the Antipodes in an Australian exercise of sweeping the board which pointed an accurate finger at who would win the Gold Medal at Rome later in the year. The result was by no means cut-and-dried, however, until the show-jumping

Bill Roycroft and Our Solo.

had been completed, and, indeed, on the eve of day two, Anneli Drummond-Hay had only to jump a clear round to win her first Badminton on her own horse, Perhaps, which she had bought for £15 only eighteen months before. However, a foot in the water and a fence down relegated her to third place behind the Australians, Bill Roycroft with Our Solo, and Laurie Morgan on Salad Days, who had each jumped clear. Australian riders also filled fourth and tenth places.

Ted Marsh's Blue Jeans, this time ridden by Capt. Arthur finished fifth, but would undoubtedly have been higher placed had not a child run into the path of the horse and forced him to pull up; no damage was done except for loss of precious time. Riding Samuel Johnson, Frank Weldon again scored a double maximum on the speed and endurance section and could have taken third place but for expensive faults in the show-jumping which put him down to seventh.

Interestingly, with the same dressage score as Our Solo, Martin Whiteley and his own Peggoty won the Little Badminton, with the 1959 runner-up, Mrs J. O. McMillen and Robinwood, filling the same position.

Our Solo

This Australian-bred horse was one of the handful of small horses which has been brilliant over the big Badminton courses. In early life, he was destined for pony racing but, when he stopped growing at 15 hh, he exceeded the height limit and was kept instead to help with cattle droving to save petrol in post-war years. He was later sold on as a child's pony but, proving too strong, he came to the attention of 6 ft 2 in. Bill Roycroft who bought him for polo and had two successful seasons with him.

Turning to combined training, Our Solo gave Bill Roycroft 'a very good start to many years of exciting eventing'. Their first major victory, the 1960 Badminton, was the prelude to greater things, and in the autumn of that year they helped their team to the Gold medal at the Rome Olympics. Roycroft's contribution was remarkable: sustaining a bad fall on the cross-country which resulted in concussion, a broken collar bone and a badly injured shoulder, he remounted to complete the course. He was whisked away by helicopter to hospital as soon as he finished, but made good his escape to come back and jump a clear round to victory the next day.

Our Solo returned to Australia and was retired in 1961, spending his well-earned retirement doing light work on a ranch in Victoria.

1961

Australia returned to Badminton in the shape of Laurie Morgan and Salad Days who, after helping his team to win the Olympic Gold Medal at Rome, vowed to take the Whitbread Trophy home as well.

After the year of respite from the weather, 1961 was nearly as bad as 1959, with a glutinous cross-country course which tested to the limit the fitness, stamina and endurance of horses and riders; one horse, Landfall, completed the course but the penalty was too severe – it died of a broken blood vessel soon after.

For the first time the start and finish was confined to a 'box' – a Badminton innovation – and the course began to take on a more modern look.

The dressage, which was led by Jeremy Beale on Fulmer Folly, was a near disaster for Laurie Morgan who discovered, only the day before, that he had to perform a different test from the one he knew. Salad Days himself had had only ten days' dressage schooling after competing in a hunter chase! Despite the fact that his test was 'not all that could be desired',* he nevertheless finished the day in a fairly strong position. Morgan knew that few, if any, horses would catch him on the cross-country, as Salad Days was at the very peak of fitness – fitter even than at the Olympics. As it proved, only one horse got near him, St Finbarr ridden by the Badminton veteran, Harry Freeman-Jackson, who had been sixth after the dressage and moved to within the crucial 10 penalties before the show-jumping. In third and fourth place at the end of day two was Michael Bullen on Col. V. D. S. Williams' two horses, Cottage Romance and Sea Breeze, but a fall on each of them in the cross-country put him too far behind to catch the leaders and he stayed in those positions, Sea Breeze having stayed fourth throughout the competition while Cottage Romance, which had been his Olympic mount, was second after the dressage. Both St Finbarr and Salad Days completed the eleven-fence course with no jumping faults and Morgan's ·75 time faults, which he had reckoned to incur for the sake of accuracy, could not prevent him from winning the coveted trophy, the receipt of which, from HM the Queen, 'was one of the happiest moments of my life'.

Equal tenth after the dressage in the Little Badminton, Capt. J. P. E. Welch, on Mr Wilson, went on to win his section.

Michael Bullen: third on Cottage Romance in 1961.

'. . . one of the happiest moments of my life.' Laurie Morgan, seen here in 1956, receives an award from the Queen.

Salad Days

Another Badminton winner with racehorse breeding, Salad Days continued to race, even when at the top of his eventing career, thus proving Laurie Morgan's claim that he was the best all-round riding horse in the world. Winner of the Australian Three-Day Event in 1958 and 1959, Salad Days was second in his first Badminton in 1960 before going on to win the team Gold at the Rome Olympics. After his Badminton win, Salad Days was 'retired' in England and fittingly ended his days at Badminton as the Duchess of Beaufort's hunter.

*L. Morgan, *The Horseman's Year*, 1962.

Winner of the 1961 Little Badminton, Capt. J. P. E. Welch on Mr Wilson.

Laurie Morgan on Salad Days.

Michael Bullen and Sea Breeze: third in 1962 after a close battle with Frank Weldon.

1962

In the usual pattern of sunshine after rain, this year's Event was bathed in the sun throughout. Not since the days of Sheila Willcox and High and Mighty had the Event been such a foregone conclusion and, barring accidents, everyone's money was on Anneli Drummond-Hay and Merely-a-Monarch, who had won the inaugural Burghley Three-Day Event the previous autumn. Badminton proved to be the climax of this combination's eventing career. Setting a standard in the dressage which no one could begin to catch, they led throughout and, despite one fence down in the show-jumping, they finished the Event forty-two points ahead of Frank Weldon, on Young Pretender, who had had a battle for second place with Michael Bullen on Sea Breeze. Another lady rider won the Little Badminton: Australian Penny Crofts took advantage of a last minute ride on H. Graham Clark's Priam which she had never ridden before to take first place after a close contest with Capt. J. R. Templer's M'Lord Connelly.

The League Against Cruel Sports had got in on the act of condemning eventing and had singled out Capt. Norman Arthur, warning him not to beat his horse unmercifully: ironically, he was eliminated for a refusal which might have been avoided by more positive use of his stick.

Merely-a-Monarch

Regarded by many as one of the greatest event horses of all time, fate certainly played a hand in Monarch's early career. Anneli Drummond-Hay who, following in her sister Jane's footsteps, had become successful in combined training, was looking for a new horse to event. An advertisement in *Horse and Hound* brought a terrific response, most of which were no-hopers, but which also included details and photo of a three-year-old. The youngster would probably never have received a second glance but for the fact that, some weeks later, the owners wrote asking for the photograph back. Anneli was impressed by the picture and went to view, and subsequently buy, the three-quarter

Mrs P. Crofts of Australia rode Priam for the first time to win the 1962 Little Badminton.

Anneli Drummond-Hay and Merely-a-Monarch.

thoroughbred × quarter Fell horse for £300 – a lot at the time. Monarch's early training was a steady battle with his lack of confidence and Anneli Drummond-Hay exercised extreme patience with him through all stages of his development. Gradually he was beginning to attract notice; after winning the Army Horse Trials at Tweseldown he won Foxhunter show-jumping contests at Taplow and Richmond, also gaining show ribbons at the latter in the hunter classes. Later in the same year he won the Spillers Combined Training Championships at the Horse of the Year Show: and he was still only five years old.

That winter preparation began for Monarch's first assault on Badminton, for that was his owner's goal. A mysterious injury sustained in his box a fortnight before the Event meant that Badminton had to be deferred for a year, but the eventing world was intrigued by this 'perfect' horse when he won the inaugural Burghley, where his dressage was sheer brilliance.

Badminton 1962 arrived: Monarch was supremely fit – he even outpaced two racehorses at a pre-event gallop – and as the Badminton report in *Horse and Hound* put it, it was 'Merely-a-Monarch first, the rest nowhere'. It was the pinnacle and end of his eventing career. For some time Anneli had been attracted by the show-jumping ring, partly because she feared the physical risks to her valuable horse in eventing. She had been offered various sums up to £25,000 for him and even a blank cheque, but she refused them all.

Thus, turning her attentions to show-jumping, Anneli Drummond-Hay achieved legendary success on Monarch, both nationally and internationally, despite turmoils over ownership. However, Monarch's brilliant career was dogged by ill-health. He nearly came back to Badminton again, in 1965, when the ownership problems had been resolved in a happy partnership with Col. Tom Greenhalgh. In preparation, they romped home to win Crookham, but after a training gallop Monarch burst a blood vessel in the back of one eye and had to be rested for the whole summer.

They returned to show-jumping where, after a two-year struggle, Monarch came back into winning form and later, in 1970, their Olympic hopes having been frustrated, they won the Queen Elizabeth Cup at the Royal International, eight years after winning Badminton.

Monarch now lives in happy retirement with Col. Greenhalgh in Northamptonshire.

1963

Again the pattern repeated itself. Following the terrible 1962–3 winter, Badminton shrunk to a one-day event and, even then, weather conditions were appalling, with horses floundering in the deep going on all phases.

A young man making his début at Badminton was Richard Meade, on his own horse Barberry, and he managed a creditable second to Miss Susan Fleet on The Gladiator, who had been eighth the previous year.

Sgt. Ben Jones won the Junior Stakes (Little Badminton) on Master Bernard.

1964

During a period of chaos in the combined training world the previous year, there was no great confidence in our Olympic prospects until Capt. James Templer and M'Lord Connelly added the CCIO at Munich the previous autumn to their earlier Burghley victory. Thus Badminton proved an interesting and successful occasion, especially so for James Templer, who added the Whitbread Trophy to his winning run.

Badminton served the whole of Europe as the only major trial prior to the Olympics, and the Germans sent over some riders to compete *hor concours*; indeed, one of them, Ludwig Goessing, produced the best dressage test. The first score to count, however, was returned by Jeremy Smith-Bingham on By Golly, closely followed by Susan Fleet on The Gladiator, who was, as usual, strong in this section. A Danish rider, Audre Jungersen was third, half a point ahead of Richard Meade on Barberry.

It was not a vintage Badminton and many British riders came to grief on the cross-country. Not so Capt. Templer who, finishing the first day in seventh place, gained maximum points on the steeplechase and was fastest on a cross-country which saw no maximum scores in an Olympic year when riders were obviously unwilling to press their horses unduly hard. By Golly went both clear and fast to take second place and although Tony Cameron, on Black Salmon, from Ireland rode a faster round, he could not make up sufficient ground on a poor dressage score and had to be content with third place which, despite three show-jumps down, he held to the end. The order also remained the same for Capt. Templer and Jeremy Smith-Bingham. Harry Freeman-Jackson on St Finbarr jumped a clear round, into fourth place, while the erstwhile holder of that position, Michael Bullen on Young Pretender, incur-

Second in 1964, Jeremy Smith-Bingham and By Golly.

Sheila Willcox made her come-back on Glenamoy and won the 1964 Little Badminton.

red thirty jumping faults to drop back to sixth, but came up from seventh to fifth on his second horse, Sea Breeze. Disappointingly, The Gladiator had to be withdrawn before the show-jumping when standing fifth, owing to a leg injury.

In the Little Badminton, Sheila Willcox made her eventing comeback on Glenamoy, a horse on which she hoped to earn her ticket to Tokyo, as the decision had been made to allow women to compete in the Olympic Three-Day Event, largely due to her own success and that of Anneli Drummond-Hay. The Little Badminton was secured, but not so the much worked-for Olympic ride which eluded her, as it did Anneli Drummond-Hay, throughout her career.

Capt. James Templer on M'Lord Connelly.

Bill Roycroft and Stoney Crossing finished the 1965 Event in sixth place, after coming third to Arkle and Mill House in the Cheltenham Gold Cup only weeks before.

M'Lord Connelly

After Merely-a-Monarch's withdrawal from the eventing scene, M'Lord Connelly enjoyed considerable success. A 16.1 hh Anglo-Arab gelding by Connetable, and a half-brother to Jennie Loriston-Clarke's Desert Storm, M'Lord Connelly took his owner, Capt. James Templer, to victory in many national horse trials, hunter trials and show-jumping competitions, including the Prince of Wales Cup at the Royal Tournament. 1962–4 proved the height of Connelly's eventing career with victories at the European Championships at Burghley in 1962, the International Championship at Munich in 1963 and Badminton in 1964. Not surprisingly Capt. Templer and Connelly were chosen for the Olympic team in Tokyo in 1964, but three stops on the cross-country put them out of the most important competition of their career. Turning their attentions to show-jumping, they also shone in this field.

1965

The fifteenth Badminton was not entirely a British affair. Although the entry was down on the previous year's pre-Olympic test, international entries were well in evidence and dominated the higher placings. Popular Australian rider, Bill Roycroft, winner of the 1960 event caused a great stir by declaring rides on *three* horses: the first time anyone had contemplated such a task and one which has been emulated only once since.

In the first year of David Somerset's and Col. Frank Weldon's organization, the new course, which broke much new ground, restored the status of the premier Three-Day Event and, indeed, appeared too severe to many in the post-Olympic year.

Major Eddie Boylan of Ireland, who had made his début at Badminton in 1949, took a four point lead in the dressage, on his big 17 hh Durlas Eile over Sheila Willcox on the Little Badminton winner, Glenamoy. Once again, Harry Freeman-Jackson returned on St Finbarr and finished the first day in third position. A safe cross-country round by the leader maintained his position but Bill Roycroft meant business and lost no time on any of his three mounts. Eldorado, which he had ridden in Tokyo, moved up from thirteenth to sixth while Stoney Crossing, which had finished third to Arkle and Mill House in the Cheltenham Gold Cup weeks before, finished day two in third place. Roycroft's third mount, Avatar, stood second behind Martin Whiteley on his novice horse, The Poacher, in the Little Badminton and they finished the Event in the same order.

The Great Badminton show-jumping proved critical and Bill Roycroft's sole clear round on Eldorado was not enough to catch Major Boylan, who had two fences down, but it did edge him ahead of Sheila Willcox who, despite a careful round, had one fence down and incurred time faults to finish third. Bill Roycroft's chaser was less at home in the show-jumping ring and thirty jumping penalties dropped him down to sixth. While Ireland won the title – for the second time only – the public's admiration was undoubtedly with the gallant Roycroft who had ridden a total of forty-seven miles over the toughest cross-country course in the world, in one afternoon.

Maj. Eddy Boylan on Durlas Eile.

Durlas Eile

This big brown 17 hh gelding by Artist's Son was six before he was bought and broken by the Irish Army who hunted and show-jumped him. However, they found his potential in the latter field was limited and he was sold to Major Boylan. In his hands, Durlas Eile was soon winning combined training events with the first major success coming at Burghley in 1964 where they finished fourth. The following spring, after a brilliant dressage and fluent cross-country, they snatched the Badminton victory from Bill Roycroft. This was the opening to a career which included the first World Championship-winning team at Burghley in 1966 and the individual European Championship at Punchestown in 1967, as well as finishing a close second to Celia Ross-Taylor at Badminton in the same year.

Durlas Eile was sold to Canada before the Mexico Olympics for a reported £19,000 which then was a record for a three-day event

Major Derek Allhusen and Lochinvar. A cricket score in the show-jumping relegated them to 11th in 1967.

horse, and represented his new country at those Games where the Canadian team finished eighth.

1967

Fortunes fluctuated widely in this first Badminton for two years and the show-jumping exerted a strong influence on the final results.

Durlas Eile looked set to take his second consecutive title when his beautifully relaxed test put him into first place after the dressage. Behind him were the Frenchman Michel Cochenet on Artaban and Celia Ross-Taylor riding at her first Badminton on Jonathan whose dressage was very accurate and obedient but lacked Durlas Eile's brilliance.

The competition was still wide open before the speed and endurance, the climax of which was the biggest cross-country course to have been seen at Badminton; ironically the fence which caused the most problems was the familiar Coffin. An early 'casualty' was Pollyann Hely-Hutchinson on Count Jasper who, but for a 20-penalty hesitation at the Quarry, would have taken the Whitbread Trophy, with a near-maximum bonus. Eddy Boylan took a safe clear round to remain in the lead while, with a maximum bonus, Derek Allhusen on Lochinvar moved up from tenth to second. Celia Ross-Taylor remained in third position, but a fall at the Park Wall and a stop elsewhere on the course put Artaban out of the race.

On the final day excitement rose as, for the first time, the remaining competitors jumped in reverse order. Only six clear rounds were jumped, the first to matter being Jane Bullen's on Our Nobby, who moved up from tenth to fifth. Also clear was Pollyann Hely-Hutchinson who took third place while one fence down and time faults left Miss S. Clifford and Mazaretta in their overnight position, fourth. Next to go was Celia Ross-Taylor on Jonathan, whose clear round meant that both Lochinvar and Durlas Eile also had to jump clear to retain their positions. This was not to be, however, for Lochinvar finished with a cricket score which relegated him to eleventh overall, while Durlas Eile, surprisingly, had two fences down, thus letting Jonathan slip through to win.

Celia Ross-Taylor and Jonathan.

Unpopular with many, the Little Badminton section was discontinued.

Jonathan

Another Badminton winner to get off to a somewhat unpromising start, Jonathan – the offspring of Amigo and My Fair Lady – was wild from birth and his dam refused to feed him. The idea had been to produce a small horse of about 15 hh but when at last Jonathan began to thrive, he reached a full-grown height of 16.1½ hh. He was sold as a yearling for £15 and, when eventually bought by Celia Ross-Taylor, was schooled by her for eventing in just six months, including a month with Capt. Eddie Goldman. They soon became one of the most successful combined training combinations of the 1960s – in 1966 they won the Calcutta Light Horse and the Tony Collings award for the most points gained during the year – with the Whitbread Trophy, appropriately, crowning their success.

Jonathan is still alive and well in his retirement, but cannot bear to be put out to grass for he hates to be ignored by visitors.

The Americans entered several horses in 1968. Team captain Michael Plumb on Plain Sailing.

Mark Phillips and Rock On: fourth in his first Badminton.

1968

In Olympic Year the course was advertised as the biggest ever and the entry too was one of the biggest. With fifty-five running, the dressage was again divided into two days; performances on the first were disappointing but the second day produced a much higher standard with the lead going to Staff-Sgt. Ben Jones on Foxdor. The Americans had brought over several horses for their Olympic trial and the team captain, Michael Plumb, moved into second place on Plain Sailing.

The cross-country course was big, but the going was good and most fences jumped well, despite one or two which caused particular apprehension on the walk-round. On the day, it was a 3 ft 9 in. post and rails just beyond the Keeper's Rails ditch which caused most trouble, and nearly all the early competitors were eliminated there, causing a few complaints among the crowd, but nevertheless 50 per cent of the field completed the second day, giving due emphasis to the Olympic trial. Indeed fitness of both horse and rider was the keynote and the fittest looking horse on the course was the diminutive Our Nobby who, with his young rider, Jane Bullen, gave the only double maximum bonus of the event, moving up from twenty-third to second in the process. Staff-Sgt. Jones gained maximum points on the steeplechase, was slower on the cross-country but just managed to retain the lead by a narrow margin from Nobby, Mark Phillips on Rock On and Richard Meade on Turnstone, in third and fourth respectively. Major Allhusen with Lochinvar was also within ten points of the leader and the stage was set for an exciting final. With a clear round each, Jane Bullen took her first Whitbread Trophy at the age of twenty – the youngest competitor then to have won – and Richard Meade moved up to second. Ben Jones slipped two places and behind him were Mark Phillips and Derek Allhusen. Interestingly, the first five riders were those selected to go to Mexico, with Mark Phillips as reserve, and their súccess is, of course, history.

Our Nobby

Yet another inauspicious start in life by this 15 hh horse who went on to help Britain win

Jane Bullen and Our Nobby.

the team Gold in Mexico. A premature foal, Nobby was born into a wintry world while his dam's owners were abroad. Fortunately the local blacksmith spotted and rescued the small weak-looking colt and took him to the RSPCA who cared for him. As a four-year-old, he was raced at Bath but, still undersized and not really fast enough, he changed hands – via a Welsh shepherd – and found himself in the Bullens' yard near Badminton. He was five years old, in poor condition, but showed a brilliant, natural ability to jump; as a 'welcoming gift' however, he developed Canadian Pox which swiftly passed to the whole yard. Recovered, he began to improve beyond all recognition, although with his strength came a nappiness which had to be cured before fifteen-year-old Jane was allowed to ride him. With all the problems resolved, Jane Bullen went on to have a very successful career in the Pony Club on her pony – for he had a life certificate for his height – but he grew up with her and by the time she was ready for adult competition, Nobby had grown to 15 hh!

'I suppose you would class Nobby as a rather weedy thoroughbred,' says Jane, 'but he was as tough as old boots and speed was nothing to him; he was terribly fast and a fantastic jumper.' Indeed, he once jumped nearly 36 ft on the Crookham steeplechase!

Thus their Badminton début in 1967 saw them finish fifth, to be followed a year later with a well-earned and highly popular victory, putting them on the short list for the Mexico Olympics where, in gruelling conditions, they finished eighteenth overall individual and won the team Gold Medal.

1969

Badminton's coming of age was a vintage event with four fine days and the going perfect. Forty-eight horses were declared, including two ridden by Bill Roycroft, back again with Warrathoola and Furtive, and Badminton 'veteran' Bertie Hill who came back on his own Chicago III. The end of the first day of dressage saw Debbie West and Don Camillo in the lead but this horse failed the vet that evening leaving Richard Walker, the reigning European Junior Champion, and the 15.1½ hh Pasha in the lead. The next day however, experience held the stage and Sheila Willcox's mark of 48·33 on Fair and Square was quickly toppled by Richard Meade and Barberry's 39·33; Staff-Sgt. Ben Jones and The Poacher's 44·69 and finally Bertie Hill's immaculate and untouchable 30·33 on Chicago.

Thus at the end of the dressage four Olympic Gold medallists led the field; Bertie Hill, Richard Meade, Ben Jones and Bill Roycroft – four riders representing each Olympic Games since the inception of Badminton.

Sadly a fall on the steeplechase put Bertie Hill out of the running while Barberry, not his old self, had a refusal at the Cats Cradle, then a fall in the Lake, and Richard Meade retired. Even more surprising, The Poacher was retired before the start of the cross-country, while Sheila Willcox who was fifth in the dressage had an uncomfortable ride on Fair and Square which it was thought broke down on landing over Huntsman's Leap and then took a fall over the post and rails out of Huntsman's Close. Only Bill Roycroft survived and, despite a refusal, moved up to

Angela Martin-Bird and Grey Cloud: second in 1969.

second. The field was thrown open and Richard Walker's maximum on the steeplechase and +70·8 on the cross-country brought him from ninth to first position ahead of Bill Roycroft, who also held third place on Furtive. Fourth after two days was Mary Gordon-Watson on Cornishman and, behind her, Angela Martin-Bird on Grey Cloud, whose clear round in the show-jumping moved her up to second overall

Richard Walker and Pasha.

when Cornishman knocked up a penalty of 26·25 to drop to ninth and Bill Roycroft had a fence down apiece on his two mounts to finish third and fourth. Richard Walker's cool judgement earned him a clear round and victory, to become the youngest ever winner at Badminton.

Pasha

Like Our Nobby, Pasha was also foaled in Beaufort country, in the same year, and, like the former, became a member of the Beaufort Pony Club team. By an Arab sire and out of a Suffolk Punch mare (an accomplished hunter!) Pasha was unmanageable in the hunting field but showed potential in the show-jumping ring and competed in various events before being sold for £150 as a child's pony. He finally came into Richard Walker's hands in 1965 and the combination gained their first major victory with the European Junior title. The Badminton victory followed in 1969, automatically selecting them for the senior team's assault on the European Championships at Haras du Pin where they also helped the team to win the title.

1970

Lorna Sutherland made history in this year by becoming the first – and only – girl ever to have completed Badminton with three horses: a feat achieved only by herself and Bill Roycroft.

The real honours, however, went to the popular combination of The Poacher and Richard Meade, who each marked up victory at Badminton for the first time. They opened their account well with a superlative test which put them firmly in the lead, ahead of Bertie Hill on Chicago, Judy Bradwell on Christopher Robert and Cornishman, sandwiched between Lorna Sutherland's mounts, Gypsy Flame and Popadom.

The going was fair but rather dead and only one maximum bonus was scored on the steeplechase – Bridget Parker on Cornish Gold – and none on the cross-country, which featured for the first time several combination fences. Lorna Sutherland had a refusal on each of her first two horses but the most

Lorna Sutherland on Gypsy Flame, the most difficult of her three 1970 rides.

difficult of the three, Gypsy Flame, jumped clear into fifth position. Cornishman, too, had a clear round to take fourth place, with Bertie Hill on Chicago, who was lucky to get away without penalty when he got off-course at the Quarry, third at the end of day two. The Poacher and San Carlos, ridden by Capt. R. McMahon from Ireland, returned classic cross-country rounds, finishing first and second respectively.

Jumping in reverse order on day three, the biggest shock came when Bertie Hill inadvertently took the wrong course when he stood to take third place at least, and was eliminated. Thus Gypsy Flame and Cornishman moved up a place each to fourth and third, while the real battle developed between Richard Meade and Ronnie McMahon. The latter jumped clear and the pressure was on Meade and The Poacher who, like the experienced combination they were, jumped with great confidence to take the Whitbread Trophy.

The Poacher

Of unknown breeding, Poacher's known career began at Exeter market where he was bought by Shelagh Kesler (now Mrs Bobby Coonon), who recognized his great potential. She schooled him on to one-day events and he was quickly upgraded to intermediate. He went to Badminton as a five-year-old simply because his owner was competing on another

Second in 1970: Capt. R. McMahon on San Carlos.

Richard Meade riding The Poacher.

horse and had no one to leave him with. His future owner, Martin Whiteley, who had bought his Little Badminton winner, Peggoty, from Miss Kesler, remembers seeing Poacher then and noting how nice he looked.

Poacher was then sold on, to be hunted side-saddle in the Heythrop country, where he gained notoriety as a runaway and again bumped into, almost literally, his future owner who was down for a day's hunting. At this stage, Martin Whiteley decided that he would be interested if the horse came on to the market and, sure enough, a month later, after Poacher had collided with a car and put his owner in hospital, he was for sale and eventually came to Martin Whiteley, in the autumn of 1964.

Looking after Poacher while his owner was away at the Tokyo Olympics, Michael Herbert finished the Chatsworth event rather better than planned and their win upgraded Poacher to Advanced. The following spring saw Martin Whiteley and Poacher take the Little Badminton title and, although they were asked to join the team for the European Championship in Moscow, Poacher was not ready for such competition and was especially inexperienced over banks.

Badminton, 1966, was cancelled but Poacher was one of twelve horses allowed to run, as an individual, at the first World Championships at Burghley, where he finished fifth. At the European Championships, in 1967, Poacher finished second to help the British team win their first title in ten years and sights were firmly on Mexico 1968. Poacher was allowed to miss Badminton that year but all horses on the short list were asked to go to Burghley. Sadly for Martin Whiteley, in addition to an old back injury, he had lost too much weight prior to the event and was unable to hold his horse, who was extremely fit, and the Olympic ride went to Staff-Sgt. Jones whose mount, Foxdor, which was owned by Martin Whiteley's mother, had died weeks previously. Ben Jones immediately set up a rapport with Poacher and the Mexico ticket and subsequent Gold Medal was theirs. The dressage at Mexico was a near disaster when Poacher, upset by the applause as the horse two places in front of him completed its test, got free and bolted back to the stables. Fortunately he was quickly retrieved and went on to perform one of the best tests of his life.

After Mexico, Poacher was given a season's hunting with the Grafton and tackled Badminton again the next year with Ben Jones, but unfortunately had to be withdrawn after leading the dressage, owing to lameness.

In 1970, the ride was given to Richard Meade who crowned the old horse's career by taking him to victory at Badminton, and the same combination took the runners-up award at the World Championships that autumn. In 1971, Richard Meade rode Poacher to team victory at the Burghley European Championships, after which the horse was retired to Everdon, where, cared for by Mrs Anne Hawkins, wife of the Joint Master of the Grafton, he enjoyed three seasons hunting before he became unsound and was retired to the Park where he was admired by many visitors (including the author). The Poacher died in 1977 with a unique record behind him. He competed in six CCIOs, in five of which he finished in the first five (Individual), and in five winning British teams – these victories divided between three riders. He was the only horse to have won both Little and Great Badmintons and, says Martin Whiteley, 'he was the most genuine and reliable horse I have ever ridden'.

1971

Once again bedevilled by the weather, the Badminton speed and endurance section commenced after twenty-four hours of continuous rain which played the usual havoc with the course and the Park. At the request of the FEI, the scoring system was based entirely on a penalty system, as used for one-day events.

HRH Princess Anne made her début in the great event on Doublet and immediately established herself in second place to Lt. Mark Phillips and Great Ovation after the dressage in which the judging was severe. In third place was the Swedish Army's Sarajevo ridden by Sgt. Jan Jonsson, fourth Miss A. Morrell on Sandpiper, and they were followed by two of the Mexico Gold Medal team, Cornishman V and Lochinvar, the latter to be eliminated, unfortunately, on the cross-country.

The course, though big and longer than the previous year, was rather more straightforward. Mary Gordon-Watson put in a fast steeplechase and cross-country on Cornishman, despite the difficult going, and although she collected twenty penalties for a refusal at the second rails of the Coffin she moved up from fifth to second at the end of two days. She was closely followed by the 1969 winner, Richard Walker and Upper Strata in third place, with HRH Princess Anne in fourth. The final day's jumping resulted in some slight reorganization with the ten penalties apiece of Doublet and Upper Strata allowing Debbie West on Baccarat through to third place with her own clear round. Cornishman had one fence down but just managed to hold second place – by 3·2 penalties – and although Great Ovation had two fences in hand, he and his co-owner Lt. Phillips, jumped a classic clear round to take the Whitbread Trophy.

Mark Phillips and Great Ovation.

Great Ovation

A dark bay thoroughbred gelding by Three Cheers (a Cesarewitch winner), out of Cyprus Valence, Great Ovation was bred by Mr C. Payne-Crofts in 1963. Proving too slow for 'chasing, he was eventually bought as a three-year-old by Mr Peter Phillips and his sister, Miss Flavia Phillips, from Mr Leslie Scott, through Bertie Hill. A very good looking horse and a winner in the show ring, Great Ovation was a slow starter as far as eventing was concerned; indeed, Miss Phillips recalls that he was 'so uninspiring' that he was nearly sold shortly before he won his first Badminton in 1971 when still a comparative novice. The win made Capt. Phillips and Great Ovation an automatic choice for that autumn's European Championships at Burghley, where they helped the British team into first place. The following year (Olympic year), Great Ovation and Mark Phillips took the Badminton title for the second time, narrowly beating Richard Meade, and went on to represent Britain in Munich where they again helped the team to international honours; this time the coveted Olympic Team Gold Medal. Poised for his third Badminton victory with the top dressage score in 1973, Great Ovation unfortunately went lame on the roads and tracks and had to be withdrawn. He retired from eventing in 1974 after a short but remarkably full career and now lives at Miss Phillips' yard from where he was still enjoying his hunting at sixteen years old.

1972

A classic battle developed between Great Ovation and Laurieston, ridden by Richard Meade, in the pre-Olympic Badminton, so vital for the selectors. Mark Phillips again took the lead in the dressage but Laurieston was close on his heels and a slightly faster steeplechase and cross-country by the latter put him fractionally ahead. Average times were slow over the big course which was designed with Munich in mind, but Hazel Booth and Mary Poppins II went fastest of all, going clear round the steeplechase and moving up from equal thirty-first to third! Richard Meade was fourth at the end of day two on his second horse, Wayfarer II, while Bridget Parker on Cornish Gold moved up from eleventh to fifth.

Bridget Parker and Cornish Gold: third in 1972 and a member of the Olympic Gold Medal winning team.

Competing in 1973 was Hydrophane Coldstream, here with Mr J. N. Kersley.

Jumping in reverse order as usual, tension was high as Mark Phillips jumped clear and Richard Meade could not afford to give an inch. Slowly and deliberately he, too, collected no jumping faults, but the one-and-a-quarter time faults were too expensive a mistake and he lost the event by ·65 penalties. Hazel Booth dropped right back to ninth with three fences down and Richard Meade collected twenty faults on Wayfarer putting him eighth overall, thus allowing the clear rounds of Bridget Parker, Debbie West on Baccarat and Lucinda Prior-Palmer on Be Fair – in her first Badminton – through to third, fourth and fifth respectively.

That autumn the team, consisting of Great Ovation, Laurieston, Cornish Gold and the experienced Cornishman V, took the team Gold Medal at Munich, with the individual award going to Richard Meade.

1973

The first Badminton after the Olympics was considered generally to have been the most severe course ever and came in for a good deal of criticism. Inspired by the Munich victory, the crowds were bigger than ever.

Cornishman V made his last appearance in a three-day event and would have won but for an unlucky fall; despite this, they were still the only combination not to be penalized for time, and finished sixth overall. Indeed there were many falls but the most surprising incident came when Rachael Bayliss and Gurgle the Greek passed unscathed *under* the Stockholm fence. Nevertheless, there were eight clear rounds and Lucinda Prior-Palmer finished day two comfortably in the lead from Marjorie Comerford on The Ghillie and, just behind, Richard Meade on Eagle Rock – an unexpected last minute ride.

Lucinda made no mistakes to take her first Whitbread Trophy, but The Ghillie's thirty penalties put them down to seventh, letting Eagle Rock through to second place with Virginia Thompson and Cornish Duke third and Merlin Meakin (who had been Merely-a-Monarch's groom) on Lynette, fourth.

Be Fair

There is little concerning this remarkable horse that has not already been written in his owner's biography of him.

Lucinda Prior-Palmer on Be Fair.

This 16·2hh chestnut thoroughbred was the unplanned progeny of Sheila Willcox's Fair and Square who, as an uncut colt, had been turned out with a supposedly barren mare appropriately named Happy Reunion!

Bought for £525, by female intuition as much as anything, Be Fair immediately turned into a problem horse for his fifteen-year-old owner, Lucinda Prior-Palmer. That she persevered with him through the Pony Club and the junior international team to win both Badminton and the European Championships only to finish his career, tragically, at the Montreal Olympics when he slipped an Achilles tendon, is history.

Lucinda describes Be Fair's story as a 'fairy tale', but it is a fairy tale that would not have come true but for a great deal of hard work, perseverance and determination on the part of his owner. Lucinda says of him: 'He has to be the best horse I've ever ridden. Not for sheer ability, because I think I've ridden better, but he's had that marvellous instinct of self-preservation and for that I worship him and have the utmost confidence in him.'

Be Fair is now in retirement, receiving only those visitors he chooses to meet.

Princess Anne on her second string, Goodwill, incurred no further penalties after the dressage to finish fourth.

1974

HRH Princess Anne returned to Badminton on Doublet to perform an outstanding dressage test which put her into the lead after that section, but she had to retire after a fall on the steeplechase. Great Ovation made a final appearance at Badminton and retired at the Bullfinch, but Mark Phillips' other ride, HM the Queen's Columbus, consolidated his good dressage with a clear cross-country within the Optimum Time. His dressage score was indeed an advantage as no less than five others managed the same feat across country, including Princess Anne on her second string, Goodwill. When all the leaders, bar Chris Collins on Smokey VI, jumped clear on the final day, five had incurred no further penalties after the first day: Mark Phillips on Columbus (first), Janet Hodgson on Larkspur (second), HRH Princess Anne on Goodwill (fourth), Debbie West on Baccarat (seventh) and Hugh Thomas on Playamar (eighth). Bruce Davidson on Irish Cap from the USA – who went on to win the World Championships that autumn – finished the Event in third place,

Capt. Mark Phillips and Columbus with the Whitbread Trophy.

Mark Phillips and Favour: third in 1976.

having gained time penalties on the steeplechase.

Because of the enormous crowds which were now expected, the speed and endurance section reverted to Friday, but happily for most spectators reverted back again for the next Event.

Columbus

A 17 hh grey gelding by Colonist II out of Princess Alexandra's hunter mare Trim Ann, Columbus was originally ridden by HRH Princess Anne but he proved too strong for a lady rider and was offered to Mark Phillips. In the spring of 1973, a series of falls caused people to tell Mark Phillips he was a fool to continue to ride such a dangerous horse, but he kept confidence to the extent, at that unlikely stage, of placing a bet with Mike Tucker that he would finish in the first three at the 1974 Badminton: they did better – they won.

The Badminton success led to selection for the World Championship team for Burghley in September 1974. The road to Burghley was fraught with lameness problems, but coming on form for the event, the partnership cruised around Bill Thompson's course to finish in the lead. Tragically, however, Mark Phillips had to watch victory taken from him when, at virtually the last fence on the cross-country, Columbus slipped his Achilles tendon and subsequently had to be withdrawn lame. The trouble recurred despite an operation, thwarting hopes that Columbus might go to the Montreal Olympics. However, after a sabbatical of three years, Columbus came back in 1979, first to jump round the Grand National course at Aintree with Mark Phillips in a preview for that great steeplechase, and then to finish third at Badminton.

1976

The 1975 Event had been abandoned after the first day's dressage owing to the terribly wet weather which had reduced the Park to a morass, while the 1976 pre-Olympic Event combined triumph with tragedy. In contrast to the previous year, the Silver Jubilee Badminton took place in fine spring weather and interest was naturally centred around those horses likely to go to Montreal.

Janet Hodgson took the lead after the dressage to finish the event in sixth position and, although many riders managed a clear round over the interesting new course, there were surprisingly none within the Optimum Time. The fastest clear round was Lucinda Prior-Palmer's on Mrs V. Phillips Wideawake, who went into the show-jumping with a fence in hand from Hugh Thomas on Playamar, then Mark Phillips on Favour, Richard Meade on Jacob Jones and Clarissa Strachan on Merry Sovereign, all of whose positions remained unaltered. Lucinda thus chalked up her second Badminton victory which was marred when, shortly after receiving their awards from the Queen, Wideawake collapsed and died while on his lap of honour.

Wideawake

A 16 hh bay gelding by Hereward the Wake, Wideawake joined the Prior-Palmer yard in 1973. He was full of ability, had scope and speed, but was independent and somewhat reckless at his fences. It was only in the autumn before the culmination of his career that Lucinda Prior-Palmer felt they were seeing eye to eye and their combined ability brought them through to victory in the Badminton of 1976 after 'an inspired performance as near to perfection in all-round horsemanship as one could wish to see', wrote Mary Gordon-Watson in *Horse and Hound*, in that year's Badminton report.

While still receiving the fruits of victory, however, Wideawake staggered and fell in the main ring at Badminton to die from acute heart failure.

Lucinda Prior-Palmer on the ill-fated Wideawake.

Karl Schultz and Madrigal went into the lead with an incredibly low dressage score.

1977

Lucinda Prior-Palmer's 'hat-trick' year was one of real April weather and her dashing speed and endurance, which she completed unpenalized on George, took place at the end of the Saturday afternoon in a downpour.

In a year when qualifications had been tightened even further, into the lead after the dressage went Karl Schultz on Madrigal of Germany who incurred an incredibly low 28·8 penalties. This was nearly ten marks ahead of Lucinda on George, who had come into her hands only three weeks before the Event, behind whom was Aly Pattinson on Carawich.

An early shock on the cross-country day was the departure of both Richard Meade on Tommy Buck and Mark Phillips on Persian Holiday, the latter when a rein broke coming out of Huntsman's Close, while Karl Schultz dropped right back with a stop and time

Lucinda Prior-Palmer on George, winning for the third time.

faults. Diana Thorne on The Kingmaker scored the only other completely clear speed and endurance, apart from the winner, and moved into third place still four show-jumping fences behind Lucinda, under the new system of only five penalties for a jump down. She was breathing close down the neck of Aly Pattinson whose ten penalties dropped her down to fifth overall, letting The Kingmaker through to runner-up position. Carawich's mistake also gave third place to Lucinda on her second string Killaire, while Jane Holderness-Roddam on Warrior moved into fourth position.

George

Bred by his owner, Mrs Elaine Straker, George was by St Georg, the German dressage horse, out of Winifrith, by Cottage Son, which Mrs Straker had bought from Sir Douglas Blackett of Northumberland and rode in one-day events herself.

George proved a very ugly yearling and he was nearly sold for £50. However, he was kept and Mrs Straker broke and schooled him herself for her second son, Nicholas, who introduced him to eventing and went on to compete in the Junior European Championships at Eridge with Mrs Straker's third son, Matthew. Here he was the only horse out of ten nations to finish the event with only his dressage score.

Matthew Straker rode George at Badminton and Burghley in 1976, but the following year business and army commitments in the family meant that George was without a rider, and Mrs Straker offered him to Lucinda Prior-Palmer. Accepting the ride with a recommendation from Mark Phillips who had ridden George successfully in one-day events, Lucinda went on to win Badminton in 1977 and the European Championships at Burghley the same year, a unique double victory. Lucinda says of him: 'I admired him beyond belief and he is one of the most fantastic event horses I've ever been lucky enough to sit on . . . at Badminton I loved riding him and he felt like a horse ripe to win.'

George is now back home in Yorkshire and competes in team 'chases with various members of the Straker family. He was in the winning team at Hickstead in 1978 and completed a successful 1979 season. Lucinda visited George for a day's hunting with him in the 1978/79 season and found him still the 'magic carpet' of the equine world.

1978

The biggest-ever crowd – 150,000 on the Saturday – saw the smallest entry (forty-two) for some years tackle a big but fair cross-country which easily lived up to the high standards Col. Frank Weldon sets himself.

After a somewhat doubtful start the sun shone over the remainder of the Event and the dressage section ended with Jane Starkey on her reliable Topper Too eight points in the lead from Jane Holderness-Roddam on Warrior. After a brief two months' introduction with his new ride, Bleak Hills, Richard Meade conjured the very best out of the horse to finish third after the dressage and then went on to inspire him into a clear and reasonably fast cross-country to retain their position. Jane Starkey also jumped clear but Topper Too incurred too many time penalties for her to keep the lead and she was pushed back into fourth place by Warrior's fast clear round and the even faster, unpenalized round of Lucinda Prior-Palmer on Village Gossip – the only combination to finish the Event with just their dressage score. While faults had been evenly spread around the course, which included several new fences, it was the more familiar Stockholm fence which caused the greatest number of problems.

Twenty-seven survivors went through to the final day's test including Helen Cantillon, her arm encased in plaster having broken it in three places after a fall at the Sunken Road, but she bravely carried on to complete the competition. Tension increased as those in contention completed their rounds. Felday Farmer and Elizabeth Boone jumped clear to move into fourth ahead of John Watson and Cambridge Blue from Ireland, who incurred five penalties, while Topper Too moved up to third as a result of his own clear round and Bleak Hills, three fences down which relegated Richard Meade to sixth. Lucinda Prior-Palmer, lying second, jumped clear, poised to take victory from Jane Holderness-Roddam should the latter have down more than the one fence she held in hand, but, like the experienced, cool competitor Jane is, she secured her second Badminton victory with a clear round.

John Watson and Cambridge Blue: fifth in 1978.

Warrior

A 16·1 hh bay gelding by Warwick – thus a half-brother to Diana Henderson's The Kingmaker – and out of a point-to-point mare, Winslade, Warrior was originally owned by Mrs Firth. Mrs Howard, his present joint-owner, bought him from John Shedden with whom he had been very successful in novice events, and had won one intermediate event when ridden by Mrs Sheila Michaels. With his other joint owner, Jane Holderness-Roddam riding him, Warrior won Burghley in 1976 and finished fourth at Badminton the following year, going on to be a member of the winning British team at the European Championships at Burghley, finishing fifth individual. That autumn Warrior 'doubled' for Magic Lantern in the film 'International Velvet'.

The 1978 Badminton victory earned a ticket to Lexington for the World Championships, where an inspired dressage put Warrior and Jane into second place, but the notorious Serpent fence on the cross-country was their downfall and they were eliminated.

Warrior came back to Badminton in 1979 and jumped clear across country but sustained a leg injury and was withdrawn before the show-jumping.

Jane says of Warrior: 'He's a tremendous character and just loves the "big time", hence he considers himself the Red Rum of Badminton. I think he has, without doubt, given me three of the best rides I've ever had around the cross-country at Badminton, although little Nobby gave me by far the speediest.'

Jane Holderness-Roddam and Warrior.

Sue Hatherley and Monacle, a very close second in 1979.

Lucinda Prior-Palmer and Killaire setting a record fourth win.

1979

The weather threatened throughout the thirtieth anniversary Event which proved to be a real history maker with Lucinda Prior-Palmer shattering the records to take her fourth win on yet another different horse, this time Mr Charles Cyzer's Killaire, on which she finished third in 1977.

Judy Bradwell on Castlewellan took the lead after the dressage, but Lucinda was hot on her heels, only 2·2 penalties behind with Killaire, and Topper Too was again up with the leaders in third.

Making his comeback was Columbus, with Capt. Mark Phillips, whose dressage left him towards the middle of the field but a penalty-free speed and endurance put him right up in contention, to lie in fourth place at the end of two days, behind James Wofford and Carawich of the U S A. The only other rounds clear of both time and jumping penalties were ridden by Sue Hatherly on Monacle, who moved into second place, and H R H Princess Anne, riding Goodwill in his last three-day event, who made tremendous strides to rise from near the bottom of the list to sixth. Killaire's good dressage paid dividends, for he is not a galloping horse, and he only just managed to retain the lead. Usually one of the fastest across country, Chris Collins had a crashing fall on the steeplechase on Radway and was taken off to hospital.

Twenty-two horses remained in the hunt for the final day's test which exerted more than the usual influence: only four clear rounds were jumped and the final placings changed accordingly. Mark Phillips and Columbus jumped clear to gain a place on Carawich who had two down, while the U S A suffered another pitiable change in fortunes when Karen Sachey on High Kite was eliminated at the last fence on the show-jumping when well within the top twelve. Sue Hatherly jumped clear and then had an agonizing few minutes watching Lucinda jump her round, with no fences in hand. But it was Lucinda's Badminton and not even the nudged brick in the wall decided to bring about her downfall.

A remarkable record was thus achieved by this brilliantly talented young rider who, one can confidently suppose, will not stop at four!

Killaire

Irish bred by Carnatic, this 16·3 hh bay gelding was show-jumped in Ireland by Richard Iggulden before Mr Charles Cyzer bought him in 1973. Over the next three years he was schooled and competed successfully by Marabeth Camacho and came to Lucinda Prior-Palmer's yard for Burghley in 1976 where they finished second.

In 1977, they came third at Badminton and Ledyard, U S A, and were placed at Boekelo, Holland, in 1978. Lucinda felt that Killaire, although a generous, kind horse, would never win a three-day event, but the consistently high standard shown in each phase at Badminton in 1979 (which is indeed as it should be) brought the well-earned victory.

'Any day I would take more pleasure out of winning Badminton because I love it.' Lucinda Prior-Palmer.

Appendix 1
Armada Dish Awards

Armada Dishes have been awarded to the following riders for completing Badminton five times:

Presented in 1964

Capt. H. Freeman-Jackson (Ire)
Capt. Ian Dudgeon (Ire)
Col. Frank Weldon
Capt. Norman Arthur
Mr Michael Bullen
Capt. Martin Whiteley
Miss Anneli Drummond-Hay
Mr E. E. Marsh
Mr Douglas Nicholson
Mr Brian Young

Presented in 1965

Capt. Jeremy Beale
Miss Virginia Freeman-Jackson (Ire)
Miss Sheila Willcox
Miss Penny Moreton (Ire)

Presented in 1967

Capt. the Hon. Patrick Connolly-Carew (Ire)
Miss Jennifer Graham-Clark

Presented in 1969

Major Derek Allhusen

Presented in 1970

Capt. Tim Ritson
Miss Celia Ross-Taylor

Presented in 1971

Miss Lorna Sutherland
Mr E. Thompson

Presented in 1972

Mr Richard Meade
Mrs Barbara Hammond

Presented in 1973

Mr Richard Walker
Mr Michael Tucker
Mr Bill Roycroft (Aus)

Presented in 1974

Miss Mary Gordon-Watson

Presented in 1976 (1975 cancelled)

Miss Hazel Booth
Mr Christopher Collins
Capt. Mark Phillips
Miss Debbie West

Presented in 1977

Mr Richard Meade
Mrs Marjorie Comerford

Presented in 1978

Miss Lucinda Prior-Palmer
Mrs Jane Holderness-Roddam

To be presented in 1980

HRH Princess Anne Mrs Mark Phillips
Miss Sue Hatherly
Miss Clarissa Strachan

Appendix 2
Score Sheets 1949-79

1949

Owner, horse and rider	Dressage	Speed and Endurance: Penalty (Time + Jumping)	Speed and Endurance: Bonus	Show-Jumping	Total
1. Mrs Home Kidston's Golden Willow (J. Shedden)	90	–	63	10	37
2. Lt.-Col. J. H. Dudgeon's Sea Lark (I. H. Dudgeon)	114·5	–	51	–	63·5
3. Brig. L. Bolton's Titus III	95·5	20	42	31·5	105
4. Miss Preston's Lucky Chance (Lt.-Col. P. Leech)	89	20	24	34·5	119·5
5. Miss V. L. Machin-Goodall's Neptune	172	–	54	10	128
6. Miss G. Chrystal's Remus (Capt. T. Collings)	56	70	9	34·5	151·5
7. Lady Leigh's Minster Green (Maj. J. J. Crotty)	146	–	18	40	168
8. H. Coriat's Fritzy (Earl of Westmorland)	125	100	27	10	208
9. Sgt.-Maj. L. Lungley's Nuthatch	137	120	27	20	250
10. Lt. E. A. Boylan's Cool Star	114·5	160	–	10	284·5
11. J. R. Hindley's Stealaway	130	170	24	13·5	289·5
12. Lt.-Col. C. P. D. Legard's Varne	104	390	–	43	537
13. W. Stokes' Dandy Dick	233	340	15	20	578

22 ran

1950

Owner, horse and rider	Dressage	Speed and Endurance: Penalty (Time + Jumping)	Speed and Endurance: Bonus	Show-Jumping	Total
1. Miss G. Chrystal's Remus (Capt. T. Collings)	44·5	–	30	12·75	27·25
2. Mrs Fanshawe's Kingpin (Capt. J. Shedden)	85	–	75	20	30
3. Lady Leigh's Minster Green (Capt. P. F. Arkwright)	80·5	–	69	20	31·5
4. P. McCann's Lily (Miss P. Hildebrand)	59	–	33	10	36
5. Mrs Home Kidston's Golden Willow (Capt. J. Shedden)	95·5	–	57	1·75	40·25
6. J. R. Hindley's Stealaway	83·5	–	66	34·75	52·25
7. Lt.-Col. the Hon. C. G. Cubitt's Eildon (I. H. Dudgeon)	119	–	48	20	91

8. Mrs A. M. D. Thompson's Salome (Miss E. Knox-Thompson)	124·5	20	39	11	116·5
9. Household Cavalry's Guinea Fowl (S. C. M. Thompson)	91	80	51	22	142
10. Mrs Church's Quetta (Mrs J. Watherston)	119	20	60	65·75	144·75
11. Millfield School's King Willow (Maj. R. Hern)	103·5	60	45	40·75	159·25
12. Lt.-Col. R. Heathcoat-Amory's Kiel	167·5	–	27	21·75	162·25
13. Marquess of Linlithgow's Orion (J. W. Kirkpatrick)	183·5	40	51	50·5	223
14. Miss I. Touche's Balalaika	200·5	60	57	20	223·5
15. Miss S. Poile's Freddie	125·5	93	–	33·25	251·75
16. Maj. J. Miller's Stella	143	80	9	62·5	276·5
17. Maj. W. V. Burdon's Ollo	112·5	200	–	10·75	323·25
18. Miss V. L. Machin-Goodall's Neptune	102·5	300	36	1·25	367·75

30 ran

1951

Owner, horse and rider	*Dressage*	*Speed and Endurance*		*Show-Jumping*	*Total*
		Penalty (Time + Jumping)	*Bonus*		
1. Capt. H. Schwarzenbach's Vae Victis	80·5	–	9	10	81·5
2. Miss J. Drummond-Hay's Happy Knight	128·5	20	48	–	100·5
3. H. M. Van Loon's Nerantsoula	106	–	39	42·25	109·25
4. Col. H. Bühler's Werwolf (Lt. A. S. Bühler)	134·5	20	45	4·75	114·25
5. Capt. Naylor-Leyland's Torloisk (A. C. M. Thompson)	173·25	–	75	20	118·25
6. Capt. A. Blaser's Mahmud	48·75	60	24	40·25	125
7. Maj. J. Miller's Stella	157	20	51	10	136
8. O. Schwarz's Euphrona	129·5	60	63	10·5	137
9. Col. H. Bühler's Richard (Capt. H. Bühler)	108	60	36	20·25	162·25
10. S. Koechlin's Tambour	78·25	80	48	59·5	169·75
11. Mrs J. R. Baker's Starlight (Lt.-Col. D. N. Stewart)	119·5	50	24	40	185·5
12. W. Brake's Badger	183	60	33	–	210
13. J. R. Hindley's Stealaway	114·75	60	54	89·75	210·5
14. T. Holland Martin's Gold Pot (Maj. L. Rook)	136	110	24	10	232
15. Col. H. Bühler's Uranus (Capt. H. Bühler)	94·5	130	18	32	238·5
16. Miss M. Naylor's Rowena (Miss S. Flenry)	204·25	40	15	11	240·25
17. H. Freeman-Jackson's Cuchulain	198·25	30	15	41·75	255
18. Miss S. Dickson's Seretse (Capt. W. J. Frisby)	222	60	27	30·75	285·75
19. Maj. E. S. Jenkins' Steadfast III (Lt.-Col. J. Crawford)	156·25	90	12	62·25	296·5
20. Lt.-Col. J. H. Dudgeon's Navan (I. H. Dudgeon)	196·5	220	21	–	395·5
21. R. N. Hall's Rocket	138	410	–	84	632

38 ran

1952

Owner, horse and rider	Dressage	Speed and Endurance: Penalty (Time + Jumping)	Speed and Endurance: Bonus	Show-Jumping	Total
1. Capt. M. A. Q. Darley's Emily Little	151·25	20	45	–	126·25
2. Mr & Mrs P. A. Hutton's Dandy (B. Young)	135	–	27	20·25	128·25
3. Brig. L. Bolton's Greylag	120·25	20	42	30·5	128·75
4. Lt.-Col. J. H. Dudgeon's Hope (I. H. Dudgeon)*	149·5	20	36	0·5	134
5. Miss P. Moreton's Vigilant	100·25	40	33	31	138·25
6. H. Freeman-Jackson's Cuchulain	160·25	40	51	–	149·25
7. E. E. Marsh's Abundance (J. Shedden)	139	40	27	–	152
8. Lt.-Col. H. M. Llewellyn's Lionheart (Lt. W. R. Thompson)	152·5	30	36	10	156·5
9. Miss V. Pardoe's Garth Royal	129·75	80	18	43·75	235·5
10. Miss M. Roberts' Fitz (Maj. R. Hern)	121	130	9	–	242
11. H. Wainwright Yates' The Master (Miss P. McCormick)	156·25	100	9	20	267·25
12. Lt. C. W. D. Morgan's Heavy Weather	148·75	225	–	–	373·75
13. Lt.-Col. J. H. Dudgeon's Abbeyfeale (Miss J. Drummond-Hay)	81·75	340	15	–	406·75
14. Col. A. B. J. Scott's Lady Diana (Lt.-Col. D. N. Stewart)	152·75	250	33	40	409·75
15. Lt. J. Cameron-Hayes' Water Gypsy	126·25	340	–	10	476·25

* An error was later discovered which eliminated Ian Dudgeon and caused everyone else to move up a place.

26 ran

1953

Owner, horse and rider	Dressage	Speed and Endurance: Penalty (Time + Jumping)	Speed and Endurance: Bonus	Show-Jumping	Total
1. Mrs J. R. Baker's Starlight XV (Maj. L. Rook)	81	–	96·3	10	+ 5·3
2. Maj. F. W. C. Weldon's Kilbarry	89	–	60	10	39
3. Capt. H. Schwarzenbach's Vae Victis	87	–	38·1	–	48·9
4. J. Asker's Iller	84·5	–	71·4	40·75	53·85
5. Miss V. L. Machin-Goodall's Neptune	142·5	–	78·6	–	63·9
6. J. R. Hindley's Speculation	138	–	67·6	10·25	80·75
7. Lt. C. W. D. Morgan's Owenmore	122	40	66·9	10	105·1
8. Brig. L. Bolton's Flanagan	127·5	20	45·9	10	111·6
9. King's Troop R.H.A's Heavy Weather (Lt. C. W. D. Morgan)	142	20	46·2	–	115·8
10. Mrs A. Huot's Sunbeam	175	–	40·2	10	144·8
11. Miss V. Pardoe's Garth Royal	141·5	5·1	12	20	154·6
12. Capt. M. A. Q. Darley's Emily Little	145·5	40	39·3	10	156·2
13. H. Freeman-Jackson's Cuchulain	149·5	60	68·1	21	162·4
14. Millfield School's King Willow (Maj. R. Hern)	171	–	29·4	63	204·6
15. Lt. Andrea Zindel's Bussira	143	60	11·7	20	211·3
16. R. Dennis' Lohengrin (Lt. N. Arthur)	207·5	40	63·3	30·25	214·45

17. Miss M. Hough's Bambi V (A. E. Hill)	118	180	63	0·25	235·25
18. Mrs Edwards' Jimmy E (Miss S. Poile)	150	65·3	–	21	236·3
19. Miss D. Mason's Tramella	125	122·7	12	10	245·7
20. H. Wainwright Yates' The Master (J. J. Beale)	142·5	90·8	0·9	30	253·4
21. Porlock Vale Riding School's Top Sawyer (B. Young)	164	92·3	23·4	20.75	253·65
22. Miss P. Molteno's Carmena	181	75	60	22·5	258·7
23. Lt. H. Schätti's Topas	113·5	128·1	13·2	40	268·4
24. Cornhill School of Equitation's Salome (Miss E. Knox-Thompson)	133	180	45·6	20	287·4
25. Capt. W. J. Frisby's Epijune	201·5	119	27	30·25	323·75
26. Miss M. Whitehead's Ardnagee	195	241·1	–	40·75	476·85

40 ran

1954

Owner, horse and rider	*Dressage*	*Speed and Endurance*		*Show-Jumping*	*Total*
		Penalty (Time + Jumping)	*Bonus*		
1. Miss M. Hough's Bambi V	104	20	59·7	–	64·3
2. Maj. F. W. C. Weldon's Kilbarry	135	–	89·1	20	65·9
3. Miss D. Mason's Tramella	106	20	56·4	–	69·6
4. Capt. A. J. Castle's Late Final	152·67	–	79·2	20	93·47
5. H. Freeman-Jackson's Brown Sugar	156	–	52·8	10	113·2
6. Lt.-Col. J. H. Dudgeon's Spahi (I. H. Dudgeon)	130·67	40	50·1	–	120·57
7. Capt. G. L. Wathen's Strathcona	153·34	20	48·9	–	124·44
8. Porlock Vale Riding School's Killultagh (Lt. N. Arthur)	190·67	20	76·2	–	134·47
9. E. E. Marsh's Crispin	177·34	20	74·1	24	147·24
10. Miss J. Bennett's Sandy Boy	180·67	60	79·5	–	161·17
11. Miss A. E. Holland's Tudor Gal (Maj. L. Rook)	169·37	20	44·7	20	164·67
12. Miss P. Molteno's Carmena	128·67	80	66·6	30	172·07
13. Brig. L. Bolton's Redwing	154	12·6	4·8	30	191·8
14. Maj. P. H. Jackson's Zulu	187·34	72·4	35·4	10	234·34
15. Capt. G. G. R. Boon's Halberdier	196	41·3	–	–	237·3
16. King's Troop R.H.A's Water Gypsy (Maj. D. P. H. Dyson)	130	110·6	12·6	10	238
17. Miss Harms-Cooke's Maximillian (Miss D. Faber)	181·34	60	30	30	241·34
18. Lt.-Col. W. Lewicki's Skilly	146	114·7	14·4	–	246·3
19. Miss J. Carlisle's Sandpiper	209·34	60	49·2	30	250·14
20. Miss P. Sutcliffe's Tessa	127·34	15·3	1·5	40	259·64
21. G. Lee Morris' Can Can (Miss P. Sutcliffe)	198	87·5	–	21·25	306·75
22. Miss J. B. Johnson's Gransden Lady (B. Young)	147·34	158·3	–	40	345·64
23. Mr & Mrs R. E. Wetherall's Locksley (Mrs R. E. Wetherall)	198	93·6	–	80	371·6
24. J. C. Brady's May Morning (B. L. Green)	246·67	153·9	–	40	440·57

36 ran

1955

Owner, horse and rider	Dressage	Speed and Endurance: Penalty (Time + Jumping)	Speed and Endurance: Bonus	Show-Jumping	Total
1. Maj. F. W. C. Weldon's Kilbarry	79·334	–	84·01	–	+ 4·676
2. Miss J. Johnson's Radar (Lt.-Com. J. S. K. Oram)	97·334	–	60·23	–	37·104
3. A. E. Hill's Countryman III	114	20	90	10	54
4. L. R. Morgan's Gold Ross	132·666	–	73·54	–	59·126
5. German Olympic Committee's Trux Von Kamax (O. Rothe)	108	–	53·8	20	74·2
6. A. S. Bühler's Uranus	100	–	33·31	10	76·69
7. Swedish Army's Jubal (Capt. H. V. Blixen-Finecke)	82	80	91·92	10	80·08
8. L. H. Dudgeon's Charleville	145·334	40	84·01	–	101·324
9. H. Bühler's Richard	144	2·4	19·89	–	126·51
10. H. Freeman-Jackson's Brown Sugar	186·666	–	54·9	–	131·776
11. Mrs V. L. Boon's Neptune	132·666	60	62·45	10	140·216
12. Miss A. Holland's Tudor Gal (Lt.-Com. J. S. K. Oram)	107·334	80	57·99	20	149·344
13. Miss S. M. Willcox's High and Mighty	130·666	60	48·1	10	152·566
14. M. Bühler's Tizian	146·666	21·3	–	–	167·966
15. Mrs J. R. Baker's Starlight XV (Maj. L. Rook)	139·334	60	30·46	–	168·874
16. Maj. H. S. Killick's Take a Chance (Capt. W. J. Frisby)	163·334	20	9·43	–	173·904
17. Maj. Drummond-Moray's Freya (Miss A. Drummond-Hay)	152·666	31·8	2·13	–	182·336
18. Miss S. Clifford's Second Son	164·666	40	37·91	20	186·756
19. E. E. Marsh's Crispin	140·666	80	51·98	20	188·686
20. Miss J. Bennett's Sandy Boy	168	26·3	–	–	194·3
21. King's Troop R.H.A.'s Water Gypsy (Maj. D. P. H. Dyson)	145·334	70	–	21·25	227·584
22. Maj. J. N. D. Birtwistle's Delagyle	166	120	63·16	10	232·84
23. J. Beale's Simon	266	20	81·83	40	244·17
24. Capt. M. F. Whiteley's St Nicholas	238·666	–	38·67	55·75	255·746
25. Kamax-Werke's Sixtus Von Kamax (M. Huck)	137·334	139·8	17·91	10	269·224
26. R. N. Hall's Copperplate (Miss L. Touche)	188	100	35·99	30	282·01
27. Capt. H. Schwarzenbach's Vae Victis (Lt. A. Zindel)	150	133·5	–	–	283·5
28. E. E. Marsh's Leprechaun	126·666	171	14·12	–	283·546
29. Maj. M. Smallwood's Steel Worker	222	80	45·68	30	286·32
30. Maj. D. Susanna's Aristos	134·666	169·6	4·76	30	329·506
31. Italian Army's Falchidar (Sgt.-Maj. G. Molinari)	184·666	177·1	19·46	10	352·306
32. Maj. F. De Leone's La Primarosa (Lt. G. Gutierrez)	220	133·9	–	10	363·9
33. Italian Army's Taquilo (A. Cupuzzo)	200·666	219·2	30·85	–	389·016
34. H. Coriat's Torloisk	245·334	186·9	36	36	432·234

51 ran

1956

Owner, horse and rider	Dressage	Speed and Endurance: Penalty (Time + Jumping)	Speed and Endurance: Bonus	Show-Jumping	Total
1. Lt.-Col. F. W. C. Weldon's Kilbarry	56·22	–	108	–	+ 51·78
2. Miss S. M. Willcox's High and Mighty	57·78	–	108	–	+ 50·22
3. L. R. Morgan's Gold Ross	73·33	20	107·69	20	5·64
4. HM the Queen's Countryman III (A. E. Hill)	125·44	–	108	10	27·44
5. Lt.-Col. J. Hume Dudgeon's Copper Coin (Miss P. Moreton)	120·78	–	91.87	–	28·91
6. Miss A. Drummond-Hay's Trident	125·44	–	95·57	–	29·87
7. Maj. J. N. D. Birtwistle's Delagyle	123·9	60	99·01	–	84·89
8. Miss G. Morrison's Just William	183·78	–	108	10	85·78
9. Equestrian Federation of Australia's Radar (B. Crago)	104·44	20	44·9	10	89·54
10. E. E. Marsh's Wild Venture	179·56	–	99·88	10	89·88
11. Equestrian Federation of Australia's Brown Sugar (W. W. Thompson)	143	–	52·8	–	90·2
12. H. Freeman-Jackson's Cellarstown	181·44	–	96·22	10	95·22
13. Equestrian Federation of Australia's Marcus Adair (E. Barker)	174·44	–	73·67	10	110·77
14. Lt.-Com. J. S. K. Oram's Copperplate	137·11	60	79·6	10	127·51
15. Miss J. Bennett's Sandy Boy	205·56	–	76·16	20	149·4
16. Capt. M. F. Whiteley's St Nicholas	190·78	20	75·79	20	154·99
17. Equestrian Federation of Australia's Dandy (B. Crago)	152·67	12·6	15·09	10	160·18
18. Equestrian Federation of Australia's Radiant III (D. J. Wood)	147·22	60	34·46	10	182·76
19. Lt.-Col. J. Samuelson's Ignatius (J. H. Dudgeon)	215·67	–	63·35	57·25	209·57
20. Miss R. Greville Williams' Eveone	202·9	13·2	11·02	10	215·08
21. Miss V. Engelmann's Master Dene	223·44	–	24·75	30	228·69
22. Mrs G. Fasenfield's Charleville (Comdt. Mullins)	215·67	60	26·84	20	268·83
23. Mrs J. W. Prins' Oyster Hill (J. W. Prins)	287·67	–	41·04	30	276·73
24. Miss I. Touche's Hunting Stewart	285·67	–	68·97	70	286·7
25. Miss V. Gilligan's Jungle Queen	158·9	160	31·37	–	287·53
26. Miss J. Somervail's Duncormack	162	80	23·54	100·25	318·71

35 ran

1957

Owner, horse and rider	Dressage	Speed and Endurance: Penalty (Time + Jumping)	Speed and Endurance: Bonus	Show-Jumping	Total
1. Miss S. M. Willcox's High and Mighty	24·33	–	103·7	–	+79·37
2. Lt.-Col. J. Hume Dudgeon's Red Sea (Miss P. Moreton)	50·33	–	103·91	–	+53·58
3. E. E. Marsh's Wild Venture	44·67	–	108	20	+43·33
4. Miss G. M. Morrison's Benjamin Bunny	63·33	–	108	10	+34·67
5. I. H. Dudgeon's Charleville	48·33	–	84·01	10	+25·68

6. Mrs T. F. R. Bulkeley's Pampas Cat (Miss K. Tatham-Warter)	32	20	97·01	22·25	+22·76
7. King's Troop R.H.A.'s Scamperdale (Capt. R. W. Scott)	69	–	102·26	11·75	+21·51
8. Miss P. Molteno's Bandoola	55·67	–	84·75	10	+19·08
9. H. Freeman-Jackson's Cellarstown	57·33	20	103·5	10	+16·17
10. J. G. Henson's Souvenir II (W. G. Henson)	72·67	–	101·33	20	+ 8·66
11. Mrs J. W. Prins' Oyster Hill (J. W. Prins)	85·67	–	95·43	30	20·24
12. Miss V. Engelmann's Master Dene	48·67	–	31·9	10	26·77
13. Miss M. Hough's Bambi V	51	20	36·45	10	44·55
14. Miss J. Berry's Woolpack	63·33	4·8	21·43	–	46·7
15. Miss V. Freeman-Jackson's Liscarroll	67	20	49·52	10	47·48
16. Capt. S. D. Pettifer's Vanity	69·67	20	49·12	10	50·55
17. Miss Y. Stedman's Boldevil	53·33	20	23·37	32	50·96
18. Miss S. Clifford's Dispatch	60·67	40	54·98	10	55·69
19. J. J. Beale's Fulmer Folly	59·67	20	37·02	20	62·65
20. J. M. Barrington's Rio Grande	69·67	60	75·79	20	73·88
21. King's Troop R.H.A.'s Watchman (Capt. J. C. C. Sworder)	65·67	60	32·31	–	93·36
22. Miss M. C. Wallace's Star XV	73·33	42·3	20·24	10	105·39
23. D. R. Somerset's Countryman	58	80	101·44	77·75	114·31
24. Miss R. Charrington's Raglan	72	40	34·85	40	117·15
25. Miss L. G. Kidman's Killala (Miss A. Kidman)	56	133·1	–	20	209·1

38 ran

1958

Owner, horse and rider	*Dressage*	*Speed and Endurance* *Penalty (Time + Jumping)*	*Bonus*	*Show-Jumping*	*Total*
1. Miss S. M. Willcox's High and Mighty	37	–	115·2	10	+68·2
2. Maj. D. Allhusen's Laurien	70	–	101·2	–	+21·2
3. R. T. Whiteley's Pluto (Miss A. Drummond-Hay)	62·33	–	88·4	20	+ 6·07
4. Com. J. S. K. Oram's Copperplate	81·67	–	96	10	+ 4·33
5. Miss V. Gilligan's Jungle Queen	65	20	106	20	+ 1
6. E. E. Marsh's Wild Venture	59·67	20	90·4	10	+ 0·73
7. D. Somerset's Countryman III	91	–	105·2	20	5·8
8. Miss G. Morrison's Benjamin Bunny	112·67	–	107·2	10	15·47
9. S. H. Walford's Absalom	113·33	–	86	–	27·33
10. Miss E. Colquhoun's Dear Brutus	100	20	87·6	–	32·4
11. Capt. J. M. Cavanagh's Landfall	104·67	–	90	20	34·67
12. Andrea Zindel's Choral	102·67	20	86·8	–	35·87
13. Miss A. Kesler's Samuel Johnson	82·67	20·8	62·4	–	41·07
14. Miss V. Freeman-Jackson's Liscarroll	112	–	76	20	56
15. D. Nicholson's Souvenir	103·33	20	82·4	20	60·93
16. H. Freeman-Jackson's Sonnet	104·33	20	38·4	10	95·93
17. Mrs E. S. Collins' Boldevil	112·67	60	83·6	10	99·07
18. King's Troop R.H.A.'s Watchman (Capt. J. R. T. Phipps)	125·67	20	52·8	10	102·87
19. Mrs P. J. Brocklehurst's Pepy (Miss J. Kent)	110	60	84	40	126
20. Lt.-Col. J. Hume Dudgeon's Just Maggie (Miss P. Moreton)	102	80	82·4	40	139·6
21. Miss R. Greville Williams' Top Twig	132·67	60	68·8	20	143·87

22. Mme Clement's Violette (M. Cochenet)	91·67	66·8	15·2	10	153·27
23. Capt. M. F. Whiteley's Happy Wanderer	118·33	40	–	–	158·33
24. D. Bolton's Cottage Romance	148	–	9·6	20	158·4
25. J. Le Roy's Garden	91·67	140	48·8	–	182·87
26. M. Allhusen's Dachs	118·67	81·2	11·2	–	188·67
27. Mrs G. Booth's Marlay Password (Miss A. Coulton)	104·33	49.6	–	40	193·93
28. Miss J. Carlisle's Mick	146·67	60	68	60	198·67
29. Miss V. Pardoe's National Provincial	113·67	100	52	60	221·67
30. J. M. Barrington's Rio Grande	130·33	120	24·8	95	320·53
31. Capt. C. W. D. Morgan's Steel Fortune	127·67	284	37·6	20	394·07
32. Mr & Mrs L. E. Allen's Forsha (Mrs Allen)	108·67	492	–	55	655·67

57 ran

1959 Great Badminton Championship

Owner, horse and rider	*Dressage*	*Speed and Endurance*		*Show-Jumping*	*Total*
		Penalty (Time + Jumping)	*Bonus*		
1. Mrs. J. Waddington's Airs and Graces	38·34	–	34	–	4·34
2. D. Somerset's Countryman III	95·34	–	88·4	10	10·94
3. E. E. Marsh's Wild Venture	80	–	68·8	10	21·2
4. Maj. D. S. Allhusen's Laurien	69	–	38·8	–	30·2
5. Mrs N. Marshall's Samuel Johnson (Col. Weldon)	101·34	–	68·4	10	42·94
6. E. E. Marsh's Blue Jeans	87·66	20	63·2	–	44·46
7. J. J. Beale's Fulmer Folly	62	–	26·4	10	45·6
8. H. Freeman-Jackson's St Finbarr	99	–	49·2	10	59·8
9. Lt.-Col. F. W. C. Weldon's Fermoy	97	20	46·8	–	70·2
10. Miss E. Colqhoun's Dear Brutus	92·56	40	43·2	–	79·46
11. J. Le Roy's Garden	93	2·6	20	30	85·4
12. R. T. Whiteley's Pluto (Miss A. Drummond-Hay)	68·34	60	57·8	30	100·74
13. Miss C. Graham Menzies' New	95	13	18·8	20	109·8
14. Capt. J. M. Cavanagh's Landfall	91·5	25·2	–	10	110·6
15. Miss R. Woollard's Ken Tikhi	118	20	33·6	10	114·4
16. France's Gitan B (M. Cochenet)	59·34	8·8	9·6	60	118·54
17. Miss J. Carlisle's Mick	135	–	20	20	135
18. H. Freeman-Jackson's Sonnet	112	32	4·4	10	149·6
19. Miss M. C. Wallace's Star	86·34	67·2	23·2	30	160·34
20. D. Nicholson's Souvenir	109	0·8	22·8	30	177
21. France's Harka (Lt. B. Stible)	82	82	–	20	184
22. Miss J. D. Stevens' Athleague	130·34	70·4	–	20	220·74

24 ran

1959 Little Badminton Event

Owner, horse and rider	Dressage	*Speed and Endurance* Penalty (Time + Jumping)	Bonus	Show-Jumping	Total
1. Miss B. E. Shaw's Double Diamond (Miss S. Kesler)	121·66	–	54·8	10	76·86
2. J. A. Crofts' Robinwood (Mrs J. O. McMillen)	98	–	60·8	40	77·2
3. S. P. Taylor & Mrs P. J. Diggle's Free As Air (Mr Goddard Watts)	111·6	–	37·6	10	84·06
4. Col. V. D. S. Williams' Frigorifico (Capt. J. Arthur)	39·34	67·2	18·4	10	98·14
5. Capt. M. F. Whiteley's Happy Wanderer	84·66	29·6	14	–	100·26
6. D. Nicholson's Merry Messenger	82·34	40	26·4	10	105·94
7. D. Nicholson's Sandyman (P. Nicholson)	80·34	20	24	30	106·34
8. Mr & Mrs A. Owen's Marcus Adair (B. Young)	65	23·6	–	30	118·6
9. Miss M. C. Newton's Troubadour	57·66	88·8	–	10	156·46
10. Mr Van de Vater's Tobruk	75·34	43·6	–	40·5	159·44
11. Col. D. L. Darling's Trinity	90·34	49·6	–	60	199·94
12. Miss I. Touche's Tartan	99·34	110	–	10	219·34
13. Col. V. D. S. Williams' Cottage Romance (D. Bolton)	78	145·2	–	10	233·2
14. Mrs W. G. Henson's Dark Elegance	161	60	46	70	245
15. D. Nicholson's Thame (B. J. Amer)	89·34	260	38·4	40	350·94
16. Col. R. E. Coaker's Deception	113	228·8	–	10	351
17. Miss C. Ross Taylor's King Midas	74	300·8	–	10	384·8
18. Maj. G. L. Wathen's Tolrock	92·34	328·8	24	–	397·14

27 ran

1960 Great Badminton Championship

Owner, horse and rider	Dressage	*Speed and Endurance* Penalty (Time + Jumping)	Bonus	Show-Jumping	Total
1. Equestrian Federation of Australia's Our Solo (W. Roycroft)	90·33	–	123·6	–	+33·27
2. Equestrian Federation of Australia's Salad Days (L. R. Morgan)	88·33	–	108	–	+29·67
3. Miss A. Drummond-Hay's Perhaps	69·67	–	107·6	20	+17·93
4. Equestrian Federation of Australia's Mirrabooka (N. J. Lavis)	86·67	–	109·6	10	+12·93
5. E. E. Marsh's Blue Jeans (Capt. N. Arthur)	100	–	131·2	10	+11·2
6. J. J. Beale's Fulmer Folly	86·67	–	94·4	–	+ 7·73
7. Mrs N. Marshall's Samuel Johnson (Lt.-Col. F. W. C. Weldon)	96·33	–	123·6	20	+ 7·27
8. Col. V. D. S. Williams' Frigorifico (Capt. J. N. S. Arthur)	93	20	111·2	20	21·8
9. Col. V. D. S. Williams' Sea Breeze (M. Bullen)	97·67	20	104·8	10	22·87
10. Equestrian Federation of Australia's Adlai (J. W. Kelly)	86·67	60	100	20	66·67

Owner, horse and rider	Dressage	Penalty (Time + Jumping)	Bonus	Show-Jumping	Total
11. Equestrian Federation of Australia's Toscanella (B. J. Crago)	107·33	–	59·6	20	67·73
12. Mme Clement's Violette G (M. Cochenet)	99	4·8	32·4	10	81·4
13. Capt. H. Freeman-Jackson's St Finbarr	94·67	80	90·8	–	83·87
14. Capt. H. Freeman-Jackson's Sonnet (Comdt. W. B. Mullins)	113·33	–	53·6	50·5	110·23
15. Maj. & Mrs E. A. Boylan's Corrigneagh (Maj. Boylan)	105·67	80	98·4	30	117·27
16. Col. V. D. S. Williams' Cottage Romance (M. Bullen)	92·33	120	91·6	10	130·73
17. E. E. Marsh's Wild Venture (A. E. Hill)	112·33	120	99·2	10	143·13
18. Miss M. C. Wallace's Star XI	91	120	64·8	–	146·2
19. J. Le Roy's Avril	106·33	120	44	10	192·33
20. Hon. P. T. Connolly-Carew's Ballyhoo	129	100	34·8	20	214·2

24 ran

1960 Little Badminton Event

Owner, horse and rider	Dressage	Speed and Endurance		Show-Jumping	Total
		Penalty (Time + Jumping)	Bonus		
1. Capt. M. F. Whiteley's Peggoty	90·33	40	84·4	10	55·93
2. J. A. Crofts' Robinwood II (Mrs J. O. McMillen)	120·67	–	89·2	30	61·47
3. Miss R. Greville Williams' Top Twig III	98·67	–	82	50·5	67·17
4. Mr & Mrs A. R. B. Owen's Marcus Adair (B. A. Young)	112	–	50·8	30·5	91·7
5. Lt.-Col. D. D. P. Smyly's Carte Blanche	119·33	40	76·8	10	92·53
6. Miss J. Stevens' Athlcague	136·33	–	54·8	30	111·53
7. Queen's Own Hussar's Gipsy Love (Capt. M. Q. Fraser)	116·67	16	37·6	30	125·07
8. Miss H. White's Counting House	128·33	80	68	10	150·33
9. Miss C. Ross Taylor's King Midas	90·33	80	40·8	30	159·53
10. J. G. Henson's Sultana (W. G. Henson)	147	–	45·6	86·5	187·9
11. Mrs T. F. R. Bulkeley's Tilleul (Miss I. Touche)	149·67	45·6	16	10	189·27
12. Mr Graham-Clark's Hansel (Miss J. Graham-Clark)	168·67	60	35·2	20	213·47
13. Mrs W. G. Henson's Dark Elegance	144	140	66	50	268

21 ran

1961 Great Badminton Championship

Owner, horse and rider	Dressage	Speed and Endurance		Show-Jumping	Total
		Penalty (Time + Jumping)	Bonus		
1. L. R. Morgan's Salad Days	102·67	–	118·4	0·75	+14·98
2. Capt. H. Freeman-Jackson's St Finbarr	77·33	–	88·4	–	+11·07
3. Col. V. D. S. Williams' Cottage Romance (M. Bullen)	61·33	60	114·4	10	16·93
4. Col. V. D. S. Williams' Sea Breeze (M. Bullen)	76·67	60	115·6	–	21·07

5. A. R. Tulloch's Benjamin Bunny (J. G. A. Tulloch)	120·67	–	94·4	10·25	36·52
6. King's Troop R.H.A.'s Sherpa (Sgt. R. S. Jones)	103·33	–	65·6	–	37·73
7. D. Nicholson's Merry Messenger	117·33	–	90·4	11·5	38·43
8. Miss S. G. Fleet's The Gladiator	76·67	60	77·2	1	60·47
9. Mme Clement's Violette G (M. Cochenet)	106·67	–	44	–	62·67
10. Miss L. du Pont's Mr Wister	91·33	–	37·2	11·25	65·38
11. A. Le Goupil's Jacasse B	126·67	–	57·6	20	89·07
12. Lt. the Hon. P. T. Connolly-Carew's Ballyhoo	132·67	2·4	46·8	3·75	92·02
13. D. Nicholson's Sandyman (P. Nicholson)	132	16·8	40·8	12	120
14. Mrs J. O. McMillen & J. A. Croft's Robinwood (Mrs McMillen)	124·67	60	73·6	11	122·07
15. Lt.-Col. D. D. P. Smyly's Carte Blanche	112	120	53·6	2·25	180·65

27 ran

1961 Little Badminton Event

Owner, horse and rider	*Dressage*	*Speed and Endurance*		*Show-Jumping*	*Total*
		Penalty (Time + Jumping)	*Bonus*		
1. Capt. J. P. E. Welch's Mr Wilson	95·33	–	102	–	+ 6·67
2. Miss J. Wykeham-Musgrave's Ryebrooks	78·67	–	84	2·5	+ 2·83
3. Miss S. Clifford's Dispatch	108	20	80·8	–	47·2
4. Queen's Own Hussar's Gipsy Love (Lt. T. W. Ritson)	118·67	–	107·6	51·25	62·22
5. Miss C. Ross-Taylor's King Midas	75·33	60	70	2	67·33
6. P. V. Hervey's High Jinks	133·33	20	63·2	13·75	103·88
7. J. G. A. Tulloch's Botany Degree	110	60	62·4	11·25	118·85
8. Miss V. Freeman-Jackson's Granite	157·33	–	47·6	12	121·73
9. Mrs J. J. Beale's Anonymous	88	60	26·4	1	122·6
10. H. Graham-Clark's Hansel II (Miss J. Graham-Clark)	86	71·6	7·2	–	150·4
11. Mrs C. Horton's Illogan	160	30·6	8	8·25	190·85
12. O. E. Johnson's Ad Astra (Capt. M. F. Whiteley)	90·67	82·4	5·6	23·75	191·22
13. C. Parson's Quality Street (M. Skinner)	85·33	132·8	–	11	229·13
14. P. N. Simpson's Why Not	150·67	139·2	6·4	30	313·47
15. Miss P. Green's Red Dawn	88	241·2	–	11·25	340·45

32 ran

1962 Great Badminton Championship

Owner, horse and rider	*Dressage*	*Speed and Endurance*		*Show-Jumping*	*Total*
		Penalty (Time + Jumping)	*Bonus*		
1. Miss A. Drummond-Hay and Mrs A. Gilroy's Merely-a-Monarch (Miss A. Drummond-Hay)	56·67	–	118·4	10	+51·73
2. N. Gardiner's Young Pretender (Lt.-Col. F. W. C. Weldon)	95·67	–	118·4	10	+ 9·73
3. Col. V. D. S. Williams' Sea Breeze (M. Bullen)	110·67	–	118·4	–	+ 7·73

4. A. Cameron's Dignity	99·33	–	99·6	–	+ 0·27
5. Miss P. Green's Red Dawn	108·67	–	91·2	–	17·47
6. Capt. M. F. Whiteley's Peggoty	126	–	87·6	–	38·4
7. Lt. the Hon. P. T. Connolly-Carew's Ballyhoo	123·33	–	72·8	–	50·53
8. D. Nicholson's Souvenir	134·67	–	82·8	–	51·87
9. P. V. Hervey's High Jinks	140·67	–	103·2	20·5	57·97
10. Capt. J. P. E. Welch's Mr Wilson	114·67	40	93·2	–	61·47
11. Miss S. Fleet's The Gladiator	39·33	80	116·8	10	62·53
12. Lt. J. D. Smith-Bingham's By Golly	96·67	–	33·2	10·25	73·72
13. King's Troop R. H. A.'s Sherpa (Sgt. R. S. Jones)	134·67	–	44·4	10	100·27
14. Queen's Own Hussars' Gipsy Love (Capt. T. W. Ritson)	161·33	20	115·6	51·25	116·98
15. Lt.-Col. J. Hume Dudgeon's Finn (I. Dudgeon)	126·67	108	–	–	234·67

19 ran

1962 Little Badminton Event

Owner, horse and rider	Dressage	Speed and Endurance: Penalty (Time + Jumping)	Speed and Endurance: Bonus	Show-Jumping	Total
1. H. Graham-Clark's Priam (Mrs P. Crofts)	132·67	–	107·2	–	25·47
2. Capt. J. R. Templer's M'Lord Connelly	130·67	20	118·4	–	32·27
3. Miss V. Freeman-Jackson's Granite	144·67	–	76·4	10	78·27
4. H. Graham-Clark's Hansel (Miss J. Graham-Clark)	128·67	–	52·8	10	85·87
5. Miss J. Crawford's Grey Gander	182	–	70·8	–	111·2
6. Maj. J. N. D. Birtwistle's Goldwave	118	14·4	13·6	1	119·8
7. Mrs F. C. Greenwood's Anzac (P. N. Simpson)	134	40	54·8	1·25	120·45
8. Miss D. Booth's The Zephyr (Van de Vater)	139·33	24·8	24·8	10	149·33
9. T. Allhusen's Highwayman	122·67	100	54·4	–	168·27
10. King's Troop R.H.A.'s Lanark (Sgt. R. S. Jones)	96	64	8·4	20	171·6
11. C. C. Cameron's Sam Weller (Lady J. Stanhope)	138·67	61·6	58	53·75	196·02

16 ran

1963 One day event only

1964 Great Badminton Championship

Owner, horse and rider	Dressage	Speed and Endurance: Penalty (Time + Jumping)	Speed and Endurance: Bonus	Show-Jumping	Total
1. Capt. J. R. Templer's M'Lord Connelly	75	–	108	–	+33
2. J. D. Smith-Bingham's By Golly	53·5	–	70	10	+ 6·5
3. C. C. Cameron's Black Salmon (A. Cameron)	90	–	106·4	30	13·6
4. Capt. H. Freeman-Jackson's St Finbarr	96	–	69·2	–	26·8

5. Col. V. D. S. Williams' Sea Breeze (M. Bullen)	95	20	88	–	27
6. N. Gardiner's Young Pretender (M. Bullen)	95·5	–	94·8	30	30·7
7. Capt. & Mrs J. Beale's Victoria Bridge (Capt. Beale)	82·5	–	49·6	10	42·9
8. D. Nicholson's Merry Messenger	121·5	–	86	10	45·5
9. Miss B. Pearson's Easter Bouquet	112	–	76	10	46
10. H. Graham-Clark's Priam (Miss J. Graham-Clark)	101·5	–	43·6	13	70·9
11. A. le Goupil's Lutine	135	–	49·2	–	85·8
12. Vanlandeghem and Brennan's Kilbride (R. T. Brennan)	127	–	29·6	–	97·4
13. R. J. H. Meade's Barberry	61·5	100	54	10	117·5
14. M. Gabe's Iceluy (Capt. Landon)	113·5	80	46	–	147·5
15. Hon. P. T. Connolly-Carew's Ballyhoo	122·5	118·4	13·2	–	227·7
16. L. J. Carvajal Salas' Quieto	118	145·6	–	–	263·6
17. Mlle R. Cailleux's Harmonieuse	89·5	174·4	18·4	20	275·5
18. H. Schwarzenbach's Kipling (Lt. A. Schwarzenbach)	109	174·4	–	30	313·4
19. Capt. A. Jungerson's Meston	61	211·6	–	52	324·6

27 ran

1964 Little Badminton Event

Owner, horse and rider	*Dressage*	*Speed and Endurance*		*Show-Jumping*	*Total*
		Penalty (Time + Jumping)	*Bonus*		
1. Mrs J. Waddington's Glenamoy	65·5	–	86·8	20	+ 1·3
2. Lt.-Col. J. Hume Dudgeon's Lough Druid (Miss P. Moreton)	76	–	64	10	22
3. Miss C. Sheppard's Fenjirao	83	–	30·8	10·5	62·7
4. Miss M. Macdonell's Kilmacthomas	64·5	–	18·8	20	65·7
5. Miss B. Pearson's Anna's Banner	111·5	–	46·4	1·75	66·85
6. Capt. M. F. Whiteley's Happy Talk	62	60	51·2	–	70·8
7. M. Tucker's The Viking	98	20	62	30	86
8. Miss R. Oxford's Sunny Jim (Capt. Beale)	97	–	37·2	34·75	94·55
9. Miss M. Speed's Rise and Shine	90·5	60	55·6	–	94·9
10. Hon. W. R. Leigh's Marshall Tudor	101·5	20	46	20	95·5
11. C. Harty's San Michele (J. Harty)	102·5	–	60·4	58	100·1
12. Miss V. Freeman-Jackson's Mercury	97	20	38·8	30	108·2
13. Maj. M. A. Q. Darley's Lyonstar	131	40	47·2	10	133·8
14. H. Graham-Clark's French Frolic (Miss S. Kesler)	77	136·8	20	30	233·8
15. Mrs W. J. Ballard's Stranger V	127	120	50·4	30	266·6

25 ran

1965 Great Badminton Championship

Owner, horse and rider	Dressage	Speed and Endurance: Penalty (Time + Jumping)	Speed and Endurance: Bonus	Show-Jumping	Total
1. Maj. E. A. Boylan's Durlas Eile	45·5	–	98·4	20	+32·9
2. W. Roycroft's Eldorado	87·5	–	113·2	–	+25·7
3. Mrs S. Waddington's Glenamoy	48·5	–	84·8	11·25	+25·05
4. Miss M. Speed's Rise and Shine	75·5	–	104·44	10	+18·9
5. Miss C. Sheppard's Fenjirao	66·5	–	84·4	10	+ 7·9
6. W. Roycroft's Stoney Crossing	81	–	112·4	30	+ 1·4
7. Mlle R. Cailleux's Nadine D	74	–	78·8	10	5·2
8. Maj. D. Allhusen's Lochinvar	76·5	–	105·2	40	11·3
9. Miss V. Freeman-Jackson's Sam Weller	85·5	–	96	30	19·5
10. Miss J. Graham-Clark's French Frolic	89	–	75·2	10	23·8
11. Miss C. V. Nicholl's Blue Commando (E. Thompson)	89·5	–	53·6	12	47·9
12. Mrs J. Ballard's Stranger V	127·5	20	98·8	10	58·7
13. Mrs R. W. McKeever's Suzie Wong (R. W. McKeever)	132	–	92·4	32	71·6
14. Capt. the Hon. P. T. Connolly-Carew's Ballyhoo	91	36	26·4	10	110·6
15. R. Pennefather's Radar	97·5	20	24·4	43·25	136·35

21 ran

1965 Little Badminton Event

Owner, horse and rider	Dressage	Speed and Endurance: Penalty (Time + Jumping)	Speed and Endurance: Bonus	Show-Jumping	Total
1. Capt. M. F. Whiteley's The Poacher	94·5	–	76·4	20·25	38·35
2. W. Roycroft's Avatar	89·5	60	100·8	10	58·7
3. Mrs T. W. Kopanski's The Little Mermaid	88	–	18·8	–	69·2
4. Maj. & Mrs C. M. Parker's Cornishman (Mrs Parker)	87·5	20	52	20	75·5
5. T. Durston Smith's Dreamy Dasher	116·5	20	60·8	10·25	85·95
6. T. Hinde's Freeman II (Mrs A. Oliver)	56	62·4	30·4	1	89
7. M. Tucker's The Viking	101·5	60	73·6	10	97·9
8. Mrs Somers and Mrs Birkmyre's Corrinwell (E. Thompson)	127·5	20	20	10	137·5
9. Miss V. Longmore's Alouette	94·5	170·8	15·2	20	270·1

17 ran

1966 Event cancelled

1967

Owner, horse and rider	Dressage	Speed and Endurance: Penalty (Time + Jumping)	Speed and Endurance: Bonus	Show-Jumping	Total
1. Miss C. Ross-Taylor's Jonathan	39·33	–	105·2	–	+65·87
2. Maj. E. A. Boylan's Durlas Eile	31	–	106·4	20	+55·4
3. Hon. Mrs Hely-Hutchinson's Count Jasper (Miss P. Hely-Hutchinson)	50·67	20	116·8	–	+46·13
4. Miss S. Clifford's Mazaretta	52·33	–	104·4	11·75	+40·32
5. Miss J. Bullen's Our Nobby	61·67	20	118	–	+36·33
6. Lady H. Russell's Turnstone (R. Meade)	55·67	–	106	20	+30·33
7. Mrs A. B. Whiteley's Foxdor (Sgt. R. S. Jones)	59·67	–	100	10	+30·33
8. Miss L. Sutherland's Nicholas Nickleby	59·67	–	87·2	–	+27·53
9. Mrs C. M. Parker's Cornishman	69·33	–	111·2	20	+21·87
10. Capt. T. W. Ritson's Evening Echo	62·33	–	105·6	21·5	+21·77
11. Maj. D. Allhusen's Lochinvar	51·67	–	118·4	56·25	+10·48
12. Mr & Mrs M. Plumb's Foster (M. Page)	58·33	–	74·8	10	+ 6·47
13. King's Troop's Ballykarron (Sgt. E. Witts)	64·33	–	89·6	20	+ 5·27
14. King's Troop's Sir Francis (Lt. R. J. Vines)	75·33	20	118·4	20·5	+ 2·57
15. J. Shedden's Heyday (Miss B. Pearson)	58	20	83·6	11	5·4
16. Miss J. Billington's Steel Column	77	–	79·2	10	7·8
17. Maj. J. Lynch's The Regent (Maj. J. Beale)	54	–	84	40	10
18. Miss J. Fowler's Ginger Nut	62·67	20	118·4	60	24·27
19. Mrs S. Johnson's Richelieu	82	–	68·4	22·25	35·85
20. M. Whiteley's Senior Partner	58·33	–	90	70·25	38·58
21. W. Goldie's Rembrandt (D. Goldie)	70·67	40	84	20	46·67
22. Capt. the Hon. P. Connolly-Carew's Kildorrery	84·67	60	98·8	21·75	69·62
23. M. Cochenet's Artaban II	35	80	43·2	10	81·8
24. Mr & Mrs A. Kitchin's Char's Choice (P. Welch)	64·67	80	60	–	84·67
25. Miss A. Martin-Bird's Leedora	74·67	100	78·8	–	95·87
26. Miss P. Smallwood's Jeremy (Miss G. Watson)	61·67	44·4	21·6	30	114·47
27. Capt. D. Mann's Keelrow	57·33	80	72·8	50	114·53
28. L. W. Wickson's Benjamin (E. Thompson)	61·67	28	4·8	30·25	115·12
29. East Germany's Uranio (U. Vite)	57	80	28	20	129
30. Mrs R. E. Harding's Fisherman (Miss M. Harding)	75·33	60·4	12	21·5	145·23
31. J. Hollingsworth's Omar Khayyam	71	191·6	–	30	292·6

43 ran

1968

Owner, horse and rider	Dressage	Steeplechase	Cross-country: Jumps	Cross-country: Time	Show-Jumping	Total
1. Miss J. Bullen's Our Nobby	92·5	+37·6	–	+86	–	+31·1
2. Lady H. Russell's Turnstone (R. J. H. Meade)	88·5	+32·8	–	+83·6	–	+27·9
3. Mrs R. T. Whiteley's Foxdor (S/Sgt. R. S. Jones)	62	+37·6	–	+56·8	10	+22·4
4. O/C M. Phillip's Rock On	90	+37·6	–	+80·8	10	+18·4

5. Maj. D. Allhusen's Lochinvar	73·5	+37·6	–	+60	10	+14·1
6. Miss F. E. Pearson's Ballinkeele	66	+37·6	–	+49·2	10	+10·8
7. P. Welch's Char's Choice	96	+32·8	–	+53·6	–	9·6
8. Miss L. Sutherland's Popadom	86	+33·6	20	+44·8	–	27·6
9. U.S. Equestrian Team's Plain Sailing (M. Plumb)	64·5	+ 3·2	–	+32·8	–	28·5
10. Miss L. Sutherland's Nicholas Nickleby	95·5	+13·6	–	+51·6	–	30·3
11. Van de Vater and partners' Argonaut (Van de Vater)	73	+24	–	+20	20	49
12. Maj. J. Lynch's The Regent (Maj. J. Beale)	73·5	+32·8	40	+48·8	20	51·9
13. J. C. Wofford's Kilkenny	123	+37·6	40	+48·4	10	87
14. K. Higgs and Miss S. Willcox's Fair and Square (Miss Willcox)	71	+27·2	20	+12·8	20	96·6
15. Miss J. Jobling-Purser's Jenny	65	+18·4	40	+18·8	30	97·8
16. Capt. T. W. Ritson's Evening Echo	83	+32	60	+50	40	101
17. Miss S. Warwick's Brown Duke	107·5	+37·6	60	+ 0·4	–	129·5
18. L. W. Wickson's Benjamin (E. Thompson)	108·5	+ 8	20	2	30	152·5
19. A. W. Buller's Orlando	105·5	+ 8	–	27·2	30	154·7
20. U.S. Equestrian Team's Foster (M. O. Page)	82·5	+27·2	140	+14·4	–	180·9
21. Miss L. Roberts' Roewen	107	+22·4	40	50·4	10	185
22. Mr & Mrs R. Ward's Cherrybin (T. Durston-Smith)	101	+22·4	120	+23·2	10	185·4
23. Dr H. Schwarzenbach's Green Flash (A. Bühler)	99	+ 2·4	80	14·8	40	231·4
24. Mrs Kjaer and Comdt. W. B. Mullins' March Hawk (Comdt. Mullins)	113·5	+20·8	120	8·8	10	231·5

55 ran

1969

Owner, horse and rider	*Dressage*	*Steeplechase*	*Cross-country Jumps*	*Cross-country Time*	*Show-Jumping*	*Total*
1. R. Walker's Pasha	62·67	+32	–	+70·8	–	+40·13
2. Miss A. Martin-Bird's Grey Cloud	67	+37·6	–	+66	–	+36·6
3. Equestrian Federation of Australia's Warrathoola (W. Roycroft)	47·33	+35·2	20	+70·8	10	+28·67
4. Equestrian Federation of Australia's Furtive (W. Roycroft)	70·33	+37·6	–	+70·8	10	+28·07
5. Hon. Mrs Hely-Hutchinson's Count Jasper (Miss P. Hely-Hutchinson)	79·67	+37·6	–	+70	–	+27·93
6. Miss C. Ross-Taylor's Jonathan	69·33	+37·6	–	+55·2	–	+23·47
7. Miss S. Warwick's Brown Duke	87	+37·6	–	+70·8	–	+21·4
8. Benenden Riding Est's P. J. L-L. Esq. (J. Smart)	80·33	+37·6	–	+70·8	10	+18·07
9. Brig. D. Gordon-Watson's Cornishman V (Miss M. Gordon-Watson)	70	+37·6	–	+70·8	26·25	+12·15
10. Mrs J. Compton-Bracebridge's Lane Trial (R. Walker)	59	+37·6	40	+70·8	10	0·6

11. Miss L. Sutherland's Nicholas Nickleby	76·67	+32	–	+48	10	6·67
12. Miss C. Lockhart's Gamecock	63	+16	–	+40	–	7
13. Miss T. Martin-Bird's Spirdion	81	+28·8	–	+54	10	8·2
14. Miss M. S. Bedford's Tawny Port	95·67	+37·6	–	+58·4	10	9·67
15. Mrs S. Johnson's Richelieu	92	+32	–	+59·6	10	10·4
16. Mr & Mrs L. Sederholm's Alpaca (Miss C. Bradley)	69·33	+21·6	60	+67·2	10	50·53
17. Equestrian Federation of Australia's The Baron (J. Scanlon)	82·33	+23·2	60	+63·2	–	55·93
18. Miss J. Bradwell's Christopher Robert	52·33	+20	60	+35·2	–	57·13
19. Mrs J. A. Woodhouse's Corchy	85·67	+30·4	20	+22	10	63·27
20. Miss A. Morrell's Sandpiper IV	76·67	+37·6	20	5·6	–	64·67
21. Miss J. Lockett's Country Style	91	+29·6	60	+48·4	20	93
22. Lt. R. R. Horne's Blue Steel	98	+28·8	80	+68	20	101·2
23. Miss J. Skinner's Titania (Miss A. Pirquet)	75·33	+22·4	60	+22	21·25	112·18
24. Miss S. Neill's Peri	83	+36·8	80	+44	33·75	115·95
25. Capt. T. W. Ritson's Evening Echo	63	+26·4	80	+29·2	45	132·4
26. Mrs C. Horton's The Dark Horse	64	+37·6	120	3·6	20	170
27. Lady H. Russell's Flamingo (Miss S. Kozuba-Kozubska)	100·33	+13·6	120	29·6	20	256·33

48 ran

1970

Owner, horse and rider	Dressage	Steeplechase	Cross-country Jumps	Cross-country Time	Show-Jumping	Total
1. Combined Training Committee's The Poacher (R. Meade)	36	+27·2	–	+28·4	–	+19·6
2. Irish Army's San Carlos (Capt. R. McMahon)	60	+33·6	–	+41·6	–	+15·2
3. Brig. M. Gordon-Watson's Cornishman V (Miss M. Gordon-Watson)	54	+20·8	–	+30	–	3·2
4. Mrs M. Martin's Gypsy Flame (Miss L. Sutherland)	53·5	+23·2	–	+16·4	10	23·9
5. Miss D. West's Baccarat	74·5	+25·6	–	+23·6	–	25·3
6. T. Durston-Smith's Henry the Navigator	88	+24	–	+26	–	38
7. Miss M. Meakin's Lynette	65	+15·2	–	+12·8	10	47
8. W. Goldie's Rembrandt (D. Goldie)	90	+32	–	+14	10	54
9. Mrs S. Johnson's Richelieu	104	+32·8	–	+17·2	10	64
10. Miss A. Sowden's Mooncoin	104·5	+30·4	–	+ 9·2	–	64·9
11. Mrs C. M. Parker's Cornish Gold	90	+37·6	20	+ 6·4	–	66
12. Miss L. Sutherland's Popadom	54·5	+14·4	20	1·6	10	71·7
13. P. Henry's Qui Dit Mieux (D. Flament)	69·5	0·8	–	+ 8·4	10	71·9
14. Mrs M. Laurent's Skyborn (M. Tucker)	116·5	+28·8	–	+25·2	10	72·5
15. Mrs C. Horton's The Dark Horse (Miss L. Sutherland)	91·5	+20	20	+ 6	10	95·5

16. Miss R. Prout's Farewell	119·5	+30·4	–	6	10	105·1
17. M. Moffett's Demerara	91·5	+13·6	20	9·6	10	117·5
18. Mrs R. C. A. Hammond's Eagle Rock	97	+ 4·8	–	6·4	20	118·6
19. Maj. J. N. D. Birtwistle's Blitz-Krieg	102·5	+11·2	20	+ 6·8	20	124·5
20. S. T. R. Stevens' Benson	87	+29·6	80	+17·6	10	129·8
21. Miss D. West's Don Camillo	76·5	+11·2	60	+ 7·2	14	132·1
22. T. R. Sturgis' Coco	157	+18·4	–	+12·8	12·25	138·05
23. M. Phelps Jun.'s Argonaut	76	+17·6	60	26·8	–	145·2
24. Irish Army's Cinn Saile (Capt. L. Kiely)	118	+20	40	0·8	10	148·8
25. Miss F. M. Lochore's The Young Laird	82·5	+10·4	60	+ 7·6	30·5	155
26. C. D. Collins' Tawny Port	90	+16	80	2	10	166
27. J. A. H. Wolter's Puk	95	17·6	20	15·6	30	178·2
28. L. W. Wickson's Benjamin (E. Thompson)	127	1·6	40	25·2	–	193·8
29. Miss S. Faulkner's Sir Galahad	78	4	140	26·4	13·75	262·15
30. P. Henry's Quartz (J. L. Coutable)	66·5	+ 8	200	70·8	20	249·3

46 ran

1971

	Penalties					
			Cross-country			
Owner, horse and rider	*Dressage*	*Steeplechase*	*Jumps*	*Time*	*Show-Jumping*	*Total*
1. Lt. M. and Miss F. Phillips' Great Ovation (Lt. M. Phillips)	75·5	13·6	–	36·8	–	125·9
2. Brig. M. Gordon-Watson's Cornishman V (Miss M. Gordon-Watson)	88·5	8	20	29·2	10	155·7
3. Miss D. West's Baccarat	102·5	6·4	20	30	–	158·9
4. Mr & Mrs J. Compson Bracebridge's Upper Strata (R. Walker)	94·1	12	20	23·6	10	159·61
5. HRH Princess Anne's Doublet	82·5	32	–	42·4	10	166·9
6. M. Tucker's Farmer Giles	111·5	8	–	38·4	10	167·9
7. Miss A. Sowden's Mooncoin	99	18·4	–	50·8	–	168·2
8. Miss M. Rock and T. Durston-Smith's Henry the Navigator (T. Durston-Smith)	114·5	20·8	–	35·6	–	170·9
9. Mrs D. Brentnall's Mary Poppins II (Miss H. Booth)	98	16	20	38·4	–	172·4
10. G. Craigie's Deemster (Miss H. Booth)	93·5	24	20	48·4	–	185·9
11. Miss R. Prout's Farewell	131·51	13·6	20	43·6	–	208·71
12. Miss L. Sutherland's Peer Gynt	97·01	0·8	40	62·8	10	210·61
13. Mrs L. Staveley's Gainsborough IV (N. Brake)	108·5	19·2	–	84	–	211·7
14. Mrs W. Morrell's Sandpiper IV (Miss A. Morrell)	87·5	36·8	20	73·2	–	217·5
15. Miss J. Neill's Peri (Mrs S. Browne)	104	48	–	57·6	10	219·6
16. Lady H. Russell's Flamingo (R. Meade)	114·5	11·2	20	58	20	223·7

17. Capt. and Mrs C. Kendall's P. J. L.-L. Esq. (J. Smart)	102·5	20·8	60	62·4	–	245·7
18. Mrs P. Sturgis' Coco (T. R. Sturgis)	152	16·8	–	78·8	–	247·6
19. Mrs R. C. A. Hammond's Eagle Rock	110·51	40·8	–	68	40	259·31
20. W. Powell-Harris' Smokey VI	142·5	10·4	40	41·6	31·75	266·25
21. Swedish Army's Sarajevo (Sgt. Jan Jonsson)	86	23·2	80	70·8	10	270
22. C. D. Collins' Tawny Port	99·5	102·4*	20	66·8	10	298·7
23. M. Moffett's Demerara	114	25·6	100	77·2	–	316·8
24. A. W. Buller's Rob Roy	125	16·8	120	90·8	–	352·6
25. J. G. A. Tulloch's Lord Doodles	116	44	100	103·2	40	403·2
26. Dr J. H. Wigersma's Navigator (H. J. Wigersma)	118·5	13·6	160	104·4	20	416·5
27. Miss Y. Held's Range Warden (J. Zindel)	115·5	95·2	80	157·6	–	448·3
28. J. Sebire's Just Robert	119·51	44	180	116·4	20	479·91
29. C. F. Harrison's Cheal Code (Mrs W. M. Comerford)	153·5	–	240	130·4	30	553·9

* Includes 60 steeplechase jumping penalties by Tawny Port.

48 ran

1972

	Penalties					
			Cross-country			
Owner, horse and rider	*Dressage*	*Steeplechase*	*Jumps*	*Time*	*Show-Jumping*	*Total*
1. Lt. M. and Miss F. Phillips' Great Ovation (Lt. M. Phillips)	59	8·8	–	38·8	–	106·6
2. Maj. D. Allhusen's Laurieston (R. Meade)	66	2·4	–	37·6	1·25	107·25
3. Mrs C. M. Parker's Cornish Gold	79·5	–	20	42	–	141·5
4. Miss D. West's Baccarat	73·5	12	–	59·6	–	145·1
5. Miss L. Prior-Palmer's Be Fair	83	4·8	20	37·6	–	145·4
6. Hon. Mrs F. Westenra's Classic Chips (S. T. R. Stevens)	93	–	20	33·2	–	146·2
7. Mrs H. Wilkin's Wayfarer II (R. Meade)	79	4·8	–	45·6	20	149·4
8. Mrs D. Brentnall's Mary Poppins II (Miss H. Booth)	101	–	–	21·6	30	152·6
9. G. Craigie's Deemster (Miss H. Booth)	100·5	10·4	–	54	–	164·9
10. Miss J. Hodgson's Larkspur	104·5	14·5	–	46·4	–	165·3
11. eq: C. D. Collins' Centurian	101	1·6	20	52·4	–	175
11. eq: Mrs R. C. A. Hammond's Eagle Rock	85	14·4	20	55·6	–	175
13. Mr & Mrs P. Robeson's Kyte (Miss M. Meakin)	91	13·6	–	72·8	–	177·4
14. Hon. Mrs Hely-Hutchinson's Count Jasper (Mrs J. Lochore)	109	28	–	48·4	–	185·4
15. Brig. M. Gordon-Watson's Cornishman V (Miss M. Gordon-Watson)	66·5	–	80	40·4	–	186·9

16. Miss L. Sutherland's Peer Gynt	71	–	60	56·8	10	197·8
17. Mr & Mrs J. Compton Bracebridge's Upper Strata (R. Walker)	71	8	80	60·8	–	219·8
18. Switzerland's Cassagne (D. Morand)	101·5	31·2	–	90	–	222·7
19. Miss A. Morrell's Sandpiper IV (R. Walker)	90	11·2	60	71·6	–	232·8
20. Mr & Mrs O. Fox-Pitt's Knowlton Tango (Mrs Fox-Pitt)	91	28	40	82·8	0·5	242·3
21. Miss A. Collins' Think Lucky	84·5	9·6	60	74·8	20	248·9
22. Mr & Mrs M. Tucker's Mooncoin (M. Tucker)	94	9·6	80	60	10	253·6
23. Mrs M. F. Jones' Farewell	130	8	60	58·4	–	256·4
24. C. F. Harrison's The Ghillie (Mrs M. Comerford)	138·5	–	–	78	40	256·5
25. Miss J. Macdonald's Samuel Whiskers	96·5	50·4	20	83·4	10	259·3
26. Benenden Riding Est's P. J. L-L. Esq. (J. Smart)	111·5	25·6	–	112·8	10	259·9
27. Ireland's Jenny (Miss J. Jobling Purser)	74	11·2	60	126	–	271·2
28. Mrs J. Rowntree's Island Monarch (Capt. J. Lochore)	93·5	13·6	60	98	10	275·1
29. Switzerland's Retur (Capt. J. Hurlimann)	116	15·2	20	120·8	20	292
30. Switzerland's Big Boy (Lt. A. Schwarzenbach)	94	37·6	20	122·8	20	294·4
31. D. H. S. Thompson's Marcus (Miss V. Thompson)	86·5	27·2	60	120·4	10	304·1
32. Switzerland's Red Baron (Lt. M. Haurijun)	108·5	12	60	115·2	10	305·7
33. Australia's Harley (C. Roycroft)	123	30·4	100	72·4	–	325·8
34. C. Wares' Gavelacre	109	–	120	81·6	20	330·6
35. Lt.-Col. E. L. Stocker's Patrick Castle (Mrs Stocker)	144·5	64·8	–	121·6	–	330·9
36. Ireland's Benka (A. W. Buller)	114·5	15·2	60	156·4	–	346·1
37. Italy's Forgotten Fred (M. Turner)	113·5	20	120	72·4	21·75	347·65
38. Miss S. Strachan's Parlour Maid	151	27·2	60	102	10	350·2
39. Hon. Mrs P. Connolly-Carew's Tawny Port (Capt. Connolly-Carew)	106	28	140	100·4	–	374·4
40. Miss E. Colquhoun's Marguerite	115	–	160	99·6	–	374·6
41. Australia's Dépêche (R. Sands)	117·5	178*	40	48·4	–	383·9
42. Australia's Taris (B. Schrapel)	115	–	120	150	–	385
43. J. G. A. Tulloch's Lord Doodles	93·5	–	120	124	49·25	386·75
44. Mrs M. F. Jones' Rattler (Miss H. Seymour-Smith)	127	25·6	100	156·4	10	419
45. Mr & Mrs O. Fox-Pitt's Knowlton Corona (Mrs Fox-Pitt)	125	39·2	100	155·2	30	449·4
46. Italy's Camolin (Lt. Stefano Angioni)	98	16·8	80	294·4	10	499·2

* Includes 174 penalties incurred by Dépêche on the roads-and-tracks phases A and C.

60 ran

1973

Owner, horse and rider	Penalties: Dressage	Steeplechase	Cross-country: Jumps	Cross-country: Time	Show-Jumping	Total
1. Miss L. Prior-Palmer's Be Fair	42	–	–	14	–	56
2. Mrs R. C. A. Hammond's Eagle Rock (R. Meade)	60	–	–	18·4	–	78·4
3. Miss V. Thompson's Cornish Duke	58	–	–	33·2	10	101·2
4. Miss M. Meakin's Lynette	55·75	–	–	45·6	–	101·35
5. Mrs R. Jones' Farewell	69·75	–	–	34·4	–	104·15
6. Brig. M. Gordon-Watson's Cornishman V (Miss M. Gordon-Watson)	47·25	–	60	–	–	107·25
7. C. F. Harrison's The Ghillie (Mrs M. Comerford)	61	–	–	17·2	30	108·2
8. HM the Queen's Goodwill (HRH Princess Anne)	53·5	7·2	20	34	–	114·7
9. Mrs A. H. and Miss S. Hatherly's Harley (Miss Hatherly)	63·75	1·6	20	33·6	–	118·95
10. Miss P. A. Biden's Little Extra	57·5	–	20	50·8	–	128·3
11. Hon. Mrs P. Connolly-Carew's Tawny Port (Capt. Hon. P. Connolly-Carew)	54·75	9·6	–	68	–	132·35
12. Miss H. Knight's Blitz-Krieg	51·5	–	40	39·6	–	133·1
13. Miss C. Strachan's By George	51	–	20	55·2	10	136·2
14. Miss E. Profumo's Western Morn (Miss J. Bullen)	57·5	7·2	40	25·6	10	140·3
15. Miss J. Watson's Great Scot	68·75	–	–	53·2	20	141·95
16. C. Ware's Gavelacre	60·75	5·6	60	34	–	160·35
17. Mrs H. C. Straker's George (M. Straker)	69·25	–	60	36·8	21	187·05
18. Miss J. Graham's Sumatra	80·25	4·8	60	66·8	–	211·85
19. HM the Queen's Columbus (Lt. M. Phillips)	50	–	120	50·8	–	220·8
20. Miss L. Sutherland's Fairoaks	53·5	–	100	79·2	–	232·7
21. N. Engert's Mille Tonnerres	57·5	6·4	100	60·4	10	234·3
22. P. Hurlimann's Retur	51·5	–	60	108	20	239·5
23. A. Colquhoun's Belle Grey	58·5	6·4	80	100·8	–	245·7
24. H. Thomas' Playamar	58·5	28	80	96	–	262·5
25. R. F. H. Ward's Hydrophane Coldstream (J. N. Kersley)	53·5	–	180	49·2	–	282·7
26. Lt.-Col. E. L. Stocker's Patrick Castle (Mrs Stocker)	89·5	11·2	80	87·6	30	298·3
27. H. Klocke's Apoll (H. Rethemejer)	39·75	12	140	100·4	30	322·15
28. Miss J. Graham's Haze III	63	15·2	60	176	10	324·2
29. J. Sebire's Just Robert	56·75	4	180	74·4	43	358·15
30. K. Wagner's Polo	56	16·8	180	122·4	10	385·2

69 ran

1974

Owner, horse and rider	Penalties: Dressage	Steeplechase	Cross-country: Jumps	Cross-country: Time	Show-Jumping	Total
1. HM the Queen's Columbus (Capt. M. Phillips)	40·33	–	–	–	–	40·33
2. Miss J. Hodgson's Larkspur	53	–	–	–	–	53
3. B. Davidson's Irish Cap	41·67	–	–	13·6	–	55·27
4. HM the Queen's Goodwill (HRH Princess Anne)	58·67	–	–	–	–	58·67
5. C. F. Harrison's The Ghillie (Mrs M. Comerford)	46·33	–	–	12·4	–	58·73
6. Mrs H. Wilkin's Wayfarer II (R. Meade)	44·33	5·6	–	10	–	59·93
7. Miss D. West's Baccarat	60	–	–	–	–	60
8. H. Thomas' Playamar	63·67	–	–	–	–	63·67
9. C. D. Collins' Smokey VI	56·67	–	–	–	10	66·67
10. C. D. Collins' Centurian	59	–	–	13·2	–	72·2
11. Mrs R. C. A. Hammond's Eagle Rock	53·67	2·4	–	18·8	–	74·87
12. Mrs J. Geekie's Copper Tiger (Miss C. Geekie)	67	2·4	–	6·4	–	75·8
13. Mrs H. Lochore's Ben Wyvis (M. Tucker)	61·67	–	–	16·4	–	78·07
14. Mr & Mrs T. R. Sturgis' Demi-Douzaine (T. Sturgis)	64·33	–	–	6·4	10	80·73
15. Miss V. Thompson's Cornish Duke	59	4·8	20	9·2	–	93
16. J. Becchu's Ut Majeur (T. Touzaint)	40·33	–	20	39·2	–	99·53
17. Miss L. Sutherland's Fairoaks	40	14·4	–	36·4	10	100·8
18. H. Kingsley's Aeolia	63	–	20	0·4	20	103·4
19. J. M. Hawtin's Devil's Jump (Miss S. Hatherly)	61	–	20	14	10	105
20. Miss J. Graham's Sumatra	84·67	–	–	26	–	110·67
21. King's Troop R.H.A.'s Dr Sebastian (Lt. M. Wallace)	41	–	–	51·6	20	112·6
22. Mrs M. J. and Miss D. A. Thorne's The Kingmaker (Miss Thorne)	59	–	20	36·4	–	115·4
23. G. Craigie's Deemster (Miss H. Booth)	62·33	16	20	25·6	–	123·93
24. Miss J. Crossman's Touch and Go III (Miss M. Frank)	50·67	–	20	51·2	10	131·87
25. Hon. Mrs F. Westenra's Classic Chips (J. Kersley)	58	–	80	–	–	138
26. Miss A. Collins' Think Lucky	62·33	–	40	29·2	10	141·53
27. Miss M. Meakin's Lynette	53·33	–	60	32·4	–	145·73
28. Miss J. Starkey's Acrobat	52·67	2·4	60	41·2	–	156·27
29. Miss L. Prior-Palmer's Be Fair	52·33	–	80	25·6	–	157·93
30. N. Engert's Mille Tonnerres	62·67	0·8	40	66·8	–	170·27
31. Miss V. Holgate's Dubonnet	60·67	–	40	71·2	–	171·87
32. Mrs H. C. Straker's George (M. Straker)	61	7·2	60	45·2	10	183·4
33. A. le Goupil's Arthemise	45·67	3·2	100	54·8	12·25	215·92
34. Miss E. Aldous' Barman II (E. O'Brien)	83·67	44·8	20	60·8	10	219·27
35. A. Bruneau's Velox d'Escla (S. Bruneau)	92·5	6·4	60	60·4	–	223·3

36. Miss A. Rich's Kilkenny Brae	63	14·4	60	78·8	10	226·2
37. W/Com. R. C. Longsdon's Long Horsley (A. Hill)	58	–	120	28·8	20	226·8
38. R. M. M. Biden's Glider (Miss P. A. Biden)	50·33	–	160	82	10	302·33
39. Maj.-Gen. D. L. Darling's Barley Cry (Miss C. Darling)	81	–	120	44	62·75	307·75

60 ran

1975 Event abandoned after dressage

1976

	Penalties					
			Cross-country			
Owner, horse and rider	*Dressage*	*Steeplechase*	*Jumps*	*Time*	*Show-Jumping*	*Total*
1. Mrs V. Phillips' Wideawake (Miss L. Prior-Palmer)	50	–	–	18·8	–	68·8
2. H. Thomas' Playamar	58	–	–	23·6	–	81·6
3. Mrs Carpendale and Capt. M. Phillips' Favour (Capt. M. Phillips)	57	–	–	25·2	–	82·2
4. British Equestrian Federation's Jacob Jones (R. Meade)	60·33	–	–	22·8	–	83·13
5. Miss C. Strachan's Merry Sovereign	56·67	–	–	32	10	98·67
6. Miss J. Hodgson's Larkspur	48	7·2	–	43·6	10	108·8
7. Mrs Charlotte Steel's Gamble	68·67	3·2	–	43·6	–	115·47
8. Mrs and Miss Starkey's Topper Too (Miss J. Starkey)	57·33	–	–	58·4	–	115·73
9. M. Moffett's Demerara	83·33	–	–	32·8	–	116·13
10. C. Collins' Smokey VI	83·33	–	20	12·4	20	135·73
11. Miss V. Thompson's Cornish Duke	69·33	–	20	46·4	10	145·73
12. P. Mikhall's Devil's Jump (Mrs J. Holderness-Roddam)	69·67	3·2	20	29·6	30	152·47
13. Mrs and Miss Thorne's The Kingmaker (Miss D. Thorne)	66·33	–	60	22·4	10	158·73
14. Mrs S. Flood's Clonrochem (B. Mullins)	83·33	5·6	–	43·2	30	162·13
15. Mrs M. Brown's Ritudyr Rose (A. Harris)	94	–	–	65·6	10	169·6
16. R. Brake's Bampton Fair (A. Brake)	75	4·8	–	62	30	171·8
17. B. Powell's Alexander the Great	84·33	2·4	20	58·4	10	175·13
18. Mrs A. Andrew's Red Rusky (Mrs B. Hammond)	78·67	9·6	–	67·2	20·25	175·47
19. Mrs A. Bühler's West Country	66·33	–	20	84·8	10	181·13
20. Miss J. Pertwee's Bo'sun	84·67	–	20	84	–	188·67
21. Mr & Mrs T. R. Sturgis' Demi-Douzaine (T. Sturgis)	81	–	60	38·8	10	189·8
22. Comtesse de Brye's Don Carlos (J. Smart)	82·67	–	40	60·8	20	203·47
23. Mrs H. C. Straker's Ruan (N. Straker)	75·67	12·8	20	88·8	10	207·27
24. Van de Vater's Blue Tom Tit	70	12	–	96·4	30	208·4

25. Dr R. H. Foxton's B. R. M. (Miss A. Foxton)	81·33	–	20	78·8	30	210·13
26. Mrs H. Lochore and M. Tucker's Ben Wyvis (M. Tucker)	66·67	–	100	37·6	10	214·27
27. H. Kingsley's Aeolia	69	–	20	106	20	215
28. A. Ffooks' High Knowes	80·67	21·6	–	104	10	216·27
29. E. Manley-Walker's Jerrico IV (E. Thompson)	67	21·6	20	99·6	10	218·2
30. C. F. Harrison's Cheal Cloud (Mrs M. Comerford)	61·67	–	40	79·6	41·25	222·52
31. Mrs H. C. Straker's George (R. Desourdy)	90·83	–	80	23·2	30	224·03
32. Miss D. Clapham's Martha	72·33	8·8	60	68	20	229·13
33. Preci-Spark Ltd's Bleak Hills (V. Jones)	79·67	–	80	87·6	40·25	287·52
34. C. Merino's Midnight Monk	67·33	–	120	96	10	293·33
35. Mrs Hance's Olivia (Miss A. Pattinson)	48·33	4·8	100	146·6	10	309·73
36. Mrs G. Fletcher's Cornwell (Mrs R. Lacey)	89	–	140	97·2	20	346·2
37. Mrs A. J. Rowntree's Island Monarch (Lt. J. Wathen)	73·33	12	180	78·8	10	354·13
38. A. Colquhoun's Carawich (Miss A. Pattinson)	70·33	–	100	207·6	–	377·93

70 ran

1977

	Penalties					
			Cross-country			
Owner, horse and rider	*Dressage*	*Steeplechase*	*Jumps*	*Time*	*Show-Jumping*	*Total*
1. Mrs H. C. Straker's George (Miss L. Prior-Palmer)	37·4	–	–	–	0·25	37·65
2. Mrs M. I. Thorne and Miss D. Thorne's The Kingmaker (Miss D. Thorne)	59	–	–	–	–	59
3. C. A. Cyzer's Killaire (Miss L. Prior-Palmer)	47·4	–	–	13·2	5	65·6
4. Mrs S. Howard's Warrior (Mrs J. Holderness-Roddam)	48·6	3·2	–	14	–	65·8
5. A. Colquhoun's Carawich (Miss A. Pattinson)	43·8	–	–	12·8	10	66·6
6. C. Collins' Smokey VI	51·6	–	20	–	5	76·6
7. Mr & Mrs A. Olszowski's Collingwood (Miss M. Frank)	48·6	–	–	27·6	5	81·2
8. Miss F. Moore's Drakenburg	48·6	–	20	11·6	5	85·2
9. G. Nehmten's Madrigal (K. Schultz)	28·8	0·8	20	45·2	5	99·8
10. C. F. Harrison's Cheal Cloud (Mrs M. Comerford)	60·4	–	–	30·8	10	101·2
11. Deutsches Olympiade-Komitee's El Paso (H. Klugmann)	52	–	–	44·4	5	101·4
12. Mr & Mrs R. S. Pease's Pikestone (Miss J. L. Graham)	64·2	–	–	18	20	102·2
13. Maj. G. Ponsonby's Cambridge Blue (J. Watson)	61	–	20	30·4	–	111·4

14. HM the Queen's Goodwill (Capt. M. Phillips)	51	–	40	20	5	116
15. Comtesse de Brye's Don Carlos (Mrs C. Graham)	77·6	3·2	20	9·2	10	120
16. C. Collins' Radway	70·2	–	20	26·8	5	122
17. T. Gretener's Old Jameson	36·4	13·6	20	56	–	126
18. Miss J. Pertwee's Bo'sun	76·2	–	–	53·6	5	134·8
19. 2nd Lt. A. Ffooks' High Knowes	73·2	1·6	20	40·8	–	135·6
20. Miss C. Strachan's Merry Sovereign	46·6	–	80	24	–	150·6
21. Mrs O. Jackson's Island Monarch (C. Wares)	53·2	0·8	60	38·4	–	152·4
22. E. Fenwick's Scoobie Doo	71·6	14·4	40	29·2	5	160·2
23. Mrs C. Steel's Gamble	63·2	–	80	32	5	180·2
24. Mrs J. Geekie's Copper Tiger (Miss C. Geekie)	53·2	7·2	80	42·4	5	187·8
25. Miss D. Clapham's Martha	67·2	102·4	–	19·2	–	188·8
26. F.O.R.S.'s Salut (H. Melzer)	47	24	40	68·8	10	189·8
27. R. Clarke's Aloof (Miss S. Hatherly)	83·6	–	80	48·8	–	210·4
28. Maj. & Mrs I. Macdonald's Anna Maria (Miss J. Macdonald)	44·4	7·2	100	62	–	213·6
29. Mrs P. Gormley's Master Question (J. Seaman)	55·2	7·2	60	24	67·75	214·15
30. Preci-Spark Ltd's Bleak Hills (V. Jones)	72·4	16	120	118·4	5	331·8
31. Mrs J. McKnight's Irish Trick (Miss B. Perkins)	93·8	–	180	110·4	5	389·2
32. Miss P. Maher's Ballangarry	65·4	258·4	40	78·4	15	457·2

45 ran

1978

	Penalties					
			Cross-country			
Owner, horse and rider	*Dressage*	*Steeplechase*	*Jumps*	*Time*	*Show-Jumping*	*Total*
1. Mrs S. Howard and Mrs T. Holderness-Roddam's Warrior (Mrs T. Holderness-Roddam)	52·8	–	–	4·4	–	57·2
2. Overseas Containers Ltd's Village Gossip (Miss L. Prior-Palmer)	66·8	–	–	–	–	66·8
3. Mrs Starkey and Miss J. Starkey's Topper Too (Miss J. Starkey)	44·2	–	–	28	–	72·2
4. Miss E. Boone's Felday Farmer	71·4	–	–	7·6	–	79
5. Maj. G. T. Ponsonby and J. Watson's Cambridge Blue (J. Watson)	67·4	–	–	9·2	5	81·6
6. Preci-Spark Ltd's Bleak Hills (R. Meade)	53·2	3·2	–	12·8	15	84·2
7. Mrs J. Bealby's Jack Be Nimble (C. Bealby)	70·4	–	–	23·6	–	94
8. Miss D. Clapham's Martha	56·8	20	–	24	5	105·8
9. Mrs P. Gormley's Master Question (J. Seaman)	69·2	8	20	19·6	–	116·8
10. Mrs G. Fleming-Williams' Rescator	62·8	–	20	38	–	120·8
11. Dr N. Lawson-Baker and Syndicate's Monacle II (Miss S. Hatherly)	68	–	40	25·6	–	133·6

12. Mrs D. B. Pertwee's Bo'sun (Mrs. J. Sawyer)	75	3·2	–	49·2	10	137·4
13. K. T. Kearney's Dickens II (Miss V. Kearney)	73·4	17·6	–	48	–	139
14. Miss F. Moore's Drakenburg	59·6	11·2	40	30	–	140·8
15. 2nd Lt. A. Ffooks' High Knowes	80·8	15·2	20	38·4	5	159·4
16. HM the Queen's Goodwill (HRH Princess Anne)	57·8	4·8	60	24	13·25	159·85
17. Mrs M. J. Thorne and Miss D. Thorne's The Kingmaker (Miss D. Thorne)	60·4	–	100	4·4	–	164·8
18. Miss R. Bayliss' Gurgle The Greek	64·8	8·8	60	30	1·5	165·1
19. Miss E. Robinson's Montego Bay	88·2	11·2	–	63·2	5	167·6
20. Mrs J. R. Hodgson's Gretna Green (Miss J. Hodgson)	59·4	1·6	80	42·4	0·25	183·65
21. Miss C. Strachan's Merry Sovereign	56·6	0·8	80	60·8	–	198·2
22. Mrs P. A. Seymour's Touch And Go (Miss V. Wofford)	67·8	–	60	63·6	15	206·4
23. E. Bowlby's Speculator III (Miss M. Gordon-Watson)	68·8	5·6	100	56·4	0·75	231·55
24. T. Gretener's Camas Park	59·8	19·2	120	52·4	–	251·4
25. Miss J. Gilbert's Contango II	67·8	15·2	140	50·4	3	276·4
26. Miss H. Cantillon's Wing Forward	78·8	12	100	81·2	5	277
27. Miss A. Casagrande's Dayleye	88	–	160	41·6	5	294·6

42 ran

1979

	Penalties		*Penalties*			
			Cross-country			
Owner, horse and rider	*Dressage*	*Steeplechase*	*Jumps*	*Time*	*Show-Jumping*	*Total*
1. C. A. Cyzer's Killaire (Miss L. Prior-Palmer)	49·4	–	–	6·8	–	56·2
2. Dr N. Lawson-Baker and Syndicate's Monacle II (Miss S. Hatherly)	59·4	–	–	–	–	59·4
3. HM the Queen's Columbus (Capt. M. Phillips)	66	–	–	–	–	66
4. J. Wofford's Carawich	53	2·4	–	5·6	10	71
5. Miss C. Strachan's Merry Sovereign	56·4	2·4	–	13·2	5	77
6. HM the Queen's Goodwill (HRH Princess Anne)	84·2	–	–	–	5	89·2
7. Overseas Containers Ltd's Village Gossip (Miss L. Prior-Palmer)	72	–	20	–	5	97
8. Mrs Starkey and Miss J. Starkey's Topper Too (Miss J. Starkey)	49·6	–	–	53·2	10	112·8
9. B. Peterson's Monaco (N. Haagensen)	50·6	–	40	17·2	5	112·8
10. Mr & Mrs P. Lende's March Brown (Miss K. Lende)	70	–	20	12·4	20	122·4
11. Mrs G. Fleming-Williams' Rescator	75·6	4	20	24·4	5	129
12. Mr & Mrs M. Cursham's Shannagarry (M. Cursham)	94·2	–	20	13·6	15	142·8
13. Mrs J. Bewick's Schweppes (M. Bewick)	79	0·8	20	41·6	25	166·4

14.	R. Cooper's Bert (Miss J. Cooper)	57·8	–	60	46·4	10	174·2
15.	Miss J. Bradwell's Castlewellan	47·2	–	100	24	10	181·2
16.	R. Brake's Bampton Fair (A. Brake)	72·2	–	60	44·4	10	186·6
17.	Maj. & Mrs I. Macdonald's Anna Maria (Miss J. Macdonald)	58·8	11·2	40	77·6	–	187·6
18.	Miss C. Strachan's Radiel	65·6	–	80	49·6	15	210·2
19.	Mrs N. Martin-Bird and Miss T. Martin-Bird's The Mountaineer (Miss T. Martin-Bird)	99·6	–	120	36	5	260·6
20.	Mrs J. Butler's Merganser II	75·4	5·6	140	46·8	5	272·8
21.	Miss B. Clarke's Harper's Bazaar	74·2	18·4	140	53·2	10	295·8

41 ran

Index